SO MANY LOVES

SO MANY LOVES

LEO WALMSLEY

THE REPRINT SOCIETY
LONDON

THIS EDITION PUBLISHED BY THE REPRINT SOCIETY LTD.
BY ARRANGEMENT WITH WM. COLLINS SONS AND CO. LTD.
1945

TO

SAM

PRINTED IN GREAT BRITAIN
BY COLLINS CLEAR-TYPE PRESS: LONDON AND GLASGOW

Book One

I

I CANNOT SAY exactly how old I was when I started fishing, but I am sure that I was not more than four. Curious how difficult things are made for the beginner in a difficult art. He is told that a hook is dangerous because of its barb. If he gets it stuck in his flesh the only way to get it out is to cut the flesh with a knife, or remove the snood or line from the shank and pass the whole hook forwards through the wound. So he must not use a hook at all until he has acquired skill and caution in the handling of a less dangerous weapon. He must start with a bent pin.

Thus Dad (who was no angler) must have argued when I sought his help and guidance : and indeed his pessimism was justified, for on the only occasion when he had gone fishing out to sea with a local boatman he had, during a paroxysm of sea sickness, stuck a whiting hook in his finger, and he bore the mark of it for many years.

I cannot remember whether Dad helped me even with my first bent pin tackle. I doubt if he did, beyond perhaps giving me a pin from the collection he always kept stuck into the tabs of his waist-coat, and maybe a piece of string, together with an exhortation not to bother him while he was painting, or to fall in the water and get my clothes wet, as he was supposed to be looking after me. But I do remember, just as though I was there now, the patch of hard scaur in front of our village, which with the tide down on a fine summer's day, offered Dad one of his most popular " selling " subjects. It showed the red tiled cottages of the village itself perched along the edge of the sea cliff : the slipway and the old coast-guard station with perhaps a coble or two high and dry on the sand at the slipway foot with some fishermen gossiping by : and the whole of this reflected in a wide shallow pool, that Dad always managed to get into the foreground of his picture, although as he sometimes grumbled, that meant painting everything twice and the reflection, of course, upside down ! The subject was good in two ways. It

5

was just the thing that summer visitors who had enjoyed their holidays in the place would like to take home with them as a memento : and by painting it Dad would catch the eye of any one who came down the Slipway on to the beach, which meant that quite a lot of people (visitors of course) wouldn't be able to resist their curiosity to see what he was doing. Dad would be very nice to them, and if they praised his work he would drop a hint that he wouldn't mind selling it, and that he had a lot more sketches for sale in his shop, which poor Mother had to look after when he was out.

But I wasn't interested in the view or Dad's picture of it. About fifty yards seawards of where he pitched his easel was a deep cleft in the scaur called the Nick. It had been made by the fishermen so that they could pull their cobles through it at half tide when they were bound for the south side of the Bay, and save them pulling out seawards to clear the scaur ends. It formed even when the tide was out a deep weedy pool, and lying on the scaur you could look into this and see little shore crabs and shrimps and tiny fish moving along the sandy bottom or darting among the weeds, and sometimes being trapped by the red anemones which clustered the walls of the pool like flowers. But what excited me most was that there were little caves in the rock, and that if you dropped a bit of mussel or a limpet just in front of one of these, shortly, something, you could hardly tell what, would reach out of the cave and get it. So the thing to do was impale this bait on the bent pin.

What a futile apparatus it was ! I must have wept at times with exasperation. A real fish-hook is a beautiful piece of engineering. It is not merely a piece of steel wire bent and pointed and barbed. There is a precise relationship between the length of the shank and the part that is pointed, varied according to the size and type of the fish to be caught. For most sorts of commercial fishing the shank is straight and long. This facilitates rapid baiting and the unhooking of fish. For angling and for fish with small mouths like soles the shank is usually shorter in proportion, and the pointed part may be set off at a slight angle. The barb fulfils a double purpose. It holds the fish, but just as important it holds the bait. Even with a vice and pliers it requires a fair amount of skill to bend a pin into the shape of a hook. If Dad did bend mine for me then he did it with his fingers, with the pointed part as long as the shank.

To get a piece of soft limpet or mussel to stay on this long enough to lower it to the mouth of one of those little caves must have been a ticklish job. To remove the bait from the hook seemed quite a simple matter for the invisible cave dwellers, which crab or fish, must have grown fat on the easy meals I provided, without (so far as I can remember) suffering even the inconvenience of a slight prick from my pin point.

You couldn't grow up in a place like Bramblewick however without soon learning the proper way to catch fish. As I grew older, and Mother got a little less fussy about having me out of her sight alone, my education continued apace. True that the restrictions she imposed upon me would have made my advancement impossible had I been obedient. We were of course "foreigners" in Bramblewick, and she was city born and bred. She had got into her head that the scaurs and the beach generally were very dangerous. Local women gossips must have terrified her with their gruesome stories of the fatalities that had happened in Bramblewick Bay. They were not all stories of shipwrecks and fishing boat disasters. Scarcely a summer went by without some visitor being drowned while bathing, or through being cut off by the tide on the scaurs : or by falling over the cliff. The tides were very strong and there were terrible currents and whirlpools. There were also (according to one of Mother's informants) treacherous quicksands, in which long ago, a man had been known to sink from sight in a matter of minutes. This did scare me, but I was to prove that it was a yarn, at least so far as the beach was concerned, although there were plenty of bogs up the becks and on the moors capable of swallowing up a man if he was fool enough to try walking through them. Mother gave me a strict list of " bounds." I was never to venture farther along the south shore from the village than a stumpy cliff called Garry Nab. As far as this point the cliff itself was boulder clay, grown over with furze and bramble, and to her innocent mind, safe. To the north I must never go beyond another Nab called the Gunny Hole, above which was built the northern-most cottage of the village itself. Beyond this the cliffs rose abruptly to a height of 300 feet. The tide reached the Gunny Hole at half flood, and even local men going along the beach for drift-wood in winter time had sometimes been trapped, and the coastguards had to haul them up the cliff with a rope. These cliffs were also dangerous because in wet weather and after frosts, great lumps of rock fell from them, and indeed the whole village was often awakened in the middle of the night when a particularly big mass of cliff came thundering down.

These bounds I felt were fairly reasonable and in those early days they did not irk me. My chief interests were directly seawards of the village, out on the scaurs, and here in collusion with Dad, Mother had mapped out a series of bounds which had I observed them would have prevented me from fishing altogether except in the pool of my bent pin frustrations. The scaurs of Bramblewick are one of the most striking features of the whole coast. I was to know later that they owe their existence, and that the Bay itself owes its unique shape to what geologists call an anticline. The "formation" of this area of north-east Yorkshire is liassic, consisting of evenly stratified soft shales, alternating with beds of hard ironstone or limestone. At some parts these lie level, just as they were deposited in the Jurassic Seas in the days of the ammonite and the great fish crocodile. In other parts the beds dip, in some they are broken by faults or split by volcanic intrusions : and at Bramblewick they were lifted in the form of a huge and even dome which, scoured by the titanic glaciers that advanced down from the Pole to form what is now the bed of the North Sea, left eventually a curving bay with the strata arranged in lines or terraces concentric with each other and with the curve of the bay itself. The scaurs are the hard ironstone or limestone. They " lift ", towards the centre of the Bay, so that their seaward edge is high and their shore-ward side low. Thus between them, with the tide out, you get creeks or lagoons, which the tide fills before the scaurs themselves are covered. The widest of these creeks is just in front of the village, in the north corner of the Bay, and it forms the fishermen's landing. Here in summer the boats could be left moored all night. But the scaurs gave no protection against real storms, so in winter the boats had all to be hauled up the Slipway into the Dock where the lifeboat was kept.

Some of these creeks were sandy or muddy. Some had clean shale for a bed, but in all, the tide left standing pools, usually with boulders or flattish stones in them. If there was sand or mud, as in the Landing creek, you got swarms of shrimps and sand-hoppers, and of course buried in the sand, lob-worms and rag-worms. In the hard-bottomed creeks there were swarms of shore-crabs. The scaurs themselves were encrusted with acorn barnacles, and there were limpets too, and small mussels and other shell fish. All these animals were the food of the big sea fish like cod and billet and conger, which when the tide was far out, lurked in the forests of tangle, but swam shorewards up the creek as the tide flowed.

Fish like these are shy. When the sea was calm and the water clear, and it was daylight, they'd not venture into really shallow water ; therefore the best fishing places were as far down the scaurs as you could get. Dad and Mother must have known this when my bounds were fixed at the Nick. And the Nick was not the only gap there was in the scaurs. There was the Middle Nick in the next scaur to the south, and then Tom Bell Nick in the next one to this. I was forbidden even when the tide was out and the scaurs dry to low water mark to venture seawards of any of these gaps. The reason was that the flood tide came through them long before the scaurs were covered. If you stayed on the seaward side too long you were trapped. This often happened to visitors. And the local " pleasure " boatmen, like old Will Allen, and Isaac Fosdyck, and my friend Captain Bunny, used to make quite a lot of money by rescuing them. There wasn't any danger of course, but Mother didn't understand this. In fact, unless the boatmen were busy with real parties, they'd just sit in their boats, in the Landing, pretending that they didn't notice the visitors who were on the scaurs beyond the Nicks. Then when the tide was running through them, and the water was too deep for wading, they'd just pull out along the scaurs and shout to the visitors what had happened. They'd look very surprised, and sometimes frightened, and sometimes quite angry, as though they felt the boatmen had really set a trap for them, but it wasn't often they refused to pay a few coppers for being " rescued." But if you knew the scaurs, and the way the tide flowed, according to whether it was neap or spring, you could tell within a minute how long you dare stay seawards of the Nicks, and if Dad was painting in the village, or out in the country, and there were plenty of visitors about so that Mother daren't leave the shop, I didn't bother about the bounds. I just went where I liked.

But again the best time for " scaur " fishing was dusk, and in summer, even before " day-light saving," this didn't come till long

after bed-time. The only fish you could catch in daylight as a rule
were "pennocks," which are small billets or coal-fish. The
favourite place for them was Tom Bell Nick in the third scaur
south of the Landing. This scaur was not so prominent as the
others. The creek it made with the next one to the south was never
dry in neap tides. It was wide and deep with patches of clean sand,
and boulders covered with bladder wrack. There was a patch of
sand in the Nick itself, fringed with wrack which waved like long
grass in wind when the tide started to flow. That was when the
pennocks began to come in. They'd be in small shoals, and you'd
see them first among the wrack. But if you held your bait just
over the patch of sand, one of them would suddenly dart out at
it, and unless it swallowed it whole in the first bite the whole shoal
would come out and fight for it. They were pretty fish, with
greeny blue backs and silver bellies which flashed when you hooked
one. They were quite good to eat too, but a big one was only
three inches long, and you'd want at least a dozen for a meal. What
with those which got your bait, and the fish chasing off after something else while you put another bait on, and the time it took to
get the hook out of one that had got hold properly, you were very
lucky if you got more than three before the tide got so high you
had to leave the scaur altogether. Again it was no good fishing at
all until the tide started to flow, even if there was plenty of water.
But I used to have everything ready for when that happened. I'd
learnt a lot since the days of the bent pin. I had a nice long thin
hazel for a rod : a length of real whiting line which Captain Bunny
had given me, and a real hook, with a gut snood. As pennocks
never fed on the bottom, I had made a float with a piece of cork,
so that the bait would hang about a foot below the water surface.
The bait used for pennocks was limpet. You knocked these off the
scaur with a stone, pressed the tough leathery part with your thumb
so that the soft part came out, and stuck this on your hook.
Pennocks would never look at the leathery part unless they were
especially hungry.

One afternoon, I think it must have been in September for
there weren't many visitors about, and I'd been to school, I got
down to Tom Bell Nick just at low tide. I hadn't had time to
change into my " shore clothes " as Mother called them, or change
my boots and stockings for wading shoes. Tea was going to be at

five Mother said, when Dad got back from a sketching trip in the country, but to save her from worrying I'd told her I wasn't going on the shore at all. Anyway, there was hard scaur all the way down to Tom Bell Nick, so there was no need to wet even the soles of your boots if you stepped carefully.

It was just right for fishing that afternoon. The sea was calm. The tides were dead neap, and although there was no sign of pennocks when I arrived, I knew it wouldn't be long before the flood started. Being neap it would come in very slowly, so that I should have at least a good half-hour's fishing before I had to move. I had learned from experience that it paid to get a good stock of bait ready. If the fish were biting, you didn't want to leave them and hunt for limpets. I laid my tackle down on the scaur, and resisting the temptation to knock them off with the heel of my best school boots, I looked for a suitable stone and started limpeting. But when I had got a couple of good ones I thought it would be a good idea if I baited my hook, and threw it into the Nick. The float would tell me when the tide had started to flow, and of course if I saw it bobbing I would know that the fish were there. I did this, throwing it as far out as I could to the edge of the sandy patch, where the water was then about three feet deep. I laid my rod on the scaur and went on limpeting. But close to the Nick itself the limpets had got scarce. I moved on up the scaur, turning just now and again to glance at my rod.

I wasn't very worried about it. There was still no sign of the tide flowing : and I must have been about twenty yards away from the Nick when, glancing back, I suddenly saw the thick end of it jerk up, and then slither towards the water. I dropped my bait tin, and ran. I was too late to save it. Only the thick end was visible, and this was several feet out from the scaur edge, and it was moving swiftly towards the deep water of the creek, not in a straight line, but zigzag and jerking. It wasn't the prospect of losing my precious fishing gear that compelled my immediate action. No pennock was strong enough to drag my rod from the scaur, or tow it at that rate. It was a big fish, bigger than anything I had caught to date. I *did* hesitate. I looked at my best school boots, but I knew that I had not time to unlace them and take off my stockings. The tide had just started to flow. The bottom of the nick shelved from the scaur and the rod end still hadn't reached the deepest part of it. I stepped in, and was too excited to notice the shock of the cold as the water came up over my knees. I splashed forward. It was up to my thighs now. The rod end was only about six feet away. Was it out of my depth? I hesitated again when the water reached my middle, for the shock of it this time made me gasp. And it may have been then that I heard a terrified and familiar shout from somewhere behind me. I did not turn, however. The water was clear and I could see the bottom, and I guessed that I could take at least another two strides before it got too deep for me. I took them, and it was nearly up to my arm-pits, but reaching forward I grabbed the rod end, and hung on to it as I started to move backwards with the still invisible fish tugging wildly to get away. Then I certainly did hear the voice, and recognised it as Mother's. I knew she was running down the scaurs towards the Nick. I did not turn to look. The bottom was slippery, and the fish seemed to jerk stronger than ever as I dragged it shorewards. I managed to scramble out on to the scaur. I didn't bother about the rod any more. I seized the line, and hauled it in. There was a big plop, and the next moment the fish was out on the scaur, flapping and bouncing wildly, doing its best to get back into the Nick. I still pretended that I couldn't hear Mother, although actually I could hear her footsteps. I flung myself on the fish. I managed to get my fingers into its gills, and then I gave it a whack on the shale that stunned it, and I held it up, with only its tail flapping a bit, for Mother to see, so that she'd know at once that I hadn't got my clothes wet for nothing. I still pretended that I hadn't heard her shouting to me.

"Look!" I shouted, "I've caught a salmon, a real salmon. Look at its silver scales."

It was not a salmon, but it looked like one to me. And it was big enough to be one. It was about a foot long, and it must have weighed well over two pounds. Mother didn't look at it at all, and whether from fright or anger or just relief, she did not speak just then, although I guessed she'd have plenty to say when we got home. She just got hold of my free hand, and with the fish and my rod clutched firmly in the other, we hurried up the scaurs to the Slipway. The water was squelching in my boots, my wet clothes felt horrible, and I had a guilty feeling inside me too, but I could still feel the fish quivering, and every time I glanced at it I thought it was worth all the punishment I was going to get, even if Mother was going to take my fishing gear away from me for the rest of the pennock season. Anyway what were pennocks after this !

We got near to the Slipway, where as usual there was a group of fishermen, including my friend Captain Bunny. They always stared at people, and although Captain Bunny was not like that, they would laugh and mock at anything they thought out of the ordinary such as a visitor lady walking down to the beach with only a coat over her bathing dress. Mother must have hated passing them now, for of course they stared, and grinned, but when they saw my fish, they didn't mock. We had to stop, for one of them got hold of it, and they all crowded round. I don't think any of them had seen me wading into the water after it, but they must have seen us coming up the scaur from Tom Bell Nick, and as the hook was still in its mouth, they knew how I had caught it. But they all seemed puzzled about it. The man who was holding it said :

" Eh, what is't ? "

" Why it's a salmon, of course," I said proudly.

They laughed but they didn't mock. It wasn't a salmon, and it wasn't a salmon trout. One of them thought it might be a grey mullet. He'd caught one in his salmon nets years ago but he couldn't remember exactly what it had looked like. And then Captain Bunny took it from me and looked at it very closely.

"Why," he said, " it's a bass. I've never seen one caught in these parts afore, but they're common enough up south. I've caught 'em over the ship side in Plymouth Sound and Falmouth Roads. And fine eating they are too, better than a salmon. . . . You bake it in the oven, missus, with taties and a couple of onions. I'll lay you've never tasted owt better. . . . And fancy him catching a fish that no Bramblewick fisherman 'as ever set eyes on afore. You ought to feel proud of him."

Perhaps Mother did a bit. Captain Bunny was one of the few Bramblewick men she really liked. Anyway, although I had to go to bed at once and she gave me a long scolding about being un-truthful and disobedient, and doing something that was dangerous and had given her a very big fright, she didn't take my rod away, and although she did not praise me very much, she had to admit that the fish tasted very nice when we had it for dinner next day, cooked just as the Captain had suggested. And I don't think she told Dad about my wading in to get it. He said he had never tasted anything so nice, and also that he must write to the *Whitby Gazette* about such a rare fish being caught by a little boy. It was a very interesting piece of natural history. But he didn't. I suppose he was so busy with his painting that he forgot.

2

I'D BEEN FRIENDS with Captain Bunny for a long time but I think it was that fish that made us more than ordinary friends, and led to my getting a regular job as his summer " boat-boy " with the *Lydia*. Captain Bunny was quite different from the other Bramblewick fishermen. They were all gruff and gloomy, and they wouldn't let you set foot in their cobles or small boats although they didn't mind even boys helping to haul them up in bad weather. Captain Bunny had twinkling eyes and a smile for everybody. Of course he was not a real fisherman. He was only eleven years of age when he had gone as cabin boy on his own father's brig *Star of Bethlehem*, and he was mate of her when she was wrecked on the coast of Norfolk, and his father drowned. Soon after this he had become master of a top-sail schooner, the *Lydia*, and he had remained master of her for nearly fifty years, up to the time when *she* was wrecked within half a mile of where *Star of Bethlehem* had gone aground. The captain had coloured pictures of both these ships hanging in his cottage, and I don't know how many times he told me the story of each wreck, and to him the most important thing was that the second one should happen practically in the same place as the first : that after he had been rescued the second time, he'd gone to the little village churchyard and seen the graves of his father and his other old ship-mates. He'd got so fond of the *Lydia* that he couldn't bear the thought of sailing on another ship, so he had decided to retire then. But among the salvage from the wreck was the small ship's boat. He managed to get another sailing ship captain to fetch this up for him on his next north-bound voyage, and lower it over at Bramblewick Bay. The Captain was as fond of this boat as he had been of his ship. He called her *Lydia*, and he had got Dad to paint this name on her stern with two crossed flags, one the red ensign, the other the flag of the ship's owners. Most of the Bramblewick sea-captains when they retired were very wealthy, and they lived in new houses that had been built above the old village. But Captain Bunny only had a small pension, to keep himself and his grown-up daughter on. So he had to use his boat for what was called "takking summer visitors off," either pulling or fishing.

The ordinary fishermen regarded their job just as a trade and never got excited about it. If they got any pleasure out of feeling a big cod on a line, it was only by thinking of how much money it would bring. But to Captain Bunny it was a sport, and even when he had a "party" out at the whiting grounds, which meant he had to do all the baiting, as well as taking his customer's fish off the hooks, he'd manage to work a line himself. Of course, it didn't do for him to go on catching fish if they weren't catching any, for that sort of thing often happens in a boat with several people fishing. He'd have to change lines or seats then, especially if it was a lady, and if he still went on being lucky, then he would have to wind in his line altogether, but he didn't like it. Actually he didn't like "takking folks off" at all, as I discovered very soon after I had got my job. That job for which I received one penny a week plus visitors' tips consisted chiefly in keeping the *Lydia* afloat when the Captain went for his dinner or tea, or at very low tide when, in order to get customers, he would have to stand on the Slipway and ask visitors as they came down if they wanted a boat. Although she was small, she was very heavy, and if he did get a customer, it wouldn't have been much use if she had been aground with the tide ebbing, nor anchored either if the tide was flowing and all the other boats were out. What you had to do was to pull about the Landing following the tide, in or out, keeping your eye always open for the Captain's return. She had to be kept clean and tidy. If the sun was hot, you could pull out into deep water, drop the anchor, take up the bottom boards, give her a swill down with buckets of water, then bale her, put the boards back, mop the thwarts with a cloth, and give these an extra rub with a dry cloth if you saw the Captain walking down with a party, before pulling into the scaur. In the morning and afternoon if the weather was fine and the sea smooth, most of the visitors wanted a pull only.

This was sixpence an hour, half the price of fishing. We had two pairs of oars. I would take the forrard ones, and I had to keep stroke with the Captain, which I had soon learnt to do without even looking at his. Sometimes one of the customers would want to pull and I would crouch in the bow, and would be very amused watching the visitor, man or lady, fumbling with the oars, and crashing the blades against the Captain's and then catching a crab, and perhaps falling on top of me. But if I wasn't pulling I preferred to look over the bow, watching the great jellyfish swimming past : or if it was low water, and we were moving just outside the scaur ends, looking down into the tangles in the hope of seeing congers or cod or billet, or, equally exciting, bits of sunken ships.

It was pleasant enough pulling about the Bay. I was usually given a copper or two when we put the party ashore, and I was once given a whole shilling : but both the Captain and I thought it a waste of time, and I'm sure he wouldn't have taken fishing parties off if he hadn't been so hard up. It was all right sometimes, particularly if there were only one or two gentlemen who really knew something about fishing, and had their own fishing gear and were not afraid of putting a worm on a hook, or taking a fish off. But often we had parties who seemed to think the whole thing was a joke. I'd known ladies who screamed when they caught their first fish. And then when there was a bit of swell on (which is often when the fish bite best) they'd start being sea-sick, and we'd have to haul the anchor and go home just when the fish were really biting.

But there were days, even in the height of summer, when no one wanted to go " off " either pulling or fishing, and especially was this so when there was a bit of wind and the sea choppy. The Captain of course would have got some bait in case, and he'd stand on the Slipway, or sit with me in the *Lydia* for a long time before his conscience would allow him to make what was for me a breath-taking decision.

" Well," he'd say. " It looks as though trade's going to be bad to-day. We can't afford to waste all that good bait. What do you say if we gan and get a bit o' fish for our own suppers ? You keep her afloat while I gan for t' sails. There's a fairish wind. No call to sweat oursens pulling."

And then as he turned to go, he would wink at me and say :

"Now keep your eyes open for any visitors while I'm gone. We mustn't gan off on our ourn if we can make brass otherwise."

What an anxious twenty minutes it would be while he was away. How I wished that the Captain was a younger man so that he could run that long distance and up so many steep steps to his cottage. But he was nearly seventy, and although his figure was still erect, he always walked slowly, just as though he had never got used to walking anywhere but on a ship's deck, and he always rolled a bit as though the ground was unsteady. I'd watch the Slipway for his return, and if I saw some visitors stop and question any of the old men who were standing there, I'd really pray that they were not asking for a boat. When he did come he would be carrying the masts and sails over his shoulder. He might stop and exchange a few words with the old men, but I think that as soon as he was on the beach he purposely never glanced behind him in case just at the last moment something would happen. I would have everything I could think of ready, the chocks for the little masts, the rudder and tiller lying on the stern thwart ready for fixing : but there was one necessary job I could not do. The *Lydia* had no keel, so several large stones had to be laid in her bottom for ballast. It would take the Captain another terribly anxious ten minutes to carry these from the scaur, and although we both kept our eyes averted from the village, I'd be in such a state of suspense that even a sea-gull croaking would make me think that someone was shouting for a boat. But if the wind was off-shore, we would hoist the sails straight away. The Captain would be on the stern thwart, his back to the village, and his eyes to the sea, and I don't think that any visitors, no matter how rich they looked, could have shouted him back then.

Usually we only managed to steal an afternoon for a private trip like this, but once we had a whole day of it. It was the day of Whitby Regatta, and as the railway was running special cheap trains to Whitby, and the Bramblewick shopkeepers and even the fishermen were taking a holiday, it looked as though the boat-trade would be very bad indeed. I wanted to go to the regatta of course. Apart from the yacht and boat racing, there was a greasy pole, and swimming races and a firework display at night. We had all gone the year before, and I had enjoyed it very much, and as I hadn't been getting into trouble for a long time I think I could have persuaded Mother to take me, although Dad couldn't go because he was very busy on what he called a very important picture which he hoped to get into the Royal Academy. But when the Captain on the evening before suggested that we should have a whole day's fishing and sailing, I didn't think any more about the regatta except to pray for fine weather, for that would mean fine weather for us too. Mother didn't seem to worry at all when I was with Captain Bunny, although when she packed my sandwiches and a bottle of tea, she said she'd get anxious if we were not back by tea time.

My prayers had been answered for it was a perfect day. The wind was west, but not too strong. The sun was very hot with only little round clouds in the sky that never really covered it. The tides were spring too. That was not quite so good for fishing at the whiting grounds, because, except on the slack, you wouldn't be able to keep your lines near the bottom because of the current. But then the Captain had planned that we should get there just before that time. Actually the tide was about three-quarters ebb and the *Lydia* just afloat at her moorings in the Landing by the time we had got the ballast on board and everything ship-shape for off. It was no wonder the Captain never used sails except when we were on our own. Even with the mainsail (a dipping lug) there was scarcely room for a small boy in the forepart of the boat. And for some reason he never explained to me, we had to have a mizzen too. The truth was that *Lydia* was not designed for sail at all in a yachtsman's sense. She was too broad and shallow of draught even with ballast to sail into the wind. But with the wind behind her, as it was that morning, and both sails full spread, I wouldn't have changed berths with the fastest of the Whitby Regatta racers. We shot out between the two posts that mark the entrance to the Landing at what was to me terrific speed, the waves crashing at our stem, a gurgling wake behind us. What was a regatta, even a greasy pole and a firework display, to this ?

In all my memories of fishermen and sailors I can think of no one with a lovelier face than Captain Bunny's. I can see him now sitting in the stern of the *Lydia*, with his great sea-booted legs sprawled out towards me : one gnarled sunburnt hand resting on the tiller, the other on the gunwale. He wore an old cheese-cutter

hat, with green age. He was bald on top, but between the rim of
the hat and his neck was snow-white hair, which continued down
his jaws and under his chin, which, like his mouth, was clean shaven.
His face was full with a wide forehead. It was deeply lined, but not
wrinkled, and it was these lines, particularly at the corners of his
eyes and mouth, that gave him a look of perpetual benevolence. I
had known him look stern, but I had never known him angry. And
his blue eyes, which always twinkled, must have had a special
brightness in them as with the posts behind us he said to me in his
deep husky voice :

" Eh—out with the railing line. We're clear of the tangles now.
Unless we're goin' too fast it's a likely spot this for a billet or a
sprag."

We never used the railing line when we had visitors because
we'd have to be pulling, and any one who didn't know how to
" feel " it properly would most likely get the spinner caught on the
bottom and lose it. It was a very special gear, with swivels on the
lead, and between the line and the gut cast. I paid it out very slowly.
As soon as the lead went over, it felt almost exactly as though a big
fish was pulling on it, but I knew that this was just the speed of the
boat, and I wasn't going to have the Captain laughing at me by
hauling in, just as a visitor might have done. Anyway we must
have been going too fast, or it was the wrong state of tide, for I
caught nothing, and very soon the Captain was telling me to wind
in, for we were very nearly at the whiting grounds. These were
about a mile directly seawards of the village, and about a quarter
of a mile south of Low Batts cliff and point. The marks were easy
to remember. You had to get the third window of the old coastguard station just in line with one of the Landing posts, and the
chimneys of a farm above Low Batts cliff opposite to a patch of
whins on the cliff edge. It was along this cliff that the railway led
to Whitby harbour, and just as we had got the sails furled and
the anchor over, I noticed a long excursion train puffing up the
hill, doubtless full of Bramblewick people and visitors bound
for the regatta. I didn't feel a bit envious. And I didn't have
any regrets when, after half an hour's fruitless fishing, the Captain
remarked :

" Why, it looks as though all t'fish have gone to Whitby
Regatta. If they don't come soon tide will have started to flow,

and it'll be too strong for us here. What do you think we'd best do next, gan home for our dinners ? "

I knew he was joking, and I had guessed that the whiting grounds was only the preliminary to our full day of sport. All the time Captain's eyes had been roving seawards, and suddenly he gave a shout :

" Look over yonder towards High Batts. Aren't those gulls on t'watter ? Wind your line in. I'll soon have t'anchor up. They're after sprats, and where's there's sprats there'll be mackerel or billet. That'll be better sport than this."

My excitement was momentarily divided, for as I started to wind in my line on to its frame I felt a great tug.

" Wait a minute, Captain," I yelled. " I've got one. A big 'un too."

" Steady then. Don't lose him."

He was too big for me to wind the line straight on to the frame. Half-way up the line went slack, and I thought he'd gone, then it tightened again, and in a moment I saw him, a big flat fish. I swung it over the side into the boat. It was a plaice, a two-pounder. It had swallowed the hook and Captain had to get it out for me with his knife, and I'd never seen him so pleased about a fish.

" Eh——" he kept on saying. " He's a beauty. He's a beauty!"

" Don't you think we ought to stop here for a bit longer, Captain ? " I said. " Now that they've started ? "

" Nay," he answered, " not when there's mackerel about, and there's a wind like this for sailin'. Wind will very likely drop later. Then we'll be able to have another go for flatfish or whiting, up on High Batts ground where the tide won't run so strong. Let your lead over again and then wind it properly. Look at them gulls now. There's swarms of 'em ! "

Whatever regrets I might have had were forgotten as soon as we were under way again. Certainly sailing was better than pulling, and when you could fish at the same time it was better than being anchored, provided of course that you were really going to catch some fish. The thing I had against it was that we had only one railing line, and I didn't like to do all the fishing when I knew the Captain was just as fond of it as I was. But he made me hold the line, in spite of me protesting that it ought to be his turn first because of the plaice.

The wind was as strong as ever, but as we were going aslant it now, *Lydia* heeled over to leeward quite a lot, and seemed to be travelling faster than when she had been running free. She was also travelling to leeward, the Captain pointed out, apologetically. That didn't worry me, for we were making a fair enough course for the gulls, which were still wheeling about the same patch of water. We were soon near enough to see what they were. Most of them were herring gulls, but there were a number of black-backers, and kittiwakes, and lesser blackheads, and a few snow-white gannets, which were dropping down into the sea, going under a bit and then soaring up again. There were ordinary cormorants too, and guillemots and puffins (the Captain called these Flamborough Head pilots) and razor bills, but these were just singly or in odd groups some distance from the big flock, and we actually saw a guillemot come up from a dive, close by the boat, with a live sprat in its beak. It got a fright when it saw us so near and dived again, leaving the sprat floating on the surface, and it was just then I got my first bite. We'd tried mackerel fishing several times before, but I had never been lucky enough to catch one, and my, how it pulled. It made the line zigzag and at one time it rushed ahead at such a speed that the line slacked and it almost hit the boat. I thought I'd lost it, for I could actually see it flashing through the water as it bore back. Then I felt its weight again, but I nearly wept with relief when at last I swung it into the boat and saw it kicking at the Captain's feet. The spinner had three hooks, like a grapple, but they were easy to get off, and over it went again. I tried to hand the line over to the Captain, but he wouldn't take it, and before all the line was out it was grabbed by another.

"You keep on fishing," he shouted at me when I had got this one off. "We're going straight through the shoal now. Can't you smell 'em? Look, there's sprats all round us, thick together as hail-stones. Look—there's t'mackerel among 'em where that broken water is ahead."

I was really too excited to be able to look at anything properly. The gulls now were wheeling all around us, making a terrific din. I certainly could smell fish, and I could see the sprats, masses of them, and just like a shower of rain or hail, only moving flat, and I could see and hear the splashing of the mackerel as they attacked them. But no sooner was the spinner over the side than it was grabbed, and this went on until there were at least a dozen fine fish kicking on the bottom boards. We were still sailing fast however, leaving the thickest part of the shoal behind. There came a pause in the fishing. The Captain told me to make fast the line and stand by the tacks of the main-sail as we went about, and when we were running back towards the shoal (to which the gulls had now returned) he at last agreed to take the line himself, and let me hold the tiller. And then an extraordinary thing happened. Either the shoal had moved shoreward, or we had more lee-way than even the Captain had guessed, but the *Lydia's* bow just would not keep up to the course, and then worse than anything, the wind began to fall. Before, it had been steady. Now it came in puffs. Before we had got half-way to the shoal the sails started to flap, and all round us the sea, which had been quite choppy, became smooth and shiny, except in the one place where it was disturbed and broken by the jumping fish.

I am sure that any other man would have been really angry letting someone catch all the fish, and then being robbed of his turn like this. I felt terribly selfish and I dare scarcely look at the Captain as he started to haul the railing line in to stop the spinner fouling the bottom, for the *Lydia* had completely lost way, and we were starting to drift southwards with the flood tide. But all he did was laugh and say :

" Why—it's real sailorman's luck this. Just like it falling a dead calm when you're in sight of harbour, and you're in a hurry to be ashore. Never mind. We've got plenty of worms, and if we run short, we'll have a mackerel to cut up. We'll gan into High Batts whiting grounds. We'll get another breeze later, you'll see."

" But, Captain," I protested. " Can't I pull for you to get some mackerel. The shoal's still there. It isn't fair, you've let me catch everything up to now. Let me pull for you."

He laughed again.

" Nay, it would be no good. I doubt if the two of us could pull t'awd *Lydia* fast enough for mackerel, with all this ballast aboard. Come on now, we'll get sails stowed, and pull in for High Batts. Likely as not there'll be a few nice plaice waiting for us there. We'll keep the railing line over of course. We might get a codling or a billet. You needn't go fast for them, and it wouldn't be a bad idea to put a strip of mackerel on the spinner. Cod like to take a smell at a bait afore they swallow it."

I had scarcely noticed until now, how far to the south of the Bay we had sailed. We were not more than half a mile from the great cliff of High Batts, which makes the south point of it. Here, just on the bay side of the point, was a sort of cove called Spinney Hole, which was very dangerous in bad weather. It was so smooth now that the cliffs were reflected in it as perfectly as in a looking-glass, and the view was so beautiful that I half wished that Dad was here to paint it, for the heather was in bloom on the moors above the cliff, and the fields were yellow with ripening corn. But then probably he would have felt sea-sick by now, and anyway the main thing about to-day was fishing.

We stowed the sails, and started pulling straight for the cove. The gulls had now stopped screaming and were floating on the water. There was no sign of mackerel. It looked as though the sprats for the time being had swum down to the bottom. The Captain as usual pulled the after oars, and as soon as we got enough way on the boat he jerked the spinner over. He had hitched the line round a short piece of barel stuck in a thole pin, and looking over his shoulders as I pulled, I could see this stick clearly, and I did hope that in spite of our not being able to pull fast enough, he would catch a mackerel. But nothing happened for a long time, and actually I wasn't looking at it at all when the Captain gave a sudden shout, left go of his oars, and started hauling in.

"Have you got one, have you got one ?" I yelled excitedly.

"Aye. If he doesn't get off, if he doesn't get off. A good 'un too. Must be a codling. Aye, he's on yet. Here he comes."

There was a lovely splash, and the Captain swung his first catch into the boat. It was not a codling, but a big grey gurnard, and I was delighted, for I had often heard the Captain say that gurnard was his favourite fish for eating, and apart from that, I knew by having caught smaller ones at the whiting grounds that they pulled better than fish twice their size. The pricks on a gurnard are dangerous, but the Captain soon had its head under his sea-boot heel, and the hook out and the spinner over again, and as he swung it by its tail into the basket a number of sprats dropped from its mouth.

"Look," he said, "even gurnard are after 'em. If the shoal's gone down to the bottom we ought to get a lot of fish where we're going, only maybe they'll be getting so many sprats to eat they'll not look at our bait. We haven't got far to gan now. We want to be just clear of the scaur ends. There's a deep hole with mud on t'bottom."

I had never fished on the High Batts whiting grounds before. The "pleasure" boatmen never used it, because with pulling it would take too long to get there and back, and again if the wind suddenly got up from the north, they might not be able to get back at all, and have to land on the rocky shore, and perhaps get smashed up in doing so. But there was no sign of a north wind or bad weather to-day. Everything was just perfect, now that the Captain had broken his luck. He did not catch another on the railing line. Soon he stopped pulling again, and hauled it in, then he stood up, shaded his eyes against the bright sun with one hand as he gazed shorewards to get his marks, and then he told me to stop and let the anchor over. I was surprised to find by the length of cable that there was only half the depth here of the home grounds. There was very little current too, and it took us quite a time to swing round. By this time we had our whiting lines ready, and re-baited with worm. Down they went, and the Captain made his fast and wiped the sweat from his brow with his big red handkerchief.

"It must be dinner-time," he said. "What about having a drink of tea and summat to eat while we wait for 'em to start biting."

Before I could answer I felt a tug

"Have you got one?"

"Think so," I said, hauling up.

The Captain seized his line.

"Why I have. Aye. I've got one. Two by the feel of it."

"So have I," I yelled as I pulled two whiting on board.

"A whiting and a nice dab," the Captain joined in, holding up his catch. "We needn't talk about dinner yet."

"No fear, Captain. Mine had got on before I reached the bottom. There must be swarms of fish about."

I'd known this happen before at the whiting grounds, but it was never so exciting when you had visitors aboard, and you had to waste so much time looking after them, and all the time feeling that they were going to start being sick or decide that they were staying longer than they could afford. That was like being shown a basket of strawberries and only being allowed to eat one. Now we could go on fishing just as long as we liked. And it wasn't as though it was just whiting. The next fish I caught was a gurnard, not so big as the Captain's but it pulled better than two whitings. There were dabs and plaice, and the Captain caught a haddock, and I think he was very proud of it, and I was glad, although we caught so many fish that we couldn't possibly keep count of who was catching the most. It went on like this for nearly an hour. And perhaps it was as well they did stop biting then for I was aching with hunger.

I don't think we could have really enjoyed our meal then if the Captain hadn't firmly decided to haul up our lines : for, as he said, they might come back any minute. Even when we'd finished he said he was going to wait a minute or two longer as he wanted to have a pipe, and he couldn't cut his baccy proper if his hands were slimy with fish, only there was no harm in my starting. But the fish had come back and as soon as he saw me hauling up he couldn't resisting putting his live over, and he had to give up the idea of smoking until we got another slack spell at least an hour later. This spell lasted a long time. We didn't get as much as a bite, and I began to think that our day's sport was over. It was getting near tea-time too. I wondered if Mother had said anything to the Captain last night about her wanting me not to be late. I was sure that if we'd had a " party " we would be homeward bound now. My heart sank when the Captain suddenly said :

" Things are quiet now, and no mistake. We must have caught 'em all. It's a pity it keeps so calm. They must have had a queer day at Whitby Regatta, with their yacht racing. Not a breath of wind since morning." Then to my great relief he went on : " Still we might get a billet or two close in. What do you say about having a try, just pulling about the scaur ends ? I'll take the spinner off and put a couple of billet flies on, and a lighter lead. It would be better if it was getting on for dusk for a fly and with the water so clear, but we might get one."

A billet fly is simply a white feather tied to a bare hook, and the Captain explained that the fish took it thinking it was the flashing belly of a sprat or sand-eel, a mistake that was easier to make when the light was poor. We hauled the anchor. The Captain would not hear of me pulling while he fished, and said it wouldn't do for both of us to pull for, as we would be in shallow water, we'd have to watch out very carefully for the fly fouling.

He pulled in towards the cliffs. The tide was nearly up now, but the water was so still and clear that in a few minutes I could see the bottom. We were just about where the tide would ebb to at the lowest of spring tides. There were beds of tangles, and rocks and patches of sand and gravel, and quite clearly I could see dozens of big pink and purple sea-urchins clinging to the tangles, and real crabs too. And then came an extraordinary sight. Even the Captain had never seen anything like it in his life. There was a shoal of fish, all about the same size, and about a foot long, hundreds and hundreds of them, packed close together like sprats, but not moving, except to keep their heads to the current. They were lying close to the bottom about two fathoms down in what at low tide would be a creek between two scaurs, but they were so thick you couldn't see the bottom itself. They were billet. The Captain pulled so that we went up the creek, but he had pulled at least fifty yards before we came to the end of the shoal, and the flies must have passed right through them, but I didn't get even a bite. He turned, and he pulled back again. They were still there, and we went on up and down like this several times, still without getting a bite. If only we'd had a net ! I am certain we could have caught thousands in one go, for they didn't take the slightest notice of the boat passing over them. They might have been asleep.

It wasn't that we wanted billet so much. They are all right for eating, but not so good as whiting or cod. And certainly we had done well enough with the other fish. It was just that I was getting scared again that the Captain might think it time to go home when we couldn't catch a single one. Again my fears were unjustified for shortly he said :

" Why, it's no use at present. What they're doing is lying in wait for the sprats to come in. They're thinking of live sprats and nowt else, and sun's too bright and water's too clear for them to mistake a feather for one. Fish have got more sense than you'd think. What we've got to do is wait too. We can't go home when there's fish about as thick as this. We're the only boat out to-day, remember. We've got a tidy bit of fish for ourselves, but if we're lucky and the visitors have got back from the regatta, we ought to make a tidy bit of brass on the Slipway selling what we don't want. Now I think we ought to pull ashore, and give our legs a stretch. We might find a bit of kindling and light a fire and hot up our tea. It'll be better that way than cawd. What do you say to that, or are you getting tired?"

He must have known what a silly question that was for he winked, and he didn't need to tell me to wind the railing line in as he headed the *Lydia* for the shore. The sea was so smooth that it didn't matter about the shore being rocky, although it made you think what a dangerous place it would be for a small boat if the weather was rough. We got out, and carried the anchor on to the scaur. Between this and the foot of the cliff was some shingle as well as rock, and at high-water mark there was a line of washed-up weed and plenty of small driftwood dried by the hot sun. We soon made a fire and put the Captain's billy can on it. It was almost as exciting as fishing, and I was certain that Mother could not have told the Captain about our being back early, and that anyway she wouldn't be very worried seeing that the weather was so fine. When we'd had our tea the Captain sat on a big boulder, and a last was able to cut his baccy and fill his pipe in comfort, but all the time he kept looking out to sea, and I knew he was thinking of the great shoal of billet that were waiting for the sprats. We were not the only ones waiting either. From the very foot of High Batts a high scaur runs seawards, forming a sort of island until the tide is full. This was white with gulls, and suddenly we noticed them fly up screaming just as though a gun had gone off. At the same time a patch of water just a little farther out than where we had seen the billet went dark, as though a puff of wind had stirred it. The gulls came screaming over this patch, and I didn't need the Captain to tell me what it was. He had already stood up.

The sprats had come in all right. The billet were after them too, and so excited that they were leaping right out of the water. But this wasn't the only lucky thing that had happened. As well as the dark patch made by the fish there were other patches on the water. The wind was getting up again, and we could feel it as soon as we left the shore. It was still west and very gentle and warm. Not strong enough to sail by yet, but, as the Captain said, it would wrinkle the water, and make it easier for the fish to mistake our flies for the real thing. I had scarcely got the line over before I hooked a billet. It pulled well, but not quite so hard as a mackerel, although it was much bigger. When the Captain took his turn, however, he got two on at once, and I did the same my next turn. I don't know how many we got. Our basket was already full when we started and we had to drop them on the bottom boards, and soon these were hidden, for no sooner was the line over than either one or two fish were hooked, and with fly you hadn't to bother re-baiting. And quite apart from the excitement of catching was the thought that even if they only brought, say, threepence each, the Captain would make quite a lot of money when we got ashore.

Fish ! I think the whole Bay must have been packed with them on that memorable day of Whitby Regatta when all the fishermen except ourselves were on holiday. The sprats explained it. In shoals of inconceivable numbers, they were being driven in by the larger fish to shallow water and concentrated into an almost solid mass. Our oars dipped into them as into liquid silver. They splashed from the water with every stroke. The marvellous thing was that the big fish could be fooled into biting at a piece of feather, when all they had to do was open their mouths and the real sprats would practically move in. And billets were not the only big fish that were after them. We got a mackerel on the fly, and after that the Captain changed the end fly for the spinner. It didn't seem to matter now that we were only pulling. We caught more mackerel, and then we started to get codling, really big ones, so that it was about as much as I could do to pull some of them into the boat. It became quite a job to change places from the pulling thwart to the stern because of the fish on the bottom. I began to think that if we went on like this the boat would sink in spite of the Captain having thrown the ballast stones over, and still I didn't want to go home, and I'm sure the Captain didn't either, for he was just as excited as ever and he must have been glad that we hadn't any visitors with us to say the word. It was the fish themselves that compelled him to make that decision in the end. Perhaps they had eaten so many sprats that they were gorged. Anyway they stopped biting, and after we had pulled up and down the cove about half a dozen times without getting a single bite, the Captain said :

"Well, it looks as though they've finished at last. Tide's ebbing too, and we mustn't miss our moorings. And we've got to sell some of this fish when we get ashore . . . And, by Gum ! That reminds me. I promised your mother we'd be home just after tea. It must be getting on for seven o'clock by now. Come on, bo'sun. We've got a fair wind and tide. Let's up with t'sails. But we'll keep t'railing line over. There's still a chance of another codling or billet across the scaur ends ! "

3

THE SUMMER SEASON was short. The pleasure boats were always hauled up into the village the second week in September, turned bottom up, and covered with an old sail for the winter, and never launched again until July. In any case school would have put an end to my job with the Captain. Usually the sea was too rough for pennocking in the winter, and what were pennocks when you'd caught real billets and cod ? Of course the big cobles were fishing except in really stormy weather. But (so far as I knew then) the only other sort of fishing was "scaur-lining." Many of the old retired fishermen and some of the schoolboys had "scaur-lines." But not Captain Bunny, although it was he who gave me mine. He said it wasn't real sport, for of course the line was "set" and you never felt the fish bite or pull. Usually they were dead when you got them and you simply had to take them off the hooks. They were just pieces of the ordinary "long" cod lines the coblemen used, with snooded hooks a fathom apart. You fastened one end to a big stone, and stretched out the line to another stone, down or across the creeks between the scaurs as close to low-water mark as you dared, remembering that if the tides were taking off, that is, changing from spring to neap, the next ebb would not go so far down, also that the same thing might happen with a change of wind. It was no use using worms or limpets or mussels for bait, for the first things to start moving when the tide flowed were shore crabs, and they'd have the hooks bare long before the cod came in.

The only bait that wouldn't come off was scaur-cocks. This is a kind of anemone found only at low water springs. To protect itself from big fish it covers its body with grains of sand. This also helps it to hide itself from its own victims, little fish or crabs which are seized by its tentacles and pulled into its stomach very quickly. But if anything big comes along the scaur-cock pulls in its tentacles (which look just like the petals of a dahlia), shrinks its body, and looks exactly like a little heap of sand.

The biggest job in scaur-lining therefore was getting the bait. You could only do this at low-water springs. The cocks were very tough, and they were fond of attaching themselves into crevices in the scaur, and it required a lot of skill to knife them off whole. Then the sand had to be scraped from them, and you cut each one in two from top to bottom. They would go on living on the hook, and if a line was neaped for a week, you might find some of the cocks had started growing into complete anemones again, and had re-covered themselves with sand. Yes, it was exciting, setting a line, and then when the tide was up, watching the place where you had set it, with great waves breaking on the hidden scaurs at either side : and imagining some monster cod coming along, taking one of your baits, and getting caught. But it was also very worrying, for if it was a school day, the tide might be just baring the line when you were at lessons, and flowing over it when you got out. There was supposed to be a strict law among the scaur-liners never to touch anybody else's line, but there were one or two of the old fishermen I would not have trusted to walk past my line if there was a good fish on it, and if they knew I was safe at school : and as for any boy who happened to be away from school (there might be mumps or whooping cough in his family, or he might just be playing truant) I'd know for certain he'd be at my line if he'd known where I'd set it.

One afternoon I remember running down the scaurs straight after school feeling rather worried that the tide had started to flow, and because there were two big boys also down the scaurs, although they were some distance away from my line. I didn't like either of these boys. They had actually left school, and were waiting to go to sea as apprentices. They had lines of their own, but they must have been to them by now, and in spite of them being at least two scaurs away, I felt suspicious about them. Even if they hadn't found my line already they would see me going to it, and the chances were that if there was a fish on it, they'd come and take it away from me. They might even steal my line. I daren't wait for them to go away however. The tides were taking off, and unless I got to it now, and moved it farther up the scaur I might not see it again for a fortnight. So I just went on hoping they wouldn't notice me, and very soon I forgot about them for I saw something gleaming white in the very place where my line was set, close to the edge of the flowing tide. Then I saw another and another, and I thought I was going to find the biggest catch I'd ever had on a scaur-line. But when I got to the place, I heard the boys shouting and laughing at me as they ran my way. I saw that the gleaming white objects were not fish, but stinking cods' heads that had come from the local fried fish shop.

There was one on every hook. I guessed of course that they had been put on by the two boys, who now came up pretending to be very surprised, but laughing with each other. I wouldn't have felt so angry if one of them hadn't been carrying a nice cod, and if I hadn't noticed that one of my snoods was twisted, showing that there had been a live fish on it. But it was no good my showing them how angry I was, with them being so big, for that would have meant a fight, and as well as my getting a good hiding, they'd probably have taken my line or cut it up with their knives. So I said nothing, and having had their fun, they let me alone to take off the cod heads, and coil up my line. I took care never to set it in that place again however and indeed it was thanks to this that I found the best place of all for a scaur-line, north of the Gunny Hole on the forbidden side of that strictest of all boundaries. But Mother never knew.

It was here that an exciting thing happened one day. Luckily it was a Saturday and no school. A fierce northerly gale had sprung up during the previous night. The cobles hadn't dared to put to sea, and as lots of driftwood was washing up along the south shore of the Bay all the fishermen were along in that direction. The sea was so rough that I was afraid my line would have washed away, and to add to my anxiety the tide ebbed slowly, as it always did when there was a strong wind from the north. I knew where my line was by a big boulder whose top bared at about three-quarters ebb, but as the boulder was about four feet high, I couldn't even have waded to it until long after this, and I just had to wait on the scaur in the freezing cold. No one looking across the Bay that morning would have thought it possible for even fish to be alive unless they were hiding in the caves in the rocks. From Low Batts to High Batts there wasn't a patch of unbroken water, and from Spinney Hole, the place where Captain Bunny and I had fished on that lovely summer's day, the spray rose up in a great cloud, so that you couldn't see the foot of the cliff at all. I wasn't worried as to whether there would be a fish on my line or not, I was only thinking of the line itself.

But the tide did ebb until at last it was half-way down the stone, and then although it had started to snow, I decided to see if I could get it. Like the other scaur-liners, I had a gaff, a short stick with a meat hook lashed to its end. This wasn't so much for getting hold of fish as for seizing the line itself when the tide would not bare it, and the water was muddy. You scraped it along the bottom as a sort of grapple. I took off my boots and stockings. My feet were already very cold, but the funny thing was that the water seemed quite warm when I started wading in. The only thing I didn't like was the limpets and barnacles I trod on, for of course I could not see them. I got to the boulder all right. My line was set southwards from this, on smooth scaur, so I knew there was no danger of my falling into any deep holes or over the scaur edge. The first anchor stone should have been about six feet away from the boulder itself. I felt for it with my gaff and also with my feet, but I couldn't find it. I was noticing the cold now, and no mistake. My legs were trembling and my teeth had started to chatter, but I waded on to where the other stone ought to have been, grappling all the time with my gaff, but without success. I worked backwards to the boulder.

All this time the depth of the water kept changing, for the big waves having broken on the scaur ends come shorewards in what we call " runs." They are smooth but if you are wading they flood round you, and then flow back, so that one minute you may be up to your knees, and the next only to your ankles. It was when I was almost back to the boulder that a very big run came in. It came up over my knees, and if I hadn't climbed up on to the boulder itself, it would have been over my turned-up trousers. I was frightened, for it looked as though the tide had actually started to flow. I also felt very miserable, for it was clear that my line had washed away, and that I must give it up and wade back as soon as the " run " turned. And it was soon after it did turn that I saw something that made me gasp. It was the tail of a huge cod, sticking clear out of the water, on the north side and slightly shorewards of the boulder. It was flapping and alive. I forgot the cold and all my misery. I also forgot that on the north side of the boulder there was a hole, into which I went with my second stride, but although I got my trousers wet, I didn't lose my balance. I could still see the fish : more of it now as the run receded, and I could see some of my line wrapped round it, and suddenly felt a bit of that line round my ankles. The wonder was that I was not caught by some of the hooks, for of course the whole line was in a tangle, having been broken from one of the anchoring stones. I don't think that would have stopped me however. The run had nearly finished. Another, and probably a bigger one, would come in less than a minute. I struck at the middle of the cod with my gaff and hooked it. It gave a great kick but I hung on and started to drag it, line too, toward the shore. Another run did come in. The water rose almost to my thighs. The fish disappeared from sight, but I hung on desperately, and as soon as the run started back, moved shorewards again, and the next run left me and the fish high and dry on the scaur when it ebbed.

And what a fish it was ! I'd seen bigger ones landed by the cobles, but never caught on a scaur-line. It took me all my strength to move it (and the ravelled line with its one remaining stone) up to where I had left my boots and stockings. There I found that one of the runs had come almost to the cliff foot. My boots and stockings had been awash. I couldn't have got my stockings on anyway over my wet and frozen feet, which were also cut and bleeding from the barnacles I had trodden on. I remember that I actually cried with the pain when I put my boots on, and I don't know how I managed to walk along that swiftly narrowing strip of beach to the Gunny Hole, dragging the fish and the hastily coiled up line.

It was a good job that Mother did not see me as I struggled round that perilous point with the spume from the close-breaking waves thickening the driving snow. I wasn't sorry either that there was no one on the Slipway to stop me and ask questions. I didn't get into trouble at all on this occasion. For one thing we were very hard up, and Mother must have been glad to see so much food come into the house, and the size of the fish must have surprised her. But perhaps she was learning that it was no good fussing and that I could look after myself. Anyway, although she was worried about my wet things and my chattering teeth, she wasn't cross, and after I had changed and got warmed up with some hot tea, she actually allowed me to go out again and take the fish to Captain Bunny to show him, and have it weighed and also ask him if he'd like a piece for his supper.

The Captain *was* pleased. He got out his scales, and it weighed just under twenty pounds, and he had to admit that he had never caught one so big. But he said that scaur-lining wasn't a real sport. How much better it would have been if I'd hooked this on the spinner when we were railing. Think how it would have pulled. He was right, of course, but then we couldn't rail in winter time. He couldn't even launch the *Lydia* until the settled weather came in June. And I still think that scaur-lining was better than no fishing at all.

4

EVEN scaur-lining was no good in the spring and early summer, for at that time the cod go out to deep water for spawning. I had to go back to pennocking, always hoping that I would catch another bass or perhaps something even more exciting, but I never did. And again, the very thing that kept the pleasure boatmen ashore, the east and north-east winds, prevented pennocking for most days of the week and especially Saturdays. I remember such a Saturday in late spring when I started off with my pennock rod and line, not for Tom Bell Nick but for a scaur about half-way along the shore towards High Batts, where I thought I would experiment. There was deeper water than in the Nick, so there might be bigger fish. The sea was calm, but as I left the Slipway an east wind started to blow, and by the time I had got to the place the sea was already so rough that I knew it was no good trying. It was a bit late in the season for birdnesting, but I thought that if I went up Browe Beck Wood there was just a chance of my finding a water-hen's nest. I hadn't got a water-hen's egg in my collection.

There were two becks which flowed into Bramblewick Bay. The nearest one to the village was Garry Beck. This came down into a little cove, with Garry Nab (my south boundary) forming one side of it. About a hundred yards above high-water mark in the cove was the old mill and farm-house, and above this where the Mill Wood started, the Mill Dam, all this of course strictly out of bounds. But the Miller himself, and the Squire who owned it all, imposed a potentially stricter privacy here than Mother. Both were very fierce men. There were notices up by the mill itself and at all approaches to the wood, saying that trespassers would be prosecuted, and by the stream other notices saying that fishing was strictly forbidden. What made those notices more terrifying was that the Squire was also a magistrate, and that if ever a poacher was brought up at the Whitby Police Court, he always did his best to have that man severely punished. Not only that, but I had heard that he had once caught a man setting a hare trap on his land, and that he hadn't bothered to have him prosecuted, but thrashed him with a stick.

I had been in the wood many times bird-nesting, but I'd been careful not to be seen, and I don't think I had as much as thought of fishing. For one thing the trout you saw in the beck were very small, smaller than pennock. They were shy too, and always scurried under stones if you went near them.

Browe Beck, although another mile farther south of my boundary mark, and so farther out of bounds, had no mill or farm near it, and although it was supposed to be private there were no notices up. I had noticed that there were fish in it, but again they were small and shy, and I had no idea of fishing as I made my way towards it now. Indeed, I was feeling disappointed, and reluctant to abandon the scaurs for the doubtful prospect of finding a water-hen's nest. When I got to the mouth of the beck I found that the recent gales had piled the shingle and sand against it, forming a long pool, reaching quite a long way up the wood, which was not so tall as the Mill Wood, but with a thicker undergrowth of hazels and brambles. The pool was dirty. The rough seas had left a lot of wrack and tangles in it which were going rotten. But its surface was ringed with jumping fish, and I was surprised to see that they were much bigger than the trout I'd seen in the clear parts of the beck. I didn't doubt that they were trout. I knew also that quite apart from who owned the fishing you were supposed to have a licence to catch them. That did not bother me, for there was no one about, and anyway I didn't think I could catch them. I just thought I'd experiment. I knew I'd need a worm for bait. I soon found a small one under a stone, and not very hopefully threw in my line, just as if I had been pennocking. Almost instantly the float went under and out came my first fresh-water fish. It wasn't big enough to excite me very much, but it was certainly bigger than the usual pennock, and it was much prettier. It puzzled me too. It looked like a trout in many ways, yet it semeed more silvery, and it hadn't any red spots. It was a long time after that I discovered that it was a salmon smolt, and that even with a trout licence I should not have been allowed to catch it.

Actually they were greedier and easier to catch than pennocks. I was thrilled to think that I had discovered a sort of fishing that didn't depend so much on the weather. I forgot about the water-hen. I went on up the pool into the wood, and I think I must have caught well over a score when I had a sudden idea. These " trout " were plentiful and easy to catch because the pool was big and fairly deep and also rather dirty. The only thing against them was that they were all the same size, bigger than the usual pennock, it was true, but not so big as a small billet. Yet there was another pool like this, just as big and much deeper and never really clear. That was the Mill Dam. Might not the trout in that be just as plentiful but also bigger? Would the Squire have bothered to put all those notices up about fishing if the only fish to be caught were small ones such as you saw in the becks. I knew that the squire fished himself, for I had once seen him walking towards the Mill Wood with a fishing creel on his back and a rod in his hand. But I also remember that most times I had seen him he had been carrying a thick cane, probably the same one he had used for thrashing the poacher, and I tried not to think any more about the Mill Dam. But I couldn't get the temptation out of my mind and I began to lose all interest in the little " trout." I imagined myself stealing quietly down to the dam, and throwing in my line and perhaps catching an enormous trout my first try. Then I remembered that it was Saturday, and that I had actually passed the miller and his wife on the beach dressed in their best clothes, and evidently on their way to the railway station, and Whitby market. I remembered too that Saturday was Police Court day at Whitby, and the Squire would be there too. I did not know whether the court was held in the morning or afternoon, but I was certain that whenever I had been to Whitby on a Saturday with Dad or Mother, most of the farmers had come back on the five o'clock train, and that the Squire had been on it too. He travelled first class, and Dad always touched his hat to him.

I went on trying to fight the temptation, but it was no good. I caught one more " trout," then I lapped the line round my rod, and moved on up the wood to the shallow end of the pool, crossed the beck, and climbed up the opposite bank where there was a path which led up to the level of the cliff tops and across fields to the valley of Garry Beck. It would be safer going this way than along the beach to the Mill cove. I struck the Mill Wood some distance above the dam itself, climbed the barbed wire fence close to one of the " no trespassers " notice (I took care not to look at it) and then moved cautiously through the rather thin undergrowth until at last I caught the gleam of water. Here I stopped, with my rod flat on the ground, so that if I had suddenly seen someone I could have moved away from it. The wood, deep in the valley and protected from the sea wind, was very quiet. The only sound I could hear was a cooing wood pigeon. I waited a bit, then more cautiously than ever moved down towards a clump of hazels from which I reckoned I would have a view of the whole dam as far down as the wall. I squirmed on my belly the last few feet, and having reached the clump waited again and listened before raising my head and peering downwards. And then I almost stopped breathing with fright, for just below me on the opposite side of the dam, half hidden in a clump of willows and sedge, was the Squire himself, *fishing*.

In that first awful moment I thought he must have seen me for he was not more than twenty yards away. But he hadn't. I lowered my head and started to squirm backwards, leaving my rod of course. I'd scarcely moved however when I heard a splash and a sort of grunt from the Squire himself. I dared to lift my head, and saw a sight which for the time being made me forget the peril I was in. The Squire had hooked a fish. His rod was bent into a bow. His line cutting the surface of the water from side to side, just like our railing line had done when I had caught my first mackerel. But why didn't he pull the fish in ? I could almost have shouted in my anxiety. It seemed to be hooked firmly enough. Why didn't he get it into the bank, instead of allowing it to play about like that ?

It was my first lesson in real angling. In sea fishing our concern was always that our tackle should be stout, and that having hooked a fish, to get it in as quickly as possible. It dawned on me slowly that the Squire's tackle was very light, that he was drawing the fish in towards the bank, but gradually : that every time the fish gave a rush he eased the line out a bit, but reeled in when the rush slackened. Those rushes were becoming less violent. The fish itself, although I could not see it, was getting near the bank. Suddenly the Squire bent down and picked up what looked to me like a big butterfly net. Then he stepped forwards out of the willows, and, straightening his rod, dipped the net into the water and whipped it up again, I saw the gleam of the fish in it. He took it out, and I saw it clearly, and I felt disappointed, for though it was three times as big as any of the " trout " I had caught, it was no bigger, certainly not so big as the usual billet.

But the Squire seemed pleased with it. He was a stern looking man, but he was actually smiling as he took the fish off his hook, and put it in his creel, and prepared to go on fishing again. I was still well hidden in the hazels, and I did not think of how I was going to escape. I wondered what sort of bait he was using. I found out when he suddenly cast his line forward like the lash of a whip, and a tiny black dot fell lightly on the surface of the dam close to where another trout had just jumped. I saw that it wasn't a worm but an artificial fly, the same thing we used for billet except for its size and colour. My lesson continued. I saw how he jerked it gently through the water. I could not see it, but I guessed that its movements must be very life-like. But he did not catch another fish although they were jumping in every part of the dam. He went on casting, and I thought how much more interesting this was than just throwing your worm in and waiting for the float to jerk and then go under. I thought that I must certainly try it for myself the first chance I got. Suddenly a trout plopped out of the water just underneath an overhanging branch on my side of the dam. The Squire saw it and cast his fly towards it. But this time instead of the fly falling on the water it caught on a twig of the branch. The Squire looked angry. He jerked his rod. The fly held fast. He jerked again, and then I heard him growl, for the gut cast broke close up to the line, and dropped down limp to the water.

The branch was thin, and the oak from which it grew had its roots at the edge of a low shale cliff which fell straight into the deepest part of the water. The Squire was a big man, and I knew that he would never be able to reach either the fly or cast. He must have known that too, for he took a leather case out of his pocket, clearly to find another cast. But it soon became clear that he hadn't got one. He growled again, put the wallet back, and then tried to "hook" the broken cast with the tip of his rod. I felt really sorry for him, as he went on trying without success. I wished we had been friends, because I could have got it for him quite easily. Then to crown all he got the tip of his rod fast on a twig. He jerked at it savagely, and the top joint of the rod broke. He swore then, in spite of him being a magistrate, and a warden of the parish church, and a great friend of the vicar. But I still felt sorry for him, for it must have been awful seeing the fish jumping all over the dam, and not being able to go on catching them. And yet I wasn't really sorry when at last he took what was left of his rod to pieces, put it in a cloth case, and moved away in the direction of the dam wall from which a path led down to the Mill itself, where I guessed he was going to call before going home to the Hall. As the lane from the Mill to the Hall led through the wood in sight of the dam, there was no time to waste. I moved down to the oak tree, climbed the short bending trunk and wormed my way along the slender over-hanging branch until I was in reach of the cast. It was easy to disentangle it and the fly. I swarmed back, got to the ground again, coiled up the cast and carefully stowed it in my pocket. Then I made my way cautiously back to the hazel clump, picked up my pennock rod and retraced my footsteps to the edge of the wood, where, on the field side of the notice board which I would not read, I at last felt safe. I took out the cast and gloated over it. I knew it would not be safe to try it in the dam at present. The Squire might only be a few minutes at the Mill. But he might be longer. I was tempted to go back to Browe Beck and try it there. But it was getting late, and anyway the fish there were scarcely worth catching compared with the one the Squire had caught, and which, I had no doubt, I could catch too if I dared take the risk of being found and perhaps thrashed or taken to the police court as a poacher. That was not a very nice thought, and I decided that I had better go home now. I hadn't done so badly after all. I had got enough trout for a nice meal, and for once I'd managed to keep even my shore clothes and boots and stockings dry. But all the way home I kept on taking out the Squire's cast and fly to look at it, and I knew that in spite of the risk I would not be able to resist the temptation to try it in the dam for long.

Actually I did not wait longer than till Monday. The evenings were lengthening, and after a hurried tea I set off along the beach : and no one seeing me would have guessed I was going fishing at all, for I had decided that my old pennock rod was no good for fly-fishing. I needed a new one, more slender and whippy, as near like the Squire's as I could find. There was a lane that led up from Garry Cove on the opposite side to the Mill. I walked up this and just as I got opposite the Mill I saw the Miller himself, his clothes covered with flour, standing at the door of a shed, and looking it seemed in my direction. He was as fierce as the Squire about trespassers, and I'd known him terrify summer visitors by shouting at them when they tried to walk up to the wood. But I wasn't trespassing yet, and as my hands were thrust into my trousers pockets he could not have been suspicious. I was glad indeed to see him there, well away from the dam.

I was soon in the wood, on the same side from which I had watched the Squire fishing. It seemed quieter even than it had been then, although the wood pigeon was still cooing, and as I got near the dam I heard the plop, plop of trout. I was feeling terribly excited, but also a little bit frightened, and when suddenly a pheasant got up just by my feet I jumped as though someone had hit me and my fingers were actually trembling when I started to cut the longest and whippiest hazel from that very clump where I had hidden. All the time I was trimming it I kept stopping to listen for any one coming, but I heard nothing but the pigeon and the trout, and when it was all ready, with my line made fast to it, and the Squire's cast made fast to the line, my excitement overcame my fears, and I started to move up the wood to where the dam grew shallow and I could cross, for the banks were too steep and over-grown to fish from the side I was on. I crossed and moved dam-wards again. Here was a level belt of silted mud and sand from which grew sedges and willows, so thick in parts you could not see the water. But there were gaps, and I could see the Squire's footprints in the dried mud close to these, showing where he had stood while fishing. I chose the very place where he had stood when he caught his trout and then lost his cast. The trout were jumping everywhere, quite close in too, and I saw one much bigger than the one he had caught jump clean out of the water, just the length of my rod away, and I tried to throw the fly into the middle of the ring of ripples it made.

I was to discover at once what a difficult thing it is to throw a fluffy fly and a light cast straight out, and make the fly drop where you wanted it to. Instead of going straight out, the line just went in coils which fouled the fly itself. I had taken the precaution of lapping the other end of the line round the rod from the tip to the butt. I undid all this, and made the line longer. But the result was I got the whole thing in a raffle the first cast, and it took me a long time to clear it and get it back as I had it before. I tried a shorter

line. I did get the fly into the water then, but it gave me no space
to drag it with that gentle jerking movement practised by the
Squire. The trout kept on jumping, as though to mock me. I
began to realise that there was a knack in fly-fishing that might
take me a long time to learn, but that it also had a lot to do with
the rod. Thin though my hazel was at the tip it was nothing like
so thin and whippy as the Squire's. Could I find a better one? I
thought I might find a willow that would do, and I put my hazel
down against a stump with the fly just out of the water and moved
to the nearest willow tree. And then I got a dreadful fright. I heard
voices, and then the snapping of twigs just above me in the wood.
I turned and crouched down in the sedges close by my rod. The
voices and footsteps drew nearer. I daren't look, to see who it was.
I had no need to, for I recognised one of the voices as the Squire's,
the other as the Vicar's, and I had no doubt soon that they had
come to fish, and that I was trapped.

They stopped not more than ten yards away from me on the
wall end of the dam. I could hear every word they said. I hadn't
known that the Vicar went in for fishing, although I knew he
sometimes went shooting with the Squire, when he wore ordinary
clothes except for his round collar. He was supposed to be a very
kind man. He was rich and he used to send parcels of food and
clothing to the poor people in the village and grapes from his own
greenhouse to the sick. He had been kind to Dad too, for Dad
went to church every Sunday and was also a sidesman, and although
Mother was a Wesleyan, he had sent her some grapes when she'd
been ill. Dad was even more respectful to him than he was to the
Squire, but he was strict and stern and I had always been afraid of
him. Even if the Miller and the Police Sergeant had been with the
Squire I don't think I could have been more frightened. And to
make things worse, I heard the Vicar say:

"Well, you're right about the place being full of fish. And very
nice ones too. You must have kept the poachers away this time."

And the Squire's answer:

"Poachers. Yes. Now, last summer I must have caught a
least half a dozen of them at it. Visitors, of course. Fishing with
worm too, and one of them had actually got a set line. But the
Miller keeps a sharp lookout for any one coming up the stream or
down the wood. I saw a pounder last time I was here. They grow

at a great rate, you know, when they get deep water like this and plenty of snails to feed on. Now, we'd best start down here near the wall and work upwards. Did you say you had got a cast you could lend me, and a black gnat ? I lost mine. I'll have to get the Miller to trim the branches on that side."

There was silence during which I supposed they were getting their rods ready. I crouched as close to the ground as I could, wondering how long it would be before they found me and what I would say, for I didn't see how I could possibly escape. It wouldn't be so bad, I thought, if the Squire didn't know I'd been trying to fish : if I said I was bird-nesting or looking for flowers, only there weren't any flowers near the dam, and it was long past daffodil and primrose time. If only I could hide the rod, and above all my line and the Squire's cast and fly ! They'd started fishing now for I could hear the whip of their rods. I dared to glance at my own rod. I thought that I might drag it in, cut off the line and bury this in the mud. The rod I could push in among the willows so that it would not be seen. I seized the butt of the rod, and started very gently to pull it towards me. And then an extraordinary thing happened. I had left it with the fly itself just dangling out of the water. I must have made it jerk, and look exactly like a living fly, for I saw big trout, much bigger than the one I had seen jumping, shoot up out of the water, and grab it, and the next moment I felt a terrific tug at the rod itself.

I didn't think then of the Squire or the Vicar or the peril I was in. I just couldn't help pulling the rod in, and doing my best to catch the fish. Suddenly I saw it just below me where the muddy bank slanted steeply down a distance of about two feet. It charged straight in. The cast fouled a sunken branch of the old tree trunk. It brought the fish up with a jerk. Its mouth and gills opened. I bent down, pushed my fingers in its gill slit, and gave it a jerk upwards. And as I did so my knees slipped on the soft mud. I grabbed at the log with my free hand, but I was too late to save my balance and I dived sideways into the dam.

I don't know whether I shouted, but I must have made a big enough splash to bring the Squire and the Vicar rushing to the spot. I don't know whether it was the Squire or the Vicar who pulled me out. I do know that it was the Squire who got hold of me by my left arm a moment later when I was standing on the bank, and that he was shouting at me, and shaking me just like a terrier with a rat.

"Poaching. Poaching. Setting lines, you young devil," he kept saying. "I 'll teach you."

I suppose I was crying with the double fright of falling in the dam and being caught. I daren't look at either the Squire or the Vicar, but I suddenly realised that I was still clutching the trout, and I dropped it, it was still kicking a bit, on the ground. And then it was the Vicar who put his hand on my shoulder. He said to the Squire in quite a gentle and persuasive voice :

"Don't. Don't. He's only a little boy. He wouldn't know he was doing wrong," but he said to me in a sterner voice, "Didn't you know it was wrong to fish here ? Your father and mother would be very angry about it. Setting lines too. That's real poaching. You might be had up by the police for that."

Suddenly he seemed to notice the trout, and he bent down to look at it. And then he actually started laughing.

"Why, look at this, Will," he said to the Squire. "Here's a fly in its mouth, and a gut cast. Look there's the rascal's rod. He must have caught his fish fair at any rate."

He held the trout up. But I kept my eyes on the ground, for I thought that not even the Vicar could save me once the Squire saw his own fly and cast. And then, to my great surprise, the Squire relaxed his grip on my arm, and he said in a stern but nothing like such an angry voice :

"Where did you get this fly and gut, boy ?"

I thought it best to tell him the whole truth. I said I'd been getting flowers in the wood last Saturday because it had been too rough to fish in the sea. I'd seen him lose his fly and cast in the branch, and that I would have got it for him if I hadn't been afraid of what he would have said about my being in the wood at all. I just wanted to see if I could catch a trout with a fly. I hadn't been able to throw it properly. I wasn't actually fishing when the trout got on. It just got on by itself, by accident, but once it had got on I couldn't help trying to catch it. And I didn't want to keep the fish of course.

I did dare to look at the Squire then, for both he and the Vicar were laughing, but I could hardly believe it when he let go of my arm altogether and said to the Vicar :

"Well, I'm blessed. Did you ever hear such a story. Using my own gear to catch my own trout. And a very nice trout too. A long time since I caught one so big." And then he said to me sternly but not angrily : "Now be off home with you, boy, and get your wet clothes changed before you get your death of cold. And don't let me catch you here again or I'll put a stick across your backside."

I tried to say " thank you " and I started to go, but the Squire told me to stop. He took the trout from the Vicar, removed the fly and the cast, and then handed me the trout and said :

"Here. Take your fish with you. And don't forget. No more poaching or trespassing."

Actually I did not fish in the Mill Dam again for many, many years, not for fear of the Squire but because by his sporting act he had imposed a real gentleman's obligation on me. It cost me something in restraint, particularly when somewhere round my sixteenth birthday Dad gave me a real trout rod and a tackle case full of casts and flies he had picked up cheap at a Burnharbour auction sale, for there was then no trout fishing in the district comparable with that in the dam. The becks themselves were too shallow and too over-grown for fly-fishing, and as I have said, the fish were very small. Many times I was tempted, but even when I knew the Squire was away from home I did not fall : and perhaps it was from this restraint there grew an ambition : to be one day the owner of a stream, no matter how small so long as it contained fish. To clear it, and make at least one pool as big and deep as the Mill Dam. To see that the fish in it had plenty of food like the snails that fattened the Squire's fish. To watch them year after year grow bigger and bigger ! It was a dream, and like most dreams of youth, a selfish one. My pool would certainly be well fenced and marked private.

But in my youth trout fishing, even with real tackle, was only a makeshift of a sport : something to do only when the weather was too rough for the sea and the scaurs. And to a certain degree I still feel that about it, and I think the reason is that no matter how big and well stocked a stream or river may be, you know what sort of fish you are trying to catch : that any brown trout will look like any other brown trout except for its size, and that its size even to the wildest optimist is limited. Granted that the thrill of fly-fishing is in its subtleties, that a half-pound trout in a crystal clear stream

on a sunny windless day is nobler game than a ravenous cod that
would grab a bait on a boat-hook : that river salmon fishing with
rod and line (I have never had enough money to try it) may be the
noblest and most exciting fishing sport of all. I decry neither, but
I hold that salt-water fishing has a greater potential for excitement.
Half the thrill of angling surely is anticipatory, and in the sea, that
emotion is enhanced by mystery. The chances are that when you
are fishing for cod you will catch cod : but you never *know* : for
apart from that narrow ribbon of water at the tide's edge (and this
only in daylight and in fine weather), you can never *see* what is
going on below the surface. The probabilities may be proscribed :
the possibilities are as infinite as the sea itself.

Book Two

I

SCHOOL of course interfered with any sort of fishing activities, and more so when I was granted a scholarship at the new secondary school at Scarborough. I did not win this scholarship. Dad could not afford to pay any school fees. It took him all his time to pay the rent of our cottage and the grocery bills out of his painting, although, according to him, it would only be a matter of time before he was both famous and rich. Mother I think wanted me to be either a parson or a teacher. She had heard that the County Education Committee did grant scholarships to boys who wanted to become teachers, so she wrote to the Committee, and when she was told that I was too late for the examination, she went and saw the Secretary, and argued so well that he said they might give me a special " place " if the headmaster thought I was very suitable. So I had to go to the school for an interview.

I didn't want to become a teacher, and certainly not a parson. For one thing I hated religion, which up till then had stood for everything I didn't like, such as being in my best clothes on Sunday and sitting in chapel on Sunday School (instead of being out on the scaurs or up the becks) and listening to prayers and sermons and readings from the Bible. By this time too I was well on the way to becoming an atheist. A public library had been started in the village. The Vicar had begun by giving a lot of books out of his own library, and these of course were mostly religious books and very dull. But every one was asked to give what they could spare, and in the summer a visitors' concert was held, and with the money that was raised other books were bought second-hand, and also visitors were asked to send what they could from their own homes. One gentleman who used to stay at the Victoria Hotel every summer, and was very rich, actually sent two big crates of books. These were nearly all novels and there was a great rush on them at first. Then it was discovered that many of them were " improper " and the library committee had to hold a special meeting at which

47

it was decided that no book must be issued until the honorary librarian had read it and decided that it was suitable. The librarian was a retired business man from Bradford who had come to live in the place, and as he was a lay preacher, it was felt that he was as good a judge as the Vicar as to what was right. I didn't read any of these novels. I wanted adventure books. There were a few Hentys and Ballantynes and Clark Russells. These I had read with feverish zest, often by candlelight when Mother thought I was asleep, and it must have been because I had come to the end of them and because the title sounded like adventure that I took out *The Voyage of the Beagle*. This book I believe must have come in a big parcel that had been sent by the widow of another regular summer visitor to the village. He had been a doctor and his hobby had been collecting fossils and butterflies. Nearly all his books were on natural history, and scientific subjects, and naturally the librarian could not be expected to read these to see if they were all right, and at first they did not look very exciting to me. And to Mother, who usually kept an eagle eye on my reading, the *Voyage* must have seemed harmless enough. Evidently she made no connection between it and the infamous author of *The Origin of Species*. This also was issued to me by the unsuspecting librarian, and I had nearly finished it when she chanced to pick it up and see the name Charles Darwin on the title page.

She wrapped it in brown paper and took it round to the librarian at once, holding the parcel as though it contained a bottle of deadly germs. What transpired then I never knew for certain, but Mother was a terror when her puritanical instincts were outraged, and I have no doubt that he got a severe wigging on his public responsibilities even if she did not go so far as to accuse him of trying to poison my mind by letting me have such a wicked book. Poor Charles Darwin ! Neither of them had read the *Origin* of course. And no one else in the village got the chance of reading that copy, for it disappeared, along with the *Voyage* and another of Darwin's which I had not read. But this expurgation was confined only to the name of the author, and did not embrace the rest of the deceased doctor's collection, which included Haeckel's *Riddle of the Universe*. Compared with this *The Origin of Species* was as innocent as *Pilgrim's Progress* !

I didn't want to be a teacher or a parson, and I didn't want to go to a new school. I wanted to go to sea, and in particular on a ship like the *Beagle*, catching queer fish and animals in foreign seas and countries. I had not been a bright scholar at the village school except in geography and writing compositions in anything that interested me, like fishing or birds' eggs. I hated arithmetic and spelling and history. If the headmaster of the Scarborough school (his name was Tetley) had asked me to give him the dates of the Norman kings, or do any hard sums, or parse a sentence or do some dictation, he would have had to give up straight away. But he must have been a man ahead of his time as a teacher, and a shrewd psychologist. First he was very kind in his manner, so that I did not feel afraid of him : then he made me talk about dad and mother, and my life at Bramblewick, and the things I liked doing and what I wanted to be when I grew up. I told him about fishing and my collection of birds' eggs, which included a cormorant's and a cuckoo's and a sparrow hawk's, and he encouraged me by telling me that he'd collected eggs once but he'd never found a cuckoo's : and that he liked fishing only didn't often have time for it.

I liked him, but I felt it was no use telling him any lies, and I still didn't want to go to his school. I did not tell him that I had read *The Origin of Species* and the *Riddle of the Universe*, and that I thought the story of the creation in the Bible was just a fairy tale. But I told him about the *Voyage of the Beagle*, and that I wanted to be a naturalist like Charles Darwin, and that really I wanted to go to sea at once, if only as a cabin boy. When he asked me straight out if I wanted to be a school teacher, I thought of Mother, and how anxious she was that I should go to this school, but I had to say no. Then he told me to come with him, and he took me all over the school, which as I have said was new, and as much like our village school as a cottage is like a church. Actually it was one of the first secondary schools in this country, and it had been designed and built and equipped regardless of expense. It was for boys and girls, but not Co-ed, the boys' classrooms being on the north side, the girls south of a big assembly hall on the first floor. On the second floor, reached by staircases from both wings, were chemistry and physics laboratories, a large lecture theatre, and an art room, these used alternately by girls and boys. On the ground floor was a wood-work and metal-work room for the boys : domestic science kitchens and laundries for the girls, a gymnasium, with trapezes, vaulting horses, springboards and climbing ladders, as well as a dining-room for country scholars.

I could hardly believe that this was a school, especially as being in the holidays, there were no scholars. I felt as though I was being shown round a museum when I saw the chemistry lab., with a sink and two shelves of chemicals for each student and a balance and bunsen burner, and a cupboard containing flasks and retorts and crucibles and test-tubes. The physics laboratory was equally fascinating. There were all sorts of electric machines, collections of little brass pulleys, coils of spring and wire, magnets, compasses and thermometers. There was a magic lantern in the lecture theatre, and the windows had blinds for making it quite dark. In the wood-work room were real carpenters' benches with vices and racks of tools. In the metal-work room was a forge and a lathe, and Mr. Tetley showed me some of the things the boys had made or were making. They included book-cases, and carved paper knives and trays, and model ships and steam engines and even sledges and roller skates. Finally, he took me into the school library. There were hundreds of boys' adventure books as well as plenty of books on natural history, including what was probably the first of Cherry and Richard Kearton's books on bird photography, illustrated with the most wonderful pictures they had taken by hiding in blinds and even by disguising themselves as sheep and cows. To my astonishment and delight, Mr. Tetley told me I could borrow this book and keep it for at least a week : and then he told me that he was very pleased to find a boy so interested in natural history and outdoor life, but that it was no good my thinking I could go on doing nothing but fishing and collecting birds' eggs, and that I must think seriously of how I was going to earn my living when I grew up. Although I might not want to become a teacher now I might do later, and teaching didn't mean that I'd just have to teach in a village school. If I was very clever I might in time become a university professor. Many of the world's greatest scientists and naturalists had been that. Some of them had travelled too, and explored and seen a great deal more of the world than an ordinary sailor could. And whatever I wanted to become I must be educated. All the best positions went to young men who had got university degrees. If I went to this school say for three years,

I would be able to sit for and pass the matriculation examination. That would enable me to enter a university, and if my father could not afford by then to pay the fees I might win a scholarship, even to Oxford or Cambridge, with enough money to live on as well as all the fees paid.

He was a remarkable man. He was tall and supple with loose joints so that when he walked he seemed to wave to and fro like a cat, and he kept his hands clasped behind him and his shoulders were slightly arched. He wore rubber heels on his shoes too, and although I don't think he did this on purpose he could be in a room several moments before you knew it, and if you happened to be in mischief, as, for example, mixing all the chemicals on your shelves while the chemistry teacher was out of the laboratory, or experimenting with the hot-water radiator taps, or the electric light switches during break, you'd suddenly look round and found he was watching you. But what I remember best about his appearance was his eyes. They were light grey, and he wore thick-lensed spectacles which magnified them in a peculiar way so that they seemed to look straight through you into your mind. He was religious but there was no cant about him. He was somewhat of a poet too, and a mystic. I remember that once towards the end of my ill-starred career at that school, by which time I had managed to get into the sixth form, he gave us a lecture on the appreciation of poetry. I can't remember the context, but he suddenly asked me if I believed in ghosts, and I, with an arrogant confidence born of my secret studies, said no. He smiled and a peculiar far-away look came into his eyes as he looked, not at us, but through the classroom window. "Oh," he said very slowly and quietly, and I don't think he was trying to be sarcastic. "Thus speaks the cold voice of science. But the poet says 'There are more things in heaven and earth than are dreamed of in your philosophy.' Who knows . . . Who knows!"

He aroused in me from the day of our first interview an affection that survived the many unfortunate conflicts of our association, even that episode when he gave me the choice of expulsion or a caning. I had played truant for nearly a week at a time when I ought to have been swotting for the end-of-term exams, and I had forged a letter from Mother saying that I'd been suffering from a bad cold which she thought might be the start of something infectious. Conversely, I had explained to her that school was closed because of an epidemic of mumps. I think I'd have got away with the double deception if I hadn't spelt infection wrong in my letters. I chose the caning for various reasons, not the least of them being Mr. Tetley's remark that by expelling me he would have to admit to the Education Committee that he had made a grave mistake in first recommending me for a scholarship. I felt rather proud of the fact that although he gave me a dozen strokes across my bent backside, so that I could not sit down in comfort for several days, I did not cry, and I think that must have pleased him too. But to my lasting regret I was never able to give him tangible proof that his belief in me had in any way been justified. Even then, although no one at the school knew it, he was suffering from an incurable tumour which at times must have given him great pain. He died soon after I left, and before I had written my first "scientific" article in the *Whitby Gazette*, which I would have especially liked him to have seen, for it would have given an explanation if not an excuse for my delinquency.

I had not played truant on that particular occasion to go fishing. Having found Lyell's *Principles of Geology* in the local library I had read it with as much zest as Darwin and Haeckel, and I had gone crazy on fossil hunting. The Yorkshire lias was famous for its fossils, and our own Bay was itself a very famous collecting ground. Each scaur (which hitherto I had thought of only in relation to fishing and the getting of bait) represented a definite zone in the lias formation, and had its characteristic fossils, chiefly ammonites. These had been regarded as one-time snakes by the natives of the coast and had given rise to the legend of St. Hilda, Abbess of Whitby, turning them into stone. By her holy magic she had also beheaded and neatly coiled them. It was no disproof of this legend that specimens had been found complete with heads and forked tongues, and were on sale in the Whitby jet ornament shops at fantastic prices. In such a wholesale feat of extermination even a saint might miss a few. But I knew from my Lyell that ammonites were not snakes but fossilised shells of marine animals belonging to the same family as the squid and the octopus : that the reason they had no heads was that the soft part of the animal would decompose very quickly. The specimens in the Whitby shops were fakes, and it was proved later that they were the work of the celebrated Flint Jack, who had hoodwinked even the British Museum into buying many of his "pre-historic" flint arrow and spear heads.

But on a patch of scaur close to low-water mark not far from the place where I had caught my famous cod, I had found the best proof of all that the legend of St. Hilda was false : a large and perfect ammonite, showing beyond where the shell ended the impression of what certainly resembled several octopus-like tentacles. I imagined even that on one of these were the remains of the suckers by which the squids and octopus hold their prey. The thing was imbedded in hard ironstone on the scaur top. I would have had no difficulty in getting the ammonite out with my hammer and chisel, but the impression of the body was thin, and to obtain the whole specimen in one piece meant digging out a slab at least a foot square and nine inches thick. It was a Saturday morning, with the tide already flowing. I had to be content with marking the place. Sunday morning Mother insisted on my going to chapel with her. I daren't play truant on Monday, for someone certainly would have seen me on the beach. She seemed a bit surprised when I told her at tea time that school was closed because of mumps, but she did not seem suspicious. In fact, she was really frightened and wanted to know if I had been sitting next to any of the boys who were ill, so to relieve her mind I told her it was only some of the girls who had got it. She made me gargle my throat with carbolic.

The tide only allowed me two hours each day to work on my fossil, and the stone was almost as hard as flint and would not split. In order to get my depth I had to carve a trench at least six inches wide, and it was not until Friday that I was deep enough to risk the final operation of driving my chisel under the entire slab and wedging it free. I think I was more excited then than I had ever been with fishing, but it was the same sort of excitement in a way. So far as I had been able to make out no one had yet discovered an ammonite showing its tentacles. Even Darwin himself might have been proud to have found such a thing. If only I could get it out without damage ! I would write to the British Museum about it. They would probably want to buy it. I would get a lot of money for it, and perhaps become quite famous.

Alas ! I was not to land that fish of the Jurassic Sea. Perhaps I was too excited. Perhaps I was too worried by the incoming tide, or perhaps it was an act of rough justice : for I hammered too hard. The slab did split from the solid rock, but it also split in a hundred different directions, like a pane of glass, and the vital part of it split laterally, shattering the impression of the tentacles into innumerable little chips that no one could possibly have stuck together again.

It's funny to think that what made me a failure at school was studying things like geology, and astronomy, and evolution and philosophy and other subjects which were not taught at school at all. It was not the fault of Mr. Tetley or any of the other masters, who were all very kind and patient. I was not a complete failure. I actually shone in chemistry, physics, geography and wood-work, and staggered each of my form masters in succession by being top in Scripture. This delighted Mother and made her much more hopeful about my future. I was consistently bottom or near bottom in most other subjects. I hated every branch of mathematics. History bored me. So did English, and it was years before I overcame my antipathy to Shakespeare, bred, I think, by spending an entire term on *Macbeth*, reading it piecemeal, learning disconnected speeches off by heart, doing dictation from it, analysing and parsing, but never *acting* it. Occasionally even in these subjects I would gladden the teacher's heart by showing a gleam of interest and ability. If a history lesson verged on the subject of archaeology, tumuli or flint arrowheads (such as I had already found on our moors), I was very bright. In English I shone at precis writing, and once got full marks by reducing a long-winded page of Lord Macaulay's *Warren Hastings* to a short paragraph, but this ability I think arose chiefly from a natural indolence and a desire to avoid spelling long and difficult words. I was hopeless at Latin and French, yet because fossils and birds had Latin names, I would often surprise the teacher with my vocabulary, and by adroit guessing I often made quite brilliant translations of French " unseens." My reports bore with montonous regularity such phrases as, " Has ability but lacks power to concentrate " : " Shows promise but lacks sufficient energy and interest to make progress " : " Careless and inattentive " : relieved only by the remarks of the chemistry master, Mr. Grist, and the physics master, Mr. Halliday (for both of whom I had an admiration amounting almost to hero-worship), who praised my ability and enthusiasm, especially in practical work, with the qualification that I was apt to be careless and inaccurate in any work involving mathematical calculations.

I was a fool of course, and later I was to regret my wasted opportunities, for it was a good school, unique in its day. I failed in the matric. I had the awful experience of not being able to answer a single question in the history and arithmetic papers and my sheets were blank sheets. But the Education Committee wanted their pound of flesh in return for the free schooling they had given me and saw that I passed what was known as the Preliminary Certificate Examination, which qualified me to take a post as an " uncertificated " teacher in an elementary school. As Dad's ship still hadn't come in and we were still desperately poor, I took the job as assistant in our own village school, under a " head " who had recently replaced the retired " Slogger." I loathed it, and I am certain that I would have chucked it and risked breaking Mother's heart by going to sea but for a very dramatic occurrence. The zoological departments of Leeds and Sheffield Universities had decided to open a marine biological Station in the village. They had bought the old Coastguard Station, which forms one of the village ramparts against the sea by the Slipway. They were equipping it with benches and tanks for keeping live marine animals, and they wanted someone to act as a sort of curator-caretaker, preferably someone who knew the beaches and would be able to assist in the collection of specimens. I got the job. They could only pay five shillings a week, but as there were no specified hours, I could still carry on at the school.

My position at first was little more than that of a laboratory boy. I stood in complete awe of the professors, although one of them, Professor Denny of Sheffield, didn't look a bit like what I imagined a professor should be. He was very short and dapper in smart town clothes, and in spite of him being so interested in marine animals, he would never leave the dry part of the beach or scaurs or set foot in a boat. I found out that he was really famous because, with another professor whose name I think was Myell, he had written a book about the cockroach and that this was regarded as a standard work in universities all over the world. It was the result of years of research, and I couldn't help thinking it was funny that a man should be so interested in an ugly and repulsive creature as to write a book about it unless of course, like the mosquito or the tsetse fly, it had something to do with the carrying of disease. Actually the book had nothing to do with the creature's habits but dealt with its anatomy. The cockroach was regarded as the " type " insect, just as the frog was regarded as the " type " amphibian, and the rabbit as the " type " mammal. Studying the anatomy of these animals made it easier for the student to understand the anatomy of others including man himself.

The laboratory was not intended to be a whole-time teaching establishment, but just to give a short course for the zoology students of both universities, and it wasn't just for marine biology either. The Leeds professor, Walter Garstang, specialised on birds. He certainly looked more like a real scientist. He was untidy and always wore rough tweeds and heavy boots. He didn't mind wading into pools, but the thing that interested him most was listening to the singing of wild birds. For this he would lie for hours in woods and copses, or close to streams and bogs, hiding himself just like the Keartons did to get their photographs. He could tell what any bird was just by its song, and also he could whistle these songs in the most astounding way ; and again it was funny to see him perhaps standing in front of some of his students, looking very tense and serious, and whistling the song of a blackbird to them ! I think that the professor and most of the students regarded the course almost as a holiday, for they only came for regular stays in spring and summer. I was very envious of the students. They certainly did do some work. They had microscopes. In the laboratory they dissected worms and sea anemones and shore-crabs, and made drawings and notes, but all I had to do was help collect these things and clean up after them, and I was never asked to listen to any of the lectures the professor gave. There were girl as well as men students. Some of them were going to be teachers, some of them doctors, but I don't think that any of them wanted to be real scientists and go off on expeditions as I did, and yet I was realising more and more the truth of what Mr. Tetley had said about the value of an education and going to a university. What a fool I had been not to have worked harder at school and pass my matric.

What made things worse was that I fell in love with one of the girl students. She was the sister of one of the demonstrators from Leeds, who himself had held an appointment in the University of

Chicago. Her name was Adeline. She had some Jewish blood in her. She was dark, almost Spanish looking, with lovely eyes and complexion and a dazzling smile. I did my best to attract her attention by finding her the biggest sand worms and shore crabs to cut up, but she was completely gone on a tall and athletic medical student who was a friend of her brother, and she never gave me the slightest sign that she was aware of my existence let alone of my yearning adoration.

And then in the autumn of the first year of this far from satisfying job, when the professors and students had all gone back, came Sam Wilson. The laboratory itself was in the old watchhouse, whose windows (one with a small shuttered hole for the coastguard's telescope) faced the sea. But next to this, and part of the property the universities had bought, was the chief officer's cottage, roughly furnished as a hostel for the students. I'd had a letter from Professor Denny of Sheffield to say that one of his senior students was coming to the laboratory for several months to carry out some important research work, and that he hoped I would give him every assistance. He would be living in the cottage. I had also received a letter from Sam himself, very curt and business-like, telling me the time of his arrival and asking me to buy bread and various groceries for him for which he'd settle on his arrival. These letters did not excite me very much. I had reached a sort of doldrums in my life. I had long exhausted the scientific books and treatises in the local library. I had fallen back on the novels, notably the highly-coloured romances of Robert W. Chambers, and even Charles Garvice (a better writer than most of us would care to admit), and, frustrated in my passion for the disdainful dark-eyed student, I was full of dreams and yearnings and very much in love with love. I hated teaching in the village school more than I had hated being a scholar, for I could never play truant when things got too much for me. My interest in geology was declining. There was still fishing, but Captain Bunny was dead. The *Lydia* had been sold to a Whitby fisherman to carry on his deep-sea mule. And from the time I'd started going to Scarborough school, and more so since my association with the " people " at the " lab.," I'd drawn apart from the village folk, especially the fishermen. Always a " foreigner," they regarded me now almost as a visitor. I could fish where I liked, and stay out as long as I liked without worrying Mother. I had got a real surf rod too, and I had found dozens of places along the cliffs where at high water and after dusk you could get excellent sport with cod. But I was getting sick of the whole place. I yearned for coral seas and islands, and brighter fish than cod, and more than anything for a dark-eyed, sunburnt girl, for I had also read *The Blue Lagoon*, although I had not found that in the local library !

But Sam came into my life with greater force than any love affair. I can see him now as he stepped out of the railway carriage, with a cheap suitcase and a fishing rod in one hand, a microscope case in the other, a rucksack, and at least two haversacks on his back : his round ruddy face wreathed in smiles as he saw and recognised me as the youth described to him by the professor. He dropped the suitcase and grasped my hand like a vice.

" Ah," he said. " I was hoping you'd meet me. Mind these a moment, will you ? Got a lot more things in the van. Trunk and a lot of gear. Won't be a minute, but mind—that's a super Leitz high power mike. Denny's own. Don't let any one bump into it."

He was a tornado, utterly overwhelming me. He never once stopped talking all the way down to the village except to give me time to say a quick answer to the scores of questions he literally shot at me, and I don't know whether he listened to those answers or not, but I think he did. He let me carry his suitcase, which must have been full of books by the weight of it, and one of the haversacks, which he warned me to be careful of as it contained some very special dyes. He carried the microscope and another box, but of course his heavy luggage and gear had been left for the porter.

He had never been on this part of the Yorkshire coast before, but he'd been reading a guide book and studying maps and wanted to know if that cliff was High Batts and that Low Batts, and if this was the station road we were on or the one that led down to the Dock, with the laboratory just on the side of the Slipway and not far from the lifeboat house and the post office which was marked on his map. He said he knew a lot about the village from the book he had read, but that of course wasn't the same as seeing it for yourself, and that he believed in getting everything first-hand if he could. It was like that in science. Read and listen to what other people said, but don't take anything for gospel until you could prove it for yourself. Be sceptical. Always keep your mind alert. Beware of dogma.

There was no need for me to point out the laboratory and the cottage to him. He stepped into the latter as though it was his own home, put down his things on the table, lit the gas and made an approving remark about the nice fire I had made for him. He looked at the pile of groceries I had put on the table along with the bill. He checked this carefully, and gave me the cash for it, then he lifted the lid of the kettle, saw that it was boiling, then without asking me where to find it, opened the fireside cupboard and took out the frying pan.,

" A meal first. We can talk better with our bellies full. Ham and eggs. Can't beat it. Manage two eggs ? I could eat six. But fish are nice for a change. Denny tells me the fishing here's good, and that you are the chap who knows all about it. Have a look at that rod later and tell me if it's the thing we need here, only we shan't have much time for fishing. I've got to find a Nudibranch, *Doto coronata*. There are records of it on the Yorkshire coast, but not so far from this place. Lives on a hydrozoan, *Sertularia*, found under stones close to *Laminarian* zone. I want thousands of them. But I'll tell you all about that when we've had a meal."

During that meal, which I was too bewildered to enjoy, Sam cross-examined me as to my own history. That did not prevent him from giving me a concise summary of his own. He was Yorkshire born and bred. His father owned a timber sawmill at Conisborough near Rotherham. A self-made man. Chief trade of mill was elm bobbins for otter trawls. Both father and mother very religious. Father local preacher. Two sisters, one secretary at mill, other still at school. Sam third of four brothers, elder two in mill. School career in one respect similar to my own. Scholarship to secondary school, but no fooling there or playing truant. Top most subjects most of time. Matric. easy going. Scholarship to Sheffield University. Strong on science. B.Sc. a walk-over. Could have taken teaching job at once, science in a secondary school but no teaching for Sam, if Sam could help it, least not the ordinary sort. Not enough brass in it! A professorship perhaps. Not that there was much brass in that job by itself. But it gave you a reputation. You could pick up fat fees as a consultant, and science, applied science, was the coming thing. Industry was going to depend more and more on the scientific expert, chemists, physicists, geologists, metallurgists, yes, and biologists. Even in a sawmill like

Wilson's of Conisborough you saw the possibilities. But the old man, if pretty shrewd in most respects, was a bit of a stick-in-the-mud, and resented most of Sam's ideas. Not that Sam wanted to enter the business. Too small for one thing. Hadn't in fact decided yet exactly what he was going to do in the way of money earning, but it would have to at least lead to something big, and biology at present was the thing that interested him most. He'd got a research grant and an extension of his scholarship. This Nudibranch (I had picked up enough marine biology to know that nudibranchs were sea-slugs) was infested by a small parasitic crustacean called *Splanchnotrophus* which actually attacked its host's reproductory organs and rendered them infertile. But very little work had been done on it and its life history was one of the mysteries of biology. That was the history he had to investigate during the next twelve months. There was nothing of direct economic importance about *Doto coronata* of course, or its parasite. It was not a human food and it wasn't the food of any particular fish. But anything new that could be discovered in parasitology increased the sum knowledge of the subject, and might lead anywhere, even very indirectly to a cure, say, for cancer. Apart from that the results of the investigation recorded by Sam and printed in one of the scientific journals would be a permanent tribute to his ability as a research scientist and a valuable testimonial when he came to apply for a job.

I hadn't felt so excited about anything for a long time, especially as Sam kept on referring to " us " as though it had all been arranged that I should assist him. I'd never met any one so enthusiastic and energetic, and his " bossiness " didn't worry me a bit, although I still felt bewildered. He asked me a lot of questions about the beach and the fish and other animals that were found in the pools. I was surprised to find that although he had spent only a few short holidays by the sea he knew a lot more about the smaller fish and animals than I did, and of course he called them all by their Latin names. I had to admit my ignorance, and he became very serious. He told me (what I already knew) that I'd been a fool not to have studied properly and passed the matric. and gone to a university, and that if I was going to do anything big in life I must start now and make up for lost time. I wasn't too late to pass my matric. If I could do that it might just be possible to wangle some sort of a university scholarship through my connection with the laboratory. Professor Denny had told him that I showed promise and that it was a pity that I was doing nothing but teach in a village school. Why not start studying again? Here was a chance to get a sound groundwork in zoology, so that I'd have one subject up my sleeve when I came to sit for a science degree. Anything would be possible then: naturalist on a scientific expedition, deep sea research, exploration, Colonial Government naturalist, even a job with Arctic explorers like Scott and Shackleton. Why not make up my mind to be a qualified marine zoologist? He'd teach me the elements of zoology, anatomy, physiology. He'd lend me all the necessary text books and apparatus.

We were interrupted by the arrival of the out-porter. We dumped Sam's personal baggage in the cottage, and carried the heavy packing cases into the laboratory, where also I'd got a good fire going. It was a long narrow room with a low ceiling, and it was slightly curved, following the shape of the outer walls, which were built up directly from the beach and were awash long before high water. This wall was bellied to repel the force of the waves, which in stormy weather would break and wash high over the roof. There were two windows in addition to the one with the telescope shutter. There was a wide bench like the bar of a railway refreshment room running the whole length of the front wall, with a sink at the end, and high stools for the students. There were points for bunsen burners.

In spite that he seemed to have known exactly what to expect, Sam was surprised when he saw how bright and cosy the place looked, and said it was just about ideal for any one who had to do research work. He opened all the cupboards to see what was inside them. There were winchesters of alcohol and formalin and tiny bottles of analine dyes, and plenty of test-tubes and flasks and beakers, but he said rather contemptuously that these things were just the gear required by ordinary students doing a short course in marine zoology, and we started to unpack his cases. He told me, and somehow or other it didn't seem like boasting, that the professor regarded him as his most brilliant student, and in addition to lending him his own microscope had told him to bring anything he wanted from the university laboratory. There was another microscope which, Sam explained, was of low power and just used for dissecting, and there were some wonderful mounted lenses used for the same purpose or for watching living animals. There was a microscope camera, several large glass tanks for live marine animals, scores of bottles of various chemicals, boxes of microscope slides, test tubes and dishes and flasks and beakers, and an apparatus like a grocer's bacon machine, which he said was called a microtome and was used for making slices of a specimen so thin that you could see through them with the microscope, and study the formation of the cells.

We cleared one of the cupboards of the students' things and arranged all this new gear on the shelves. Then Sam opened a case which contained nothing but books, and scientific journals and papers. One, a very big volume, was called *British Nudibranchiata* ; and Sam handled it almost as though it were sacred. He took it to the bench and opened it at a place marked with a piece of paper. There was a large coloured plate showing an animal which in shape resembled an ordinary garden slug. But instead of having a smooth back there were protuberances like branches of coral all the way down from the head to the tail, and they were beautifully mottled in pale blue and light amber and dark brown.

" There you are ! " he said dramatically. " *Doti coronata* ! Ever spotted him here ? "

I had to say no. The fact was that hitherto I had known of only one sea-slug, a fat ugly creature called the sea lemon, which indeed looked like a lemon sliced from top to bottom. I'd tried these for bait on my scaur-lines but never with success.

" Ah—I'm not surprised," Sam answered. " This is an enlargement of course. A big specimen measures only about a quarter of an inch. But the author says they're common enough on the Yorkshire coast." He turned to another plate showing another species of slug. " What about this chap, *Ancula cristata* ? "

Ancula was even more beautiful than *Doto*. Its body was a pale pearly blue. The protuberances, instead of being continuous from head to tail, formed a sort of ring in the middle of the back just like a flower, and each one was tipped with a spot of bright orange. Sam went on turning the plates. The pictures themselves were beautifully engraved and tinted. I was to learn later that from this fact alone the book, which had been published many years before, was regarded as a classic, and it was likely that the author would have made a very big name for himself as an artist if his life's work hadn't been sea-slugs. But I could hardly believe that such lovely creatures could exist on the scaurs and pools of my own Bay without my ever noticing them. There were scores of different species as unlike to each other in appearance as different species of butterflies, and nearly all were just as beautiful. Sam explained that the protuberances were of two sorts. Those that looked like tentacles contained part of the animal's digestive system, and were called papillæ. The feathery ones were gills, the word " nudibranch " meaning " naked gill." He insisted that at least half of them were common on the Yorkshire coast on rocks and in pools exposed by the tide, and that we'd have no difficulty in identifying many of them on our first expedition. Our main job of course was to find *Doto*, but it wouldn't be a bad idea to start making a record of all the animals we could find, a faunistic survey of the beach. He'd brought all the books necessary for identification. I must make a drawing of every specimen with notes of habitat, etc. That would impress Denny when it came to discussing the problem of my getting into the university. It was quite on the cards that we'd find something not recorded at all in Britain, perhaps an entirely new species. In that case it might even be given the name of its finder along with its specific name.

I was enthralled. Already I had a glamorous vision of myself as marine biologist to an expedition to the South Seas, voyaging in a white-sailed schooner : anchoring in quiet lagoons, fishing and catching all sorts of fascinating animals in the water and ashore : seeing parrots and monkeys and land crabs, natives in war canoes, and lovely Kanaka girls dancing in the moonlight !

My excitement was damped by a sudden dread that, in spite of Sam's confidence, we should not be able to find his precious *Doto coronata*. Surely if it was common I must have noticed at least one specimen the thousands of times I'd hunted the scaurs and pools at low-water mark for bait. Again Sam reassured me. He closed the book and put it very carefully on one of the cupboard shelves. Then he took a small notebook from his pocket and consulted it.

" Low water to-morrow at nine fifty-three. We're two days from full moon and the lowest springs. That gives us at least six good collecting days. Pity you've got to be at school during the week, but we've got to-morrow and Sunday. We ought to be on the beach at eight, and work the tide down. You'd better come and have breakfast with me. Any objection to working on a Sunday?"

"No," I said fervently.

"Ah. Believe in God?"

"No. Least not the god we're taught about in chapel and Sunday school."

"Correct scientific attitude. Don't believe in anything until you can prove it. Agnostic myself. Safer and more scientific than downright atheism. But I like hymns. Can you sing?"

I felt myself blushing.

"No. At least not much. I was in the local choral for one season, but got sick of it."

"Bass or tenor?"

"Bass."

"Good. I'm tenor myself. We can harmonise."

Sam opened another parcel, and to my amazement took out an accordion. He told me to pull a stool up to the fire, and he took one himself and started playing "Jerusalem the Golden," singing the air in quite a good voice. I found myself first humming and then actually singing a bass accompaniment. Sam took up the real tenor part, and when we got to the second verse I think we'd have done credit to a Salvation Army meeting. I wondered what Mother would have thought if she had seen and heard me now singing a hymn with such gusto, for I had resisted all her efforts to persuade me to join the chapel choir. Certainly she would have been surprised and pleased : and even more so if she had known that I was determined to start studying again, even the subjects I hated like history and mathematics, and sit for and pass my matric. and go to a university and make a great success of my life, if not as a teacher or a clergyman, at least as something she would be proud of.

I was as excited next day as I'd ever been at the start of a fishing trip with Captain Bunny. Sam had got a six-inch ordnance survey map of the Bay that showed every scaur down to low-water mark, and he had made a tracing of this to take with us. We were to explore the whole area systematically, marking on the map every specimen we found except, of course, such things as limpets and mussels and winkles and the common anemones. We had two large glass jars for bigger things, and corked tubes for small specimens. The tide was about half-way down and we started work on the scaur that led to Tom Bell Nick.

Although the scaurs themselves were of hard rock they were criss-crossed with narrow fissures which in places made pools several inches deep. In these grew a species of pinkish weed with hard calcareous stems that almost resembled coral. In fact its Latin name was *Coralina*.

I'd never bothered to look closely into any of these pools. They were a favourite place for the ordinary red anemone, but this was no good for bait, and you'd never find scaur cocks so far from low water. I thought Sam was wasting his time when he knelt down by one of them and started poking about in it. Suddenly he cried—

" Ah—here we are. Look at this."

He had taken a large pair of forceps from his pocket and was pointing with it to an ordinary anemone. At first I couldn't see anything to be excited about in that, but when I looked very closely I noticed that what might easily have been taken for a clump of that pinkish weed pressed against the anemone's body. Now I saw that this was actually moving very slightly and was not weed at all but an animal. Sam gripped it lightly with his forceps, popped it in a tube that he'd filled with water and held it up. For a moment it was quite still and shapeless, then it began to move and unfold itself, and I saw without Sam telling me that it was a sea-slug, one of those illustrated in the book, and noted as one of the commonest of all. I felt quite furious that a man who had lived far away from the sea all his life should come on to my own scaurs and straight away find something I had never even seen. But Sam didn't sound a bit triumphant or cocky about it.

" *Eolis papillosa*," he said. " Least I think so but we'll look it up when we get back to the lab. See what it was doing ? Browsing on the anemone. Chewing it away. Characteristic habit of nudi-branchs. *Doto* feeds on *Sertularia*, which is a zoophyte and a sort of anemone. Pretty brute, isn't it ? "

Sam was holding the tube sideways. The slug was now fully unfolded and moving with its " horns " extended, and its pappilæ erect and slightly undulating. These were not knobbed like those of *Doto*, but looked exactly like the tentacles of the anemone on which it had been feeding, and were mottled and tinted in a sort of combined imitation of that and the weed.

C

"Protective colouration and form," said Sam. "No wonder you didn't see it when you weren't specially looking. And it's the brightest colours often are the most deceptive. You've got to consider them always against their background. Red spots on a trout for example. Conspicuous enough when your trout is lying on a plate. But not against a bed of gravel . . . Wonder what else we can find in this little pool. Hang it, it doesn't contain more than two gallons of sea water. Never mind the weed, but there's at least three species apart from *Coralina*. Look, there's a gammarid, you'd call it a sand-hopper ; there's an immature shore-crab, and the shells of at least three more close to that anemone, which may have been the next one on our nudibranch's list. And look down there in that little crack. Another anemone, that's the daisy ane-mone, and close to it, see those fine red filaments that look almost like tentacles ? That's the gills of a worm, *Sabellaria* most likely. I bet we'd find more species if we examined the weed with a lens."

I was amazed, and not a little ashamed. Here indeed was the exemplification of the nursery fable of " eyes and no eyes." And to think that I was being shown all this on my own scaurs by a landsman. But I was out to learn, and in the next pool I spotted another specimen of *Eolis* before Sam, and I was as pleased as though I had hooked a big cod. I felt my stock rising too, when I found, embedded in the rock at the edge of the pool, a small ammonite and was able to give Sam its correct Latin name, which of course he did not know as he'd never taken more than an elementary course in geology. But what a dull subject geology was compared with this ! It wasn't the actual spotting and identification of the specimens that was so exciting. It was the seeing of them close up for the first time, and especially in the glass tubes and with a lens. We found a specimen of *Ancula*, the nudibranch with the orange-tipped papillæ. When it had unfolded itself in the tube and started moving I thought it looked more beautiful than any flower or butterfly I had ever seen. No wonder the man who had drawn and painted them hadn't found time to paint ordinary pictures.

I would have been quite happy to go on exploring the pools and fissures of that first scaur (every inch of which I'd imagined I knew) but the tide was ebbing fast, and Sam suddenly reminded me of the main object of our expedition. In spite of it being late in October, it was a lovely day. The sky was clear and the sun quite warm. There had been a northerly wind during the week but this had fallen away leaving only a gentle ground swell breaking on the scaur ends, where the tangles, only visible at spring tides, were beginning to show. It would have been a grand day for fishing, I thought. The rough seas would have left the water rather cloudy, and I had discovered that in such conditions you could catch cod even in daylight by casting out from the scaur ends with a surf rod and big reel. But I felt no yearning for that sort of sport, and we had hurried down almost to the end of the scaur before I remembered that I had set a line a little to the south yesterday at dinner time, intending to go to it on the night ebb. Sam's coming had put it completely out of my mind.

We left the scaur and started hunting in the bed of the now dry inter-lying creek. Here were beds of a short stumpy weed which made a sort of carpet for your feet, but wherever there were deep pools there were odd stems of tangle, the sure sign that we had reached what Sam called the Laminarian zone, *Laminaria* being the Latin name for the tangle-weed. There were plenty of flat stones here. They were pieces that had broken from the scaur top, and about as thick as paving stones. They lay invariably in shallow pools so that they did not shift even in the roughest weather : yet you could easily lift them up on edge, and by doing this you were really lifting the roof of a sort of cave.

Of course I had lifted plenty of stones before, for very often you'd find scaur cocks under them, and sometimes if they were big enough, full-sized crabs and lobsters and eels. They were also a favourite place for star-fishes and brittle stars and a tiny sea urchin which covers itself with bits of old sea-weed. And I must have noticed too that the underside of the stones were usually grown over with what looked like a fine weed and patches of a spongy crust and also a jelly-like substance. Eyes had no eyes indeed ! I'd seen only what I wanted to see, and now Sam, like a courier showing the sights of a city to a party of tourists, rattled off the Latin names of the scores of living creatures that were visible under the first stone we turned, ignoring the obvious things like small eating and hermit crabs, the butter-fish and blennies, the stars and brittle stars. The crust-like substance was actually a compound zoophyte, a colony of little polyps similar to those which build coral reefs. We'd see them just like anemones if we examined them in a glass dish of sea water under the low power microscope. The jelly-like substance was a tunicate, another compound animal and very interesting as its larvæ were free swimming like tadpoles with a rudimentary spinal column, an evolutionary link between the vertebrate and invertebrate animals. There was a species of sponge. There was a colony of tube-building worms. There were several queer shaped crustaceans not one of which I had ever noticed before, yet Sam told me their Latin names straight off, and asked me to make a note of them.

But the thing that interested him most was that fine weed-like growth which occurred in patches wherever there was room on the stone. He pulled some off with his forceps and popped it in a tube and examined it very carefully with his lens.

" Ha," he said shortly. " Thought so. _Sertularia_. Have a look at it. See the polyps ? We're getting hot on the trail."

I looked and was amazed to see that what I had always taken to be sea-weed was actually a living zoophyte. It consisted of a jointed main stem bearing at each joint, like the leaf buds of a plant, a pair of tiny cups. Some of these were empty. But most of them contained a tiny animal just like a sea anemone, with pink tentacles curling and waving very gently. Sam took the lens from me and started to search the patches of this zoophyte close up. He might have been Sherlock Holmes searching for a blood-stained fingerprint at the scene of a murder, and I felt rather like Dr. Watson, stupid and ignorant but just as excited.

" No sign of _Doto_," he said at last, " but this is _Sertularia_ all right. Let's try another stone."

We did so. We examined several in fact. All had patches of the zoophyte on them, but no sign of the creature on which so much depended. Gradually we were getting closer to the tide's edge however and to the real Laminarian zone. We came to one fairly deep pool in which there lay a slab of rock about four feet square. It would have been too heavy for one of us to move alone, but heaving together we managed to get it up on edge, and then completely over. Temporarily all thoughts of _Doto_ vanished from my mind, for under it was a magnificent lobster very much alive and kicking. For the second time that morning I felt slightly superior to Sam, for there are several ways of getting hold of a live lobster in its native element, and only one of them right. I collared it just behind the joints of its big claws and heaved it on to the dry scaur, and I soon had its claws bound with a piece of string. Sam was impressed.

"Smart work," he said. "Very smart work. *Homarus vulgaris*. Nice specimen too. You ought to dissect that. Typical decapod. Think we'd do better to dissect it for tea though. Know how to cook 'em? Devil of a long time since I tasted lobster . . . By Jove, but there's a fine patch of *Sertularia* on this stone. Let's have a look at it."

I laid the lobster safe on its back. Sam was already crouching low over the stone. And then he gave a sudden yell.

"Yes, by Jove, it's here. *Doto*. Dozens of them. Dozens of them."

I forgot the lobster myself for the time being. I crouched down on the stone alongside Sam. I think that even an expert naturalist could have been forgiven for not having noticed the objects that he was pointing to so triumphantly. To me they just looked like tiny blobs of jelly stuck on to the stalks of the zoophyte. There was not the slightest sign of life in them. But Sam teased one off very carefully, dropped it in a tube and held it up. In a few seconds, just like *Eolis*, it started to unfold and move, and under the pocket lens I saw that it was the slug he had first shown me in the book. In one respect it was different however. In addition to the beautifully tinted coral-like papillæ, there was a little white sac protruding from the back. And this excited Sam more than anything.

"*Splanchnotrophus!*" he cried. "That's the parasite's egg sac thrusting up between *Doto's* papillæ. We're in luck. Let's see if the rest of them are infested. Expect they are, even if the egg sacs are not showing. Oh, what luck."

I was certainly thinking the same thing. I had scarcely slept last night for thinking what a wonderful thing it was that Sam had come, and yet how awful it would be if he couldn't find what he wanted and had to go somewhere else to carry out his research. But we still didn't know that we were going to find a lot of them. He wanted thousands of them for his experiments. He didn't seem worried on this score however. We collected and "bottled" more than thirty specimens from that big stone, and nearly all of them carried the tell-tale egg sac. We also found three other species of slug, two of which even Sam could not identify. We turned the stone back again just as we had found it : and Sam marked its position as closely as he could on his map, before we went on to turn another. Again we were lucky, and by the time we had turned a few more there seemed no doubt at all that provided we kept close down to low-water mark we could get as many as we liked. And this was only one creek. There was the entire Bay and hundreds of similar creeks to hunt in.

I made a carrying loop for the lobster. We moved on to the south, keeping more or less parallel to the edge of the tide. We concentrated on *Doto*, but we found so many other things that I was hopelessly bewildered and I just couldn't get over the fact that I'd been exploring these scaurs almost ever since I could remember, and that at least nine out of ten things we found I'd never even seen. Of course it was largely due to the fact that I'd usually been looking for certain things like bait, and later for fossils : but I now realised that it had almost as much to do with the way that most of these animals were coloured and shaped to blend with the weed or rock on which they lived. For example, I saw something move when I turned up one stone in a pool. It moved too quickly for me to see what it was except that it was a fish. It darted towards a ledge at one side of the pool and there disappeared as though it had gone into a cave. There was no cave however. I marked the place with my eye and moved towards it, but I stared at that ledge a long time before I could see the fish itself, lying dead still and close up to a half decayed frond of seaweed which was partly brown and partly white. The fish itself (it was a father-lasher) was coloured and marked exactly like that piece of weed, and it was lying so that the brown and light patches on its body actually joined up with those on the weed. I am sure we would not have seen the fish at all but for its first startled movement caused by my lifting the stone and exposing it to the full glare of daylight. The success of protective colouring depended on the creature " freezing " into its background.

Really I needn't have been so ashamed of my ignorance, for we found quite a lot of specimens that Sam frankly admitted he could not identify without the books. He said that as soon as we had collected enough specimens of *Doto* to be going on with we'd spend a tide or so doing nothing else but collect other things, for it was clear that the hunting here was exceptionally good. I must certainly make that fauna list. Many of these animals we were finding had a commercial value. All British universities had zoological departments and marine zoology was an essential part of every zoological course. That meant a regular demand for specimens alive or preserved, for observation and dissection. These came from big marine biological stations like Plymouth and Millport and Cullercoats and Jersey, and the prices paid were pretty big, for example, sixpence for ordinary shore-crabs. It wouldn't do to start cutting the market, for these stations relied a great deal on sales to meet their heavy expenses, but if the thing was done discreetly, I might build up quite a nice little business for myself, particularly if there were animals here unprocurable at these stations. None of them, for example, had been able to supply *Doto*. What I must get into my mind, said Sam, was that although Marine biology was a very pleasant hobby, it was no good to me unless there was " brass " in it.

We went on collecting. Whether Sam was measuring every *Doto* he found in terms of ultimate " brass " or not I don't know, but we were as happy as sandboys, and so completely was I obsessed by what we were doing that I had actually started to turn a stone before I noticed that it was one of the anchor stones of my scaurline ! The tide had started to flow by now and the farther end was already awash. I called Sam's attention and we waded out along it. To my surprise there were two small codling on it, both dead of course and one of them half eaten by crabs. Sam again was impressed and delighted. He didn't bother to tell me the Latin name of the cod but just said they'd be grand fried for dinner, particularly if we could fry some potatoes to go with them, and as he was feeling pretty hungry and the tide had started to flow, we might as well pack up. We'd certainly got enough specimens to keep us going until next tide.

2

It's HARD to say which was more exciting : collecting animals or sorting them out and examining them in the laboratory. One very lucky thing happened shortly after Sam's arrival. There was a bad epidemic of whooping cough in the village and for a month school was closed. I was able to devote all of that time to marine zoology. Of course the most important thing was Sam's research on *Doto* and its parasite. What he did first was to rig up two of his glass tanks as aquaria.

To make a close imitation of natural conditions he put a layer of clean sand on the bottom, then a piece of shale we had chipped from one of the *Sertularia* bearing stones, and a few living pieces of small green weed. He kept them shaded from strong light except when he was examining them, and they seemed to settle down quite happily browsing away on the tiny zoophytes. But he could not find out much about the parasite this way. All that you could see of it was the egg sac. So most of the specimens of *Doto* had to be killed, and preserved in formalin. The next thing was to embed them in paraffin wax (melted for the purpose), like insects are embedded in amber. The wax when completely set was fixed in the microtome (the thing like a bacon slicing machine only that the knife was a real razor very finely honed), and by turning the handle slices of wax (and animal) were pared off to form a ribbon. Each slice was a cross section of the animal, so thin that it was translucent. By examining the slices in the same order as they were cut you could build up a complete picture of the animal's anatomy, or at least Sam could, only before he got to this stage the slices had to be treated with a chemical that removed the wax, then stained so that the various cells were differentiated, and finally mounted on a microscope slide and numbered.

When it came to looking at one of these sections through the microscope, I felt as confused and ignorant as an Esquimo confronted with the internals of a multi-valved radio set. It wouldn't have been so bad if it had shown only a section of the various parts and organs, say the " skin " in one layer, the muscles in another, little rings for sections of veins, solid dots for nerves. All these things, according to Sam, were visible, but so were the very cells of which they were built, and also things inside the cells. And here there was no common language into which Sam could translate his explanatory remarks, and the more excited he got himself the more technical and abstruse did he become !

But I wasn't bored even with this, and in no way discouraged, for he had given me a student's text-book on zoology, lent me a case of dissecting implements, and started me off on what he called the inter-biological course. I was dissecting dead worms and shore crabs and starfish and anemones, learning quite a lot about their digestive and nervous and reproductory and other "systems." Funny to think that with all the thousands of worms and mussels and limpets I'd put on fish hooks I'd never thought of them having hearts and veins, and livers, and kidneys, stomachs and reproductory organs and nerves, everything practically that a human being had, except a brain, or, I was glad to know, a consciousness of pain. These organs did not look like their human counterpart but they worked on the same principle and for the same purpose of keeping the animal alive and enabling it to reproduce its own species. The biggest wonder of all was how the latter process was carried out. Most people looking at a limpet or a shore-crab would assume (that is, if the problem interested them at all) that when they pro-duced their young these would be merely copies of themselves, smaller than the smallest ones you found but made the same way. Actually the young of many marine animals, of anemones for example, were just like jellyfish. They were not attached to rocks but swam free near the surface of the sea. The larvæ of shore-crabs looked like tiny shrimps, and these also were free swimming in the early stages of their existence following the hatching of the eggs, which were carried under the body of the female parent. The acorn barnacle which covered large areas of our scaurs, and looked very much like a limpet, really belonged to the crab family. Its larvæ were very similar to those of the shore-crab, shrimp-like and free swimming. And the young of sea-slugs actually had a shell which for some reason they discarded when they became adult.

It was all fascinating. It was like exploring an entirely new world. But from the first it was the living things and their habits which interested me more than the dead. I was not squeamish about cutting things up. There was no real fag in learning the long

Latin and Greek names of the various organs and their components. But to watch the animals in a tank, or in a glass dish under the low-power microscope, produced in me an indescribable delight. Looking back, I can see that it was the beauty of these animals more than anything that excited me, their shape and colour and the way they moved. I think that if I had inherited any of Dad's gift for draughtsmanship and painting I should have been content to do nothing else all my life but draw and paint them. But I had no more than a mediocre ability for either. My drawings were nothing like so good as Sam's. His at least had the merit of photographic accuracy, a quality I could never achieve.

His own research proceeded favourably. He had found the parasite itself in the microtome sections. Sea-slugs are herma-phrodites; that is, they possess both male and female reproductory organs, although they are not self-fertilising like certain plants. Two slugs must unite in order to fertilise the ova of the individual. The parasite was not unlike an ordinary crab, but it was very small, and so far Sam only had sections of it. It was actually on the female reproductory organ of the slug, which obviously it was steadily devouring. It was female itself (the male had yet to be found). It was producing eggs, and somehow or other contrived to force the sac containing these out of the slug's body, so that they could hatch in the water. By carefully removing one of these sacs from a living *Doto*, Sam had managed to secure live specimens of the larvæ. They closely resembled the free swimming larvæ of other crustaceans, that is, they were shrimp-like in shape. But they were furnished with a tooth-like protuberance at the bow end, and Sam suggested that this might offer a possible clue to the method by which the parasite entered its host; it might use the tooth for boring through the slug's body. Here, in the manner of all crustaceans and many insects, it would undergo a meta-morphosis, losing its swimming legs, and nourished by the tissue of the slug, set about the vital job of reproducing its own kind. The slug incidentally would be rendered infertile, and here was the philosophic aspect of the story. All animals fed on or were fed upon by others. It was a rule in nature that no species should become completely dominant. There was a balance which on the whole was nicely kept, and you saw it to perfection on the sea-shore. You could begin with the lowest forms of life, the tiny microscopic plants, consisting of a single cell. These formed the food of the young of most marine animals. But these young were devoured by other animals, by small fish and crabs and anemones, which in turn were fed upon by others, not necessarily bigger ones, but those provided with claws or teeth or stinging cells or speed in movement or cunning methods of trapping, such as the angler fish which buried itself in mud or sand but left exposed a worm-like filament as a bait for its prey : or the common octopus which would deliberately place a piece of fish outside its lair to attract crabs, which formed its favourite food.

The devices employed by sea animals to attain the continuation of their species were endless in their variety. Some, like the herring, attained it by a mass over-production of eggs and young. It was doubtful whether one out of ten thousand eggs hatched survived the ceaseless attacks of other fish, and sea-birds, and the hazards of the weather. And yet in spite of the vast quantities taken by fishermen, the herring population was maintained. There was a curious little animal called the worm pipe fish, quite common under the stones where we found *Dulo*, although I had never seen it before Sam's coming, which produced only about a score of eggs. These were laid by the female but in the process of fertilisation were cemented on to the body of the male, who was shaped and coloured in almost exact imitation of the stem of a certain species of seaweed. When you turned a stone the chances were you wouldn't notice him at all. He'd remain dead still among the weed he imitated. The female however was conspicuously marked and in the first moment of alarm would deliberately move into the most open part of the pool to divert attention from her mate with his precious load of eggs.

In this eternal war which went on among marine animals (the same thing happened on land only it was less obvious) it seemed that the weaker a creature was in methods of offence the stronger it was in defence : but that in neither case must it attain perfection. The sea-slugs, at least in their adult stage, seemed to enjoy a comparative immunity from the perils that assailed such things as mussels and limpets, whose shells could be crushed by the teeth of big cod, or forced open by starfish, or drilled through by dog whelks. Their free swimming larvæ certainly were vulnerable, and although not on the same scale as the herring, allowance was made by over-production of eggs. This stage passed however and it seemed that neither fish nor crab regarded sea-slugs as food. And so in the case of *Doto* nature had to apply another method of control, the internal ovary-destroying parasite.

We'd discuss things like this by the hour while we worked at the bench or sat smoking our pipes like venerable philosophers in front of the laboratory fire. When the weather was bad and the sea rough, it was like being in a lighthouse. The big waves thundered on the outer wall making the whole building tremble, and we'd see the spray swishing up over the windows and hear it splashing on the roof, and rushing down again. At high tide in such weather it wasn't safe to leave the laboratory to go into the cottage, for everything would be awash outside, and even the fishing cobles had to be hauled from the Dock far up the main street, and the cottages here had to have their ground-floor windows barred to stop flooding. On such occasions we'd have a meal in the laboratory, and when we got tired of talking, Sam would pick up his accordion and we'd sing. One night he said what a pity it was I didn't know two girls who could join us in our singing so as to make a quartette. As it happened I did know two sisters, the daughters of a sea captain who lived in what we called the Up-bank part of the village. Here close to the railway station and the Victoria Hotel were several terraces of " superior " brick villas, most of them owned by local men who had found that the mercantile marine was a much more profitable business than inshore fishing. There was a distinct social as well as a physical elevation about this community, more noticeable perhaps among the women than the men, who until they retired were away on their ships for most of the time. Both of these sisters (they were called Rachel and Jenny) had been to Scarborough school during the time I had been there, although they were paying scholars. They'd passed their matric. all right, but they hadn't gone to a university, and were just helping their mother in the home. They were both good looking, and they had good figures and dressed nicely. They were in the choir and the choral society, and for quite a time I'd been mildly " gone " on Jenny. But Rachel always stuck to her like glue, and Adeline, the dark-eyed student (for whom I still yearned at times), had completely supplanted her.

We encountered them one evening at the station where we had

gone to collect some chemicals. Sam lectured me later because in doing the introduction I had given their names the wrong way round. They were shy, and I felt nervous too, especially when Sam suggested straight away that we should go for a walk. After a lot of giggling Rachel consented. It happened to be a fine evening with a moon and we set off along Low Batts cliff top, the favourite summer promenade of the " Up-bankers." I noticed that Rachel hugged Jenny's arm tightly as we passed the last of the new villas and reached the cliff path, and during the whole walk they never separated. They were certainly both attractive looking girls, especially in the moonlight ; in fact I thought that Jenny was really better looking than my student although she was fair and blue-eyed. But she didn't stir my blood a bit, and I don't think I stirred hers, and I felt that I would have been much happier in the labora-tory. In one respect I might have been, for in answer to a polite question from Rachel as to why he was staying down in the village in winter time, Sam started talking about *Doto* and *Splanchnotrophus*, and I felt myself going hot and cold when he got down to ana-tomical details. But I don't think they understood a word of it. In spite of them having passed the matric. their only interest in the beach was the seasonal one of bathing, although even Jenny giggled with interest when Rachel reminded her of how when they were children they used to go shrimping.

The truth was that despite their villa, their education and their nice clothes and their disdain of the down-bank villagers, they were at heart true Bramblewick. Their forebears on both sides were of the same tough seafaring stock. They were hard and close and quite unimaginative. To them physically and mentally we were foreigners. I don't know whether these Bramblewick women ever fell in love in a romantic sense. Their destiny was to marry men of their own breed, officers of the mercantile marine and bear them children, sons who would go to sea, daughters who would marry sailors. Sam, too, must have sensed this complete irresponsiveness, and although he said that he thought Rachel was one of the finest looking girls he had ever met, I am sure that it would have been our last walk with them if they had not, after much giggling and self-conscious protestations that someone might hear us, and what would they think, joined us in singing. They actually consented to sit down on the end of a seat that overlooked the moonlit Bay, although Rachel still hugged Jenny's arm and Sam and I had to sit together on Rachel's side. We sang hymns, and " Ye Banks and Braes " and " Sweet and Low," and from that time onwards we got in the habit of taking them for a walk at least once a week, and in the end got as far as walking or sitting with them arm in arm, but always with them in the middle and us on the flanks. It was indeed an innocent friendship, our behaviour a model of Victorian respectability. They never came down to the laboratory of course. It would never have done for the village to know they were with us behind closed doors. Actually they would never come down to the old village at all, and if the folk down there needed anything else to convince them that I'd got " uppish " and that I was no better than a " visitor," it was there in the fact that I and " t' queer chap from t'awd coastguard station " were going about with two lassies from " Up-bank."

By now all the old pleasure boatmen of Captain Bunny's generation were dead. The fishermen themselves were thinning out, owing to the economic decline of inshore fishing caused by the development of the steam trawler. Most of the fishermen's sons I had gone to school with had joined the mercantile marine, the first step towards the ultimate building of an " up-bank " villa. There had been a temporary revival when several families of fishers from a village thirty miles up the coast had settled in the place. But these folk had been regarded as foreigners by the natives, and only two men remained—John Knaggs and the Lunns, partners in a single coble. John was old, married but childless. Henry Lunn was young with a family of five children. His two eldest boys, John and Marney, were now at the village school. They were bright and responsive scholars but erratic in their attendance. Their excuse for absence was usually that they'd had bad colds. I didn't feel it was my business to tell the headmaster (whom I didn't like anyway) that nine times out of ten they were playing truant, and for the same reason as I'd played truant myself, for fishing or bird nesting. I'd been friendly with Henry Lunn from the first, perhaps because against the powerful but subtle hostility of the village we sensed a bond of sympathy. He'd always taken an interest in my fishing, making suggestions about tackle and bait, and very often in winter time offering me a jar of skeined mussels, or queen oysters or whelks, bait which he and his partner had to buy from Hull or

Fleetwood. But even with Henry I'd detected a growing diffidence since I'd become a schoolmaster, and started hob-nobbing with the " queer folk " at the laboratory. There was no doubt that I was getting a bit superior, especially as I was now wearing, except on collecting expeditions, the flannel bags, the tweed sports coat, the open sports shirt, the fancy socks and brogues affected by the male laboratory students and by Sam himself. I wasn't worried about all this. Fishing in the ordinary angling sense had ceased temporarily to be my main passion. The finding of a rare and hitherto un-recorded nudibranch or crustacean (and we found many) was just as exciting as catching a big cod. But another reason was that Sam, in spite of him having brought a rod and tackle, had not the soul of an angler. We went on to Browe Beck one night, where, from a low jutting cliff, I had discovered a grand place for surf fishing at high tide. It was very cold with a sneaking easterly wind, and dark too, but I had brought a lantern to bait by. You don't catch many fish this way but usually they are big. Having cast well out into the surf, you prop your rod on a stone, with the light shining on the white porcelain ring on its tip, and you just watch and wait.

Sam had never tried surf fishing before. It looked simple but actually it wasn't. It had taken me weeks of practice to cast properly. You had to use a large reel because the ground was usually foul. This enabled you to wind in quickly for re-baiting. A small reel was slow, and your bare hook would have dragged along the bottom the whole way and would certainly have fouled something. You had a fairly heavy lead, with the single hook on a short snood about a yard above it. The reel had no automatic check. You could cast either sideways or overhead, but I preferred doing it sideways. You turned your back to the sea, reeled the lead in so that it was swinging clear of the ground, and checked it there with your index finger pressing on the rim of the reel. Then you swung the rod round with an upward movement, and as the lead gained its top momentum you lifted your finger and let the reel spin free, but checking it again as the lead hit the water. If you didn't do this the line would overrun the reel and rewind itself. But if you checked too soon the friction was enough to burn your finger-tip quite badly. All this of course was doubly difficult at night, and Sam, like most good teachers, was a bad learner. He saw me cast, and he thought he could do it just the same first time. He gave a terrific swing, but his lead instead of flying seawards travelled along the shore. He hadn't checked at all, with the result that his line got in a frightful mess. We cleared it and he had another try. He did check this time but he let go too soon and again he hit the shore. The third attempt certainly got the lead into the sea, and well out too, for you couldn't hear it splash, but he forgot that final braking, the line overran and fouled, and snapped, fortunately close to the lead so that we were able to clear it and fit another. I daren't suggest then that I should make the cast, but I was relieved when Sam almost humbly asked me to.

Angling, that is if you take it seriously, is a strictly individualistic and admittedly selfish pastime. I don't mind company, I don't mind teaching even if it means leaving off fishing myself in order to convey to someone else my own knowledge and experience. But the essential condition is that your companion, whether practised or a beginner, should share your enthusiasm, which implies, in this sort of fishing at any rate, an acceptance of its disciples. You can't expect every time you throw a line with a single bait into the sea to catch a fish. You can't expect when you stand or sit on a windy beach on a winter's night not to feel cold. You must be capable of watching your rod tip trembling or jerking just slightly with the movement of the sea, and of losing all concept of time : of feeling the blood congealing in your feet and hands, of your eyes and nose running, of a numbness moving slowly through your whole body, and of withstanding all this with stoic resignation, knowing that your reward will justify it, although again you mustn't lose heart if you don't get a single bite.

Sam lacked this essential quality of mind and body. His rod started to tremble as soon as I had set it down for him. I assured him that it was only the tide and the surf, but he wanted to haul it in and see that I had to persuade him to leave it. There would be no mistaking a real bite. He started pacing up and down, then beating his arms against his chest. I tried to hearten him by recounting my various experiences while fishing in this very place : how one night after I'd fished for hours without getting a single bite, I'd struck a shoal of big billet and codling, and got so many I could hardly carry them home : how on another occasion I'd landed the biggest plaice I'd ever caught, even from a boat. He listened in silence, but whenever I stopped he started whistling, and pacing up and down again, and I knew it was going to be no good, especially as neither of us got a sign of a bite, and when we hauled in the baits were still intact. It was then that Sam said :

" Do you know I'm feeling a bit worried about those sections I'm staining. Mustn't overdo 'em. Getting hungry too. What about you ? Oughtn't to waste too much time here. Anyway it doesn't look as though there's many fish about. Wonder if it will be too late to meet the girls after supper."

That was the nearest I ever got to being angry with Sam, for it was a good night and I'm certain we'd have done well if we'd waited. But I forgot my disappointment when we got back to the laboratory, where it seemed that supper was really a more urgent matter to Sam than his microscope sections. No friendship can be perfect. But I think ours came as close to the ideal as was humanly possible. The main thing anyway was work, not pastime. Sam expressed himself as delighted with my progress in zoology. As a collector he admitted I was as good as himself now I knew what to look for : and said I had the makings of a first-class field naturalist, which, if I wanted a job on an expedition, was more important than having a B.Sc. after my name, although it seemed an inflexible rule that a degree was necessary.

The only thing that troubled me was when at home late at night I picked up my old school books, the ones I'd had to study for the matric., *Longman's Arithmetic: Ransome's History: Nesfield's English Grammar: Matriculation Latin:* and tried to apply myself to the job of mastering enough of their contents to meet the ordeal ahead. I had my dark moments then, for I had only to glance into any one of them to be assailed by an acute and almost physically painful revulsion, and I knew in my heart that even if the South Seas depended on it, I should never be able to pass.

Sam realised this in the end. Even in zoology it became evident that I lacked the power to assimilate and remember facts, or to pursue any line of study which some devil inside me considered dull. My patience in watching living animals in a tank was inexhaustible, as it was when I was angling. But when it came to tracing out the nervous system of a dead and pickled dog fish, or the muscles of a frog, my interest was maintained only by the knowledge that this was a means to an end. I could understand what I saw. I could, after much practice, make efficient drawings and give all the various nerves and muscles their correct scientific names. But if Sam asked me next day to sketch what I'd done from memory, I couldn't do a thing. My mind just wouldn't work.

If he reluctantly ruled out the possibility of my passing the matric. and taking a degree, he did not lose faith in me or throw cold water on my still burning ambition to take up a scientific career. One night he became very serious and said we must really tackle the problem of my future. We must consider all the facts and possibilities, state them, get them down in writing, analyse them, formulate a *plan*. He took a sheet of foolscap, and then started asking me questions. First of all, what did I really want to be? I told him that he knew as well as I did. I wanted to travel to see the natural wonders of the world, strange people and animals and fish, especially fish. A job as a naturalist would suit me to perfection.

"Yes," said Sam. "That sounds all right. But don't forget the brass. You'd never get a job straight away as official naturalist without a degree. Your only hope would be to go as assistant, and there wouldn't be much brass in that, but it might be the back stairway to a real appointment. Don't know what you'd get on such a job. If it was a private thing, financed by some wealthy pot who wanted some publicity for himself as a benefactor of humanity, you might do well. But you must always look ahead. You want your keep and enough salary to put something by. And there's marriage to think about. Do you want to get married or not? How would that fit in with cruising in the South Seas, or exploring jungles?"

I had a sudden image of Adeline, who obviously had an interest in marine biology or why had she been studying it : and I thought what a perfect thing it would be to share such a fascinating occupation with her. Remembering *The Blue Lagoon*, my imagination took a swift romantic flight. I saw us not first as man and wife or even as lovers, but as fellow-passengers on a scientific cruise possibly under the leadership of her own brother. The situation indeed might have been as unfavourable to myself as it had been last summer. The medical student was the doctor to the expedition ; and I nothing more than a sort of laboratory boy, until the inevitable storm which would dispose of all the ship's redundant personnel and cast Adeline and me on a desert island. But I had never spoken to

Sam about my frustrated passion, and I said guardedly, that I just hadn't thought about it, but that I didn't see why the two should not be combined. There were girls who were just as interested in travel and natural history as men.

" Ha," Sam answered coldly, " but I doubt if they're normal. A woman's place is in the home. It's her destiny. You've got to look at everything from a biological point of view. The supreme test for any species of living thing is that it shall reproduce its own kind. That holds equally with *Homo sapiens*. Women want children. To them whether they know it or not, that's the fundamental purpose of marriage. That doesn't fit in with an adventurous sort of life. White women can't have babies in the jungle."

I might have said that the heroine of *The Blue Lagoon* managed even that without difficulty, but I didn't want to start an argument on such a subject and I was glad that Sam let it go. He started to write on the sheet of foolscap. Then he said :

" What we ought to do, having decided that you want to be a naturalist on a marine biological expedition, is to make a sort of balance-sheet of ' fors ' and ' againsts,' like Robinson Crusoe did. Put down on one side everything that's in your favour of getting a job, on the other side everything that stands against it. Best begin with a summary of your career though. Parents, date of birth, schools, jobs held, etc."

It didn't take long to get that down. Then Sam divided the rest of the sheet with a vertical line and wrote on one side of it Credit and the other Debit. We started on the credits, and the first thing to go down was health, which Sam said was of number one importance for a job in the tropics. It would be for a doctor to give a definite opinion of course, and the examination would be rigorous, but (and I don't think he meant it sarcastically) it wasn't likely that there was much wrong with the health of a man who could stand for hours on a freezing beach watching a fishing rod and not complaining, so he would give me full marks. There wasn't much to say about my career at the village school. Sam suggested however that when I came to apply for a job, I would be justified in saying that I had been granted a special scholarship to the Scarborough school on account of my unusual promise, and he put down " special scholarship," which certainly looked very good. I was quite frank with him as to what had happened with that scholarship. He said that we had better ignore completely the subjects I had failed in, and say, what was perfectly true, that I had excelled in science and handwork, agreeing that we had better not mention Scripture. The rest of the credits he said he could supply himself from his own observation. I was intelligent, observant, eager to acquire knowledge, quick at comprehension, and very competent at all field work. Also I was a good handyman, especially with regard to boats and their gear. That, with my theoretical and practical knowledge of geology, completed the credit side, and we started on the debit side and Sam wrote down straight away " Academic qualifications—nil." After he had done that he sat staring at the sheet of paper for a long time without speaking. Then he filled his pipe and handed me his pouch. We smoked, still in silence, and I began to feel very blue for it was clear that the single item written on the debit side out-balanced everything on the other, that I was up against an unscalable wall. Then Sam suddenly gave me a great slap across the shoulder.

" My God ! " he shouted. " I've got it. Listen. Listen. We've been thinking all the time in terms of pure science, laboratory work and research. There's another angle to science. Wouldn't interest me for obvious reasons, but it ought to be just your mark. Popular science, my boy. Writing. Articles, stories, books. There's a growing general interest in science. Ever read any of those nature stories by Bensusan and St. Mars ? And what about the Kearton books ? Don't think either of the Keartons have any academic qualifications. But don't cut into their market. Write about the things you know. Marine animals. You know the facts. Make 'em popular. You'd soon get a reputation as a naturalist. You'd make brass. Might make enough to finance your own expedition one day. South Seas, anywhere. You ought to learn photography. Illustrate your own articles and books. My God, I'm half inclined to try it myself, only I doubt if I'd ever be able to think in terms of popular science. I'd always want the precise word to describe my meaning, and the only precise words are the scientific ones. I tell you it's just your mark."

My mind was spinning.

" But I can't write," I protested.

" Rubbish. Any one can wrote provided they've got something to write about. I don't say you won't need practice. I don't suggest you begin with a book. But why not a newspaper article ? Towns-folk know damn all about marine zoology, yet all townsfolk want to spend their holidays by the sea. Show 'em how they can make their holidays more interesting : how to find things and know what they are. Damn it. Haven't you got a local paper ? I bet the editor has never guessed that this place is one of the richest collecting grounds in the country. Write a general article about the animals we've found here. Start an ' Eyes and No-eyes ' series. It would interest his summer visitor readers if no one else. You might collect them later into a book."

My mind was still spinning, but I could see there was sense in what he was saying, and deep inside me I was aware that a weight that had oppressed me for months was lifting. If this was possible there would be no need for me to swot at Latin and history and mathematics. No need to worry about the matric. or a university degree. No need for that matter to continue the duller side of my zoological studies, for the readers of a newspaper or popular magazine were not likely to be interested in things that could only be seen by laboratory dissection or with the aid of an expensive microscope. I began to feel profoundly excited. I'd read the *Jungle Books*, all the Keartons had published, and many of the Bensusan's and St. Mars nature stories. None of them touched on the ground which, thanks to Sam, I now knew pretty well. The local paper, *The Whitby Gazette*, did publish occasional articles about bird life and archaeology, and I'd got into its correspondence column myself on one occasion when someone had asked for information about the legend of St. Hilda and the ammonites. I'd given the scientific point of view. My excitement grew. Once more the future glowed with possibilities, travel, adventure, success, even fame and the love of Adeline.

" By Jove," I said. " I think it's a good idea. I think I could do it, with a bit of practice."

Sam ripped up the piece of paper and threw it in the fire.

" Bet your life you could," he said. " Easy as rolling off a log. Often thought of doing it myself, especially after reading some of this popular scientific stuff, and seeing what rubbish a lot of it is. Not all of it, mind you, but a lot of it. Reads as though the writer had got all his information from the local library. Second hand. Pot-boiling. Brass of course should be your main consideration, but no need to sacrifice accuracy. I tell you I'd like to do it myself, but my line must be pure science, academic or commercially applied."

Sam stared into the fire as he said this and I thought that for once he didn't sound quite so enthusiastic about his own work as he usually did. I wondered if my own sudden enthusiasm had made him feel rather jealous, and I was worried.

"It's a grind, you know, laboratory work, and a lot of it's very dull. I've made about a thousand sections of *Doto* and *Splanch-notrophus* to date, and about as many drawings, and still haven't filled in half the picture. Still haven't found the male parasite. And what'll happen when the job's done ? Results published perhaps in the Journal of the Royal Society. Favourable comments perhaps from about half a dozen other scientific journals, and then the thing buried away in museum and scientific libraries and forgotten. For one person who'll want to read that there'll be ten thousand will want to read a sentimental story about a dicky bird or a bunny rabbit."

It was my turn to encourage Sam. I reminded him of the real kudos his work would bring him, of its bearing on the general subject of parasitology, of what it might lead to in the shape of a big appointment, and he suddenly cheered up.

"Yes, by God, of course. And I've another batch of sections to examine to-night. I'll get on with them now. What about supper ? If you got it ready early we could go and meet the girls, then come back and work till midnight. You could start your first article."

It *was* easy. I wrote my first article that night, sent it off to the *Whitby Gazette*, and before the end of the week got a letter of acceptance, with a request that I should call on the editor the next Saturday I happened to be in town. The *Gazette* was owned by two brothers, Harry and Fred Horne. Harry, the elder, was the editor. He was a rather severe looking man, and I felt very nervous when I was taken into his office, but he soon made me feel at ease. It was like my first interview with Mr. Tetley. He asked me dozens of questions about myself, and how I had come to know such a lot about sea-shore animals, what work I was doing and what I was going to be. Then his brother Fred walked in. He was quite jolly in his manner. He said straight away that he had read my article with very great interest. He'd spent many happy hours on the scaurs at Whitby when he was a lad but had never guessed there were so many interesting things to see. But then he'd been more concerned with fishing. He still liked a bit of sea-fishing, but of course that didn't compare with salmon-fishing on the Esk. Some day perhaps I would like to come with him for a day's fishing, only of course I would not be able to fish, as the Conservators were very strict and he himself had had to wait years before he'd been able to join the river angling club, whose membership was limited. The upshot of that interview was an invitation to write as many natural history articles as I liked for the *Gazette* at a flat rate of ten shillings an article. I was given a galley proof of the one I had written, and I walked out of the office as proud as a turkey cock to join Sam, who had been waiting for me outside. I told him what had happened. He congratulated me, but I could tell by his manner that he was feeling a little bit envious, and he lapsed into an almost gloomy silence as we walked down past the fish quay to the west pier, which juts straight out seawards from the old town. It was a lovely afternoon, sunny and mild with a real spring feeling in the air. The harbour was full of fishing craft moored for the week-end, and I thought I had never seen the roofs of the fishers' cottages huddled under the Abbey cliff look so beautiful. I tried to hide my jubilance, but it wasn't easy, particularly when we came to the pier-end with its uninterrupted view of the sea, and I saw far out several large steamers and one full-rigged sailing vessel heading south. My heart beat wildly at the thought that at last there was a feasible chance of all my dreams coming true. I'd got my foot on the ladder. The *Gazette* articles were a start, and how easy the first one had been. With a bit of practice I'd soon be getting articles in real magazines. I'd write books. Soon have enough money to set off on my travels. And there was Adeline . . .

Sam suddenly said :

" I don't know whether I'm right about pure science being the best career for a man. Don't know whether it justifies all the brass and the time you spend on it. True that my training's cost me nothing. Scholarships all the way. But I wonder where it's going to lead. Wonder if I oughtn't to have gone into the timber business. Might have done if father had offered me scope. What about getting back ? Oughtn't to be wasting time here."

Again it was my job to cheer Sam up. I tried to do it discreetly, not to show him that I wanted us to celebrate my good fortune : but I suggested, seeing it was Saturday, that we might go and have a meal somewhere and then go to the Waterloo Cinema, where I had noted a Duggie Fairbanks' film was showing. There were no buses then and no trains after six, but we could walk the seven miles back. I did not even suggest that the meal and the pictures would be at my expense, but I was determined they should be, for I felt colossally rich. Sam did cheer up when we sat down to a meal of fried plaice and chips and tea, in Whitby's best cafe. He congratulated me again and again on my success, protesting that apart from making the actual suggestion that I should take up writing, it had nothing to do with him. He got full of enthusiasm for his own work, saying that his research would undoubtedly lead to him getting a very big post one day. Curiously enough there were two girls having tea in the cafe, and I recognised one as an old scholar of my Scarborough school. They weren't so pretty as Rachel and Jenny but they were smartly dressed, and as the one I knew smiled at me, I walked over to them after I had paid our bill. Sam followed, and I was able to do the introductions quite correctly. They were going to the pictures too, so it was decided we should all go together, and although both they and Sam protested, I bought all four tickets. We were lucky with pictures too. This was before the days of the long-feature film. We saw Chaplin and Duggie Fairbanks and Fatty Arbuckle, and we were all quite helpless with laughter. The Waterloo had a good orchestra too, and played a lot of tunes I liked, including Mendelssohn's " Spring Song," and *Peter Gynt*, and the incidental music from *Monsieur Beaucaire*, and that very popular ballad of the time " Just a Little Love, a Little Kiss." But what thrilled me more than anything in that programme was a short travel film showing diving for pearls in the South Seas. And I am sure if I had been alone I would have stayed for the second house and a third, if there'd been one.

Easter was approaching, and as parties from both Universities were coming to the laboratory, and the cottage would be required for the students, Sam decided that he would go home for the holidays, and he invited me to go with him. Another reason was that Professor Denny could not get away from the University, and

Sam wanted to discuss certain matters with him. I wanted to go, but I guessed that Adeline would be coming, and I said that it might lose me my job if I was absent during such a busy time, and besides I still had some articles to do. Again, I was longing to do a bit of fishing, both stream and in the sea, although at this time of the year sea-fishing is not very good. My position at the laboratory was still a humble one, but with three published articles to my credit I no longer felt humble when I thought of the professors or the students. I'd bought a new pair of flannel bags, a smart tweed sports coat (partly out of my *Gazette* money), and I felt that I was at least equal if not superior to that wretched medical student. I was relieved nevertheless, when the day before Good Friday, the parties arrived, and I saw Adeline and her brother, but no sign of my rival. That relief was sublimated into a dizzy happiness when Adeline, looking more ravishing than ever in her town clothes, actually smiled at me and shook hands and asked me how I was getting on : and that was nothing compared with what happened next day down on the beach on the first collecting expedition. It was a specially equinoctial spring tide. I scarcely knew how it happened, for I shouldn't have had the courage to contrive it deliberately, but I found myself on the same scaur as Adeline far out beyond the village. She was trying to turn over a moderately-sized stone, and I went to her assistance. She gave me another thrilling smile, and by a mircale there was a lobster under it, under-sized it was true, but very lively. I caught it and tied its claws. I told her it was undersized and that legally we should not take it but that I would wrap it in seaweed, and manage to get it past the Slipway without any one guessing what it was.

It happened to be what Sam and I called a " *Doto* " stone. I was able to point some of these out, and show Adeline the parasite egg sac, using the Latin names of course : and to point out several other animals that she did not seem to know. I could tell she was impressed, and she actually said :

" Well, what a lot you know."

" Well," I answered, " you've got to know about things like these if you're going to write about them."

She looked surprised when I said that, and echoed :

" Write about them ? I didn't know you wrote. How perfectly thrilling. Have you really had anything published ? "

" Only in the local paper up to now. But then I only started a few weeks ago. I expect I'll land the really big papers or even magazines in time, and possibly do a book. But you've got to start somewhere, haven't you ? "

" Of course you have. I long to write. But I've never done anything except for the school magazine, and it wasn't very good, I'm afraid. What do you write about, marine zoology ? "

" In a way. But of course it's got to be popularised for a local paper. No good calling that nudibranch we've just found *Dendronotus aborsense*."

She laughed.

" Of course it wouldn't. I think it's an awful bore having to learn all those long names. What interests me is that they're so beautiful. I just love watching them, particularly in these lovely pools. They're simply fascinating. I'd love to read what you've written."

It was like being in a dream. To think Adeline should really be talking to me : that she was interested in marine animals for the same reason that I was. That she wanted to read what I'd written ! I told her that I would let her read my articles of course, but that she must make allowances for my only being a beginner. They were only popular articles. She said she understood that perfectly. Then she asked if I was really taking up writing as a profession. What did I want to be ? I told her. She said she thought it sounded simply perfect, cruising round the South Seas, just the sort of life she had always dreamed of. How often she had wished that her brother instead of wanting to be a university professor, had wanted to go off on expeditions, only of course there wouldn't have been much chance of him taking her with him, although she might have got a job typing his records.

We went on collecting, or at least pretending to. I felt myself endowed with a new prodigious strength, and single-handed turned over great stones that even Sam and I would have hesitated to tackle. I didn't think much about Sam, except to reflect on how lucky I had been in not accepting his invitation. Adeline asked me what I did with myself in the winter, and didn't I find life very dull ? I had to mention Sam then, and how I had been helping him in his research and he had been helping me with my zoological studies, but I didn't say anything about the girls for I didn't want to give her the impression that I was in any way tied. And I couldn't resist saying what a disappointment Sam had been to me with regard to fishing, which hitherto had always been my favourite hobby.

" What a pity ! " she said to that. " Do you know I just love fishing, and so does my brother. We're always disappointed when we come here at this time of the year that we can't hire a boat, as they're not launched down until the summer. Isn't it stupid ? "

I told Adeline (and dear old Captain Bunny might have turned in his grave) that the best fishing here was not to be had from boats, but from the rocks, especially at the north end of the Bay and well away from the village, and after dusk. She said, without a moment's hesitation :

" Oh, how I'd love to try. Would you take me with you one evening ? I would be thrilled."

I am sure that my own voice must have trembled when I answered :

" Of course. Delighted. To-night if you like. Think I could even get you a rod, and if you're never done it before, teach you to cast the proper way. My friend left his behind him."

I'd never known the tide turn so soon as that one did, or flow so fast. We had to move shorewards, and soon we had joined the rest of the party, including the brother, who was really quite friendly to me and very amused about the lobster, which I had carefully wrapped up in weed. It didn't worry me much that all the fishermen, including Henry Lunn, were standing on the Slipway : all in their Sunday best because it was Good Friday. Even Henry, although he was standing apart from the others, stared hard at us, and I thought I detected in his eyes a rather supercilious twinkle. But it was the girl students in their short skirts and bare legs that caused the rest of them to grin and make remarks which, if inaudible to us, were evidently derisive. None of them seemed to notice my bundle of weed or suspect what was in it. I was relieved nevertheless when we reached the top of the Slipway. I hadn't fixed a definite time for meeting Adeline. I thought I could do that when we were in the laboratory. But before we turned into it there was the sound of a motor-bike coming down the road into the Dock, and suddenly it appeared—a bike and sidecar with the car full of luggage and on the bike itself a young man wearing

the blazer of Leeds University. The bike stopped, the man raised
his goggles, and both Adeline and her brother went forward to
greet him. It was the medical student. To Adeline's credit I must
say that it was clear she had not been expecting him, for I heard
her say :

" What a surprise. I thought you said you couldn't come " ;
and him say with a broad grin, " Only fixed it the last moment.
By Jove, this new bus can move. Must have averaged forty the
whole way. I'll take you for a run this afternoon."

There was no doubt that Adeline's surprise was genuine. But
there was no doubt either that she was delighted the man had come.
Her eyes were sparkling as she looked at him and his bike. I heard
her say in the same eager way she said she'd like to go fishing with
me, " Oh, I'd just love to." I knew that she had completely
forgotten my existence again, about all that she had said to me,
even about the lobster. I didn't go into the laboratory. I went
home.

I felt that I couldn't face the laboratory next day, and as neither
of the professors had come, and no one seemed to notice whether
I was there or not, I decided to go trout-fishing, not in the local
becks, but in a stream called Juggerhowe. This beck (one of
the sources of the River Derwent) starts on the south slopes of
the watershed formed by our high moors. It turns west as it
approaches Scarborough, runs through Harwood Dale and Hack-
ness and then as a slow and sluggish river travels across the
eastern part of the plain of York to enter the Ouse below Selby.
I had tried fishing Juggerhowe before, but never with success.
It was very small at the point where you reached it over the
moors, but here and there it ran into deep peaty pools, and the
fact that it joined a real river encouraged the hope that any of these
pools might contain a big trout or even a salmon.

It was a lovely sunny day. I debated with myself as to whether
I should wear my old beach clothes or my new sports coat and
flannel bags, and decided on the latter, for there were quite a lot of
visitors about, and I thought it might just happen that I should
meet someone rather attractive on my way up to the moors,
someone who might allay the pain and bitterness of my disillusionment with Adeline. It was a very slender hope, and it

did not materialise. My route took me across fields and along lanes unknown to visitors, and the only girls I saw were at the farms, and they were all ugly and repulsive.

It was a lovely day, and no mistake. The sun was really hot. The lanes were full of primroses and violets. Birds twittered everywhere, and above the fields on either side of me skylarks sang lustily, and I even imagined that I heard a cuckoo. I passed through a little copse which was ablaze with daffodils, and I thought of that poem of Wordsworth that I'd had to learn by heart at Scarborough school, but it didn't make me feel any happier. I also found myself muttering that thing about spring and a young man's fancy lightly turning to thoughts of love, only I put "heavily" instead of "lightly," for that was how I felt about it, and about the beauty of everything that was around me. I tried not to think of Adeline, but I could not stop myself imagining how perfect my expedition would have been if she had been with me. I felt sure that she would have been thrilled by the sight of those daffodils and by hearing the birds singing. I hated them for they seemed to be mocking me.

I began to cheer up however as I left the last of the fields and reached the moor. I had to climb one high hill before sighting the valley of Juggerhowe, and when I reached the top the view was entrancing. The moor stretched as far as you could see to the west. To the south it came almost to the top of High Batts cliff, and beyond this you could see miles and miles of coast to Flamborough Head. The beck itself was not visible, but the valley looked most alluring, and I thought my chances of getting some good sport were stronger than on my last trip, when the weather had been very cold. There was a group of tumuli on the hill. I dawdled a bit, looking among the worn sheep tracks for flints, and I found one that looked almost like an arrow head. But that started me thinking of Adeline again, and of how interested she would have been, and I soon hurried down the west slope of the hill and reached the Whitby-Scarborough high road, where I halted in the hope of seeing a motor car, a rare enough sight in those days. I did see one. It was going very slowly up the hill, making a terrific din, and emitting clouds of blue smoke, but I thought it looked much better than a motor-bike, and I made the half-comforting reflection that if I was a girl I'd prefer that to riding in a crazy sidecar. Some day I would certainly have one.

I pushed on, and when I caught the first gleam of water among the sedges and clumps of bog myrtle that grew thick in the valley, I forgot all my troubles for the time being. The gleam came from quite a largish pool, one which, judging by the tracks all round it, was used by the moor farmers for dipping their sheep. I approached it warily. In spite of my thinking that stream-fishing was not so exciting as sea-fishing, I could never feel cool about it, especially at the start. I saw a trout rise almost at once, and although it was nothing like so big as the ones in the Mill dam, it excited me very much, and I crept back and hastily started to put my rod together. I mounted my reel, threaded the line and attached the cast (a fine one that I had bought on my last trip to Whitby and I kept it apart from my old fly wallet.) It was dry and coiled like a spring and, in spite of my impatience to make a start, I decided to soak it first and then stretch it to straighten out the coils. While it was soaking I crept to the pool edge again and saw that a number of small grey flies were hovering over the water. I did not know the name of them but I was certain I had one very much like them in my fly wallet, and I went back to where I had left my rod and creel. The wallet should have been in the creel. It was not there however. I started desperately to search all my pockets, but already I had more than a suspicion that I had left the thing behind, and this was soon confirmed. I had walked eight miles to fish in Juggerhowe, and I had forgotten to bring my flies !

Cursing did little to relieve my feelings for there was no one to hear me. All the bitterness of my disillusionment with Adeline returned, and I really hated her. I simply would not have done such a stupid thing if I hadn't been awake most of the night thinking about her and the way she had treated me. I would not have dreamt of coming to a place like this to fish when the tides were the lowest of the year, if it hadn't been for her and her wretched man. It would be low tide now I thought, and the sea dead calm, possibly a lower ebb than I had ever seen since I'd been interested in the zoological aspects of fishing. Doubtless Adeline would be down the scaurs with the man turning stones over for her. Or perhaps they might both be looking into one of those pools which she had said fascinated her so much, pretending to be interested in marine zoology, but actually interested only in each other.

I heard the trout rise again. Savagely I turned everything out of my creel. I used this for some of my sea-fishing gear, and there was a packet of smallish whiting hooks tied to thick twisted gut. I thought that if they had been trout hooks I might have made the best of a bad job, and tried worm fishing. But if these were small for whiting, they were enormous for trout. The gut itself would be like a bit of rope falling into the water. And the water was still, and although stained with peat, very clear. Besides the sun was shining, making conditions for worm fishing completely adverse. But I had to do something to relieve the bitterness of my thoughts. I cut the smallest of the hooks off its snood and, as I had some fine silk thread, I whipped the hook on to the end of my fly cast. It looked, I thought ironically, like a boat's anchor. I moved up from the pool and found a patch of shingle over which the stream ran clear. On the side I turned over a few stones and got some earthworms, which I put in my handkerchief. It was a job getting one of them on to the whiting hook. I thought that I had never tried anything so daft and hopeless since my bent-pin days when I threw it into the pool and heard it splash, for it must have terrified the trout. But to my amazement the line had no sooner straightened than it started to jerk, and I felt a motion on the rod. I struck gently and out came a fish. I couldn't help laughing when I had got it in my hand. I think it was the smallest fish I had ever caught even on a penncok hook : it was not so big as an ordinary sprat. Yet it had swallowed the worm and quite a lot of the whiting hook. It was not a trout though. It was more silvery, had no spots, and I rightly guessed that it was a minnow, a fish rarely found in small clear trout streams, and never in our own two becks. It (and I soon discovered there were hundreds more) was here because the beck ran into a real river. It encouraged my long-held but never realised hope of finding something big. I had heard that there were " coarse " fish as well as salmon in the Derwent, and also pike, all of which fed on minnows. I began to feel better. I baited again, and promptly caught another. I crept closer to the pool and, peering down, saw that there was a shoal of them, but now no sign of trout. I did the obvious thing with the second minnow. I put it on the hook instead of a worm. The line began to jerk as before, but it was the minnows who were attacking their late shoal mate, tearing it to bits, but of course missing the hook. I was getting more excited however. I remembered that there were plenty more pools farther down the stream, and the stream itself got bigger and deeper with the springs that ran into it at frequent intervals.

I moved towards the next pool. Juggerhowe really was a lovely place. And it would have been hard to imagine anything more secluded. The valley curved first one way and then another. The level part of it through which the beck had scoured its course, was knee-deep in heather and sweet-scented mrytle. Here and there grew a stunted alder or sallow, but there were no trees on the slopes of the valley, which were clothed with heather up to their top except where there was an outcrop of naked sandstone. Wherever you looked there was no sign of human occupation. The only tracks were those made by moorland sheep, and the sheep themselves (some of the ewes with lambs) looked as wild as antelope. The sheep kept up a continuous bleating. There were no larks singing here, but I could hear the piping of curlews, the occasional chattering of grouse as the sheep put them up from the heather, and more rarely still the harsh croaking of a carrion crow.

There were more trout rising in the second pool, but they took to their lairs in the banks as soon as they heard the plop of my bait, which again was savaged by swarms of minnows. I had to go back to worm in order to catch some more of these. Their voracity was astounding. The suspicion started to grow in my mind that although minnows were undoubtedly the food of big fish, the fact that they were here in such abundance might be proof that there were no big fish to eat them : but I hadn't lost hope yet. I went on from pool to pool, and I certainly wasn't bored, for I found an adder engaged in the task of swallowing a full-sized frog, and watched it until it had completed the job ; and soon after this I saw an old ewe suddenly charge down the opposite slope of the valley and a big dog fox, that had evidently been stalking its lamb, bound out of the heather and rush towards me and get so close that I could see the look of alarm in its eyes when it saw me, and bounded off on a more discreet course.

All these things delighted me, but I could not entirely get rid of gnawing thoughts of Adeline, and I began to feel really angry with the minnows. Even if there were any big fish lurking in the depths of the pools, they were not getting a chance even to see the bait, whether worm or minnows. I came to a pool even bigger than the one where I had started. There was a big rock in the middle of it, and on the opposite side the roots of an alder twisted down into the water, giving ample cover for any size of fish. I thought I'd get over the minnow problem by weighting my bait. They were feeding near the surface and I might get it past them before they had a chance to grab it. I sat down on a clump of heather in order to fix my gear. I felt a sudden sharp pain in my backside that made me shout and almost jump into the air. I was really frightened. I thought for a moment that I had sat on an adder. But when I clapped my hand on the spot I found it was nothing worse than a bumble bee. It went on hurting like hell, and my fingers were definitely trembling when I started fixing the gear again, but now standing up. I swore. Every damn thing was going wrong to-day, and all because of that blasted woman. She had put a jinx on me. Never had I gone fishing before and forgotten any item of my equipment. Never had I been stung by such an obvious thing as a common bumble bee. And, for that matter, never had I wasted time catching fish smaller even than the pennocks of my childhood. But the misfortunes of that evil day had not ended yet. I baited the hook with the largest worm I could find, thinking that if there was a good fish lurking under the alder it would surely appreciate a change of diet from the swarming minnows. I threw it in, and it sank, and for once there was no tell-tale nibble. I watched the line. For quite a long time it was still. And then I saw it moving very steadily. It tightened to my rod-tip. The rod itself began to bend. I took the weight of it, struck, and started to reel in. It was a fish all right. I got a decided jerk stronger than any minnow. Then I felt a stronger resistance. The line tightened towards the roots of the alder, and held. I tried to disengage it. It was fast but I could still feel the fish wriggling. I slacked out from the reel, laid the rod down on the bank, crossed over the stream above the head of the pool and made my way down to the alder. I broke off a dead branch, hooked my line with it, and then traced this down to where it had fouled. And then I saw the fish, and I was utterly disgusted, for it was nothing more than a moderately-sized eel such as one could catch with a worm any time the other two becks were in spate, and from the scaurs too, for this fish was equally at home in the sea.

I was not concerned now about landing it, but only in retrieving my cast, which was securely wound round the root. In fact, I was

D

pleased when I saw it wriggle clear of the hook and disappear in the depths of the pool. But the gut was still fast and resisted all my efforts to clear it. I decided at last to tie my knife to the end of a stick and cut it as close down to the root as possible. My knife however was in my creel on the opposite bank. I retraced my footsteps towards where I had crossed, but found a place nearer the head of the pool with a stone in the middle within striking distance. If that stone had been wet and moss-grown I might have taken greater care, but it looked dry and firm to me, and anyway my years of wandering about the scaurs had made me very sure-footed. Actually, I am certain that if things had been normal that day I would have made the crossing with perfect ease. But things were not normal. A jinx was on me. My foot slipped on the stone. I lost my balance and rolled idiotically into the pool ; and when I got upright again I found that my feet were practically stuck in the bed of peaty mud that formed the bottom.

I had to laugh at myself when I got out, and peeling off my sodden sports coat, looked at my new flannel bags stained the colour of a coble sail with the peat mud (which smelt like manure) and at my once-lovely brogues : but it was ironic laughter. The water was freezing cold. The sun seemed to have lost all its power of warming. I tried to move and found that my garments were clinging to my skin like jellied ice. I thought of the eight miles walk home : the sight I'd be walking through the village, or perhaps meeting Adeline and her man, just off on a trip on the motor-bike, and I felt more like weeping than laughing as, taking a deep breath to brace myself against the feel of my clothes, I strode forwards to my rod to jerk my line from the root no matter where it broke, to collect my tackle, and start for home. I almost wished it had been an adder I had sat on instead of a bumble bee and that I was dead, for life seemed to hold nothing but disillusionment, like this stream with its inviting pools that contained nothing but silly minnows and useless eels.

It was a dreadful week at the laboratory. I did my best to avoid Adeline. This was not difficult, for the man hung on to her like a shadow. I knew that I had not imagined her real attitude towards me. I knew that she was quite indifferent. She did speak to me, but she never mentioned our proposed fishing trip or the South

Seas, and she didn't ask me for the *Gazette* articles, which I kept handy in my coat pocket in a foolish hope that she just might. She didn't even mention the lobster she'd pretended to be so excited about, which was a pity, for I would have liked to have told her that I had put it back in the sea alive. Fortunately for my peace of mind and my nearly broken heart, it was her last visit to the place, for shortly after her brother got a post at another university, and what happened after I never knew.

I was glad when the holiday was over, and the students packed up and Sam got back. I told him what had happened and he was sympathetic, but he said I must not let an unfortunate love affair upset me too much. I must think of my career. He had shown the professor some of my articles, and he had been impressed by them. The professor thought I had done a wise thing indeed in not attempting to climb the academic ladder to success. Popular science writing, provided it was honest, was a legitimate profession, and I would be doing a lot of good if I could interest the general public in the wonders of natural science. He had also told Sam that at the first opportunity he was going to discuss with Professor Garstang the possibility of giving me a more definite and dignified appointment as Curator of the Laboratory, and possibly an increase in salary. This did please me, although I suspected the idea came not from the professor but from Sam himself.

Sam however could not conceal for long a far more important piece of news. The professor had been very pleased with the progress he had made on *Duto*, and had then told him that he had been approached by the Colonial Office with regard to a post that was going to be created in the Malay States. It was nothing less than Inspector of Fisheries. They required a man with a science degree, trained in biological research, but preferably someone with commercial experience and organising ability. The salary was high, with free first-class passage out and European furlough every three years, and a house at Penang, although the Inspector would be obliged to spend a considerable proportion of his time at sea on a steam yacht which was being specially equipped with apparatus and laboratories for fishery research. Previous nautical experience was desirable but not essential.

I'll admit that when Sam told me all this I felt worse even than when I'd seen Adeline rush forward to greet her medical student.

I just felt sick with envy. The very job I wanted, better than anything I had thought of, even in my wildest dreams. I had read Conrad's *Youth*, and that word Malay conjured up a vision of romance more magical even than the South Seas. My God, fancy being obliged to do anything so completely splendid as cruising on a steam yacht in the Malayan Seas, looking for new fishing grounds and new fish, going ashore on islands such as Conrad described. And apart from the science degree and the fact that I'd had no commercial experience (not an essential anyway), I just knew that it was the job above all that I was qualified to take.

I said to Sam, weakly :

" You're going to take it of course."

He laughed.

" Good heavens ! It hasn't really been offered to me yet. Denny was just putting out a feeler so to speak. Anyway it doesn't start till next September. By then of course my *Doto* job will be finished. I asked Denny to put my name down for it tentatively. Sounds pretty good though. Shows that things are looking up in the scientific world, when they can offer all that brass for a start. Interesting work too I should think, but I don't see exactly what it would lead to. Shouldn't like the idea of being stuck out in the Malay States for the rest of my life. Don't know much about the climate, but guess it would be pretty hot. Not too good for children. You know it's just the job that would suit you, especially that yacht business. And your knowledge of boats and fishing gear would come in handy. Damn it, if only you'd got your degree ! "

I gasped, partly in astonishment, that he could even suggest that the job might have its drawbacks, more because he had voiced my own thoughts.

I said to him rather wildly :

" Do you think there's a chance of my getting a degree if I started again and worked like hell ? "

" In four years, yes. Any one with normal intelligence could do that, but this job's got to be fixed before September. No. Only hope I can see is my taking the job. Doing the whole organisation. Building it up into something really big. Getting enough power to demand an assistant naturalist and fishery expert. Choosing you, Curator of the Northern Universities' Marine Biological Station, as you will be soon if I pull the wires right. That might impress the Johnnies out there more than B.Sc., especially with my personal recommendation. If I got sick of the job, you might easily slip into my shoes. By then you could have proved yourself indispensable."

I was seized again by a huge hope. Not, God forbid, that I should ever slip into Sam's shoes, but because my faith in his ability to do the things he wanted was as great as his own. What did it matter if I was Inspector, or just another laboratory boy, so long as I got to Malaya, and sailed on that steam yacht?

I said to Sam:

"You'd never get sick of a job like that. It's just ideal. I'd come with you in any capacity. It's a marvellous country; marvellous people, the Malayans. Have you read *Lord Jim* and *Youth*? Do for God's sake tell Denny you're keen. Just make up your mind you've simply got to take it. I tell you as soon as you are fixed I'll get out there somewhere. I'll work my passage out in a tramp steamer. I tell you we've just got to do it, and I know you can do anything you've a mind to."

He was silent for a while, then he said:

"I think I will. I've got my name down anyway. Only thing that bothers me about taking a job abroad is the way things are going at the mill. Told you our chief trade is turning elm bobbins for otter trawls. Now they're starting to make these out of steel stampings. Wear better, last longer. Orders at the mill dropping. Got to strike out in new directions if the mill's going to keep up. Our material's home-grown too. Growing competition with foreign timber. Whole thing wants reorganisation, adapting to changing markets. Still I don't think father and I will ever work in harness together. He lacks the scientific mind."

"Which makes the Fishery job so perfect for you. It's science and yet it's commerce. It's the ideal job and you're the ideal man for it."

I wasn't really trying to flatter Sam. What I said was true. But it was clear there was still a conflict in his mind about it, and with my whole future at stake, I'd have stopped at nothing to sway him in the right direction. A week or so latter Denny sent him the preliminary official Colonial Office application forms. Fortunately he got a letter from home by the same mail giving some reassuring news about the mill, and to my intense relief he filled in the forms and posted them back without delay.

That was a happy spring and summer. As Adeline did not come again, the wounds healed, although it was true that I could not walk down that scaur, or look at the stones I had turned without hearing her voice and seeing her smile and feeling very bitter about the medical student. What was this however against my vision of the East, re-stimulated by another reading of *Youth*? The Colonial Office moved slowly, but soon it became clear that Sam was high favourite for the post. He had to go up to London for a personal interview and medical examination, both of which were satisfactory. But the appointment could not be confirmed until the middle of August, and it was agreed that he should complete his *Doto* research.

I still envied Sam. Apart from his academic qualifications, I could not help feeling that the job was more in my line than his. Fish and fishing interested him, but for me they were still a passion. He was always game to make a fishing trip with me, but he would not learn to cast, and although the weather was now warmer, I could not feel happy in proposing something that might bore him. I was assailed sometimes by the dreadful thought that he might get bored too with the Malayan job before he had time to scheme my joining him, but he heartened me when he discussed the practical side of it, the organisation, the problems of marketing, refrigeration, canning, the adoption of steam trawls to supplant the present primitive native methods of catching fish. He had gathered at his interview that it was the Government's desire to develop and modernise the whole fishing industry of the States. That certainly was his line, and yet I thought, although I did not tell him so, I might have done it too, provided I hadn't much to do with things like finance and keeping accounts.

I didn't tell any one I was expecting to go abroad, although I felt completely positive that I was going to follow Sam. I went on teaching, finding it not quite so irksome now that I knew I was going to chuck it soon. I went on with my academic zoological studies, for Sam said that the job he had in mind for me was assistant naturalist, and that I should be well up in laboratory technique, and I continued with my writing too, although not quite with the same zest as before, for I could not see how it was going to help me in Malaya. Again, I had written a short story about the adventures of a shore crab, modelled on a tale about a stoat by Bensusan I had read in the *Windsor Magazine*, and this had been rejected by every magazine I'd sent it to.

We got some lovely weather in July. For days on end the sea was dead calm, and the water phenomenally warm. This led to our finding many sorts of marine animals which normally do not come so far north. There was a plague of jellyfish. These caused havoc with the nets of the salmon fishers, who were also suffering from damage done by small sharks and porpoises. One of the cobles came ashore with a giant sun-fish (whose home is the Mediterranean) weighing at least a quarter of a ton, and I actually got a paragraph about this in one of the daily papers and earned five shillings for it. But it was not just the unusual weather that was bringing these big fish so far north ; it was the immense shoals of sprats. Even the oldest fishermen could not remember seeing them in such quantities. I found it rather hard to concentrate on ordinary collecting while this was happening. All day long you could see the shoals marked by clouds of gulls and gambolling porpoises out in the Bay. Then at dusk they were being driven in towards the shore, and you could stand on any of the scaurs and see the creeks between them literally jammed with sprats and the other fish that were devouring them. It made me long for old Captain Bunny and the *Lydia*, for the present pleasure boatmen had no interest in railing, which meant them pulling about all the time, and there were plenty of visitors content to do their fishing anchored at the whiting grounds for just the same money and less work.

Fortunately Sam had reached a satisfactory climax in his *Doto* research. He had found the male of *Splanchnotrophus*. He was, compared with the female, microscopically small, and he was carried by her under her " shell " when she bored her way into the sea-slug's body. Apparently he was quite helpless. As soon as she settled down she used him as a market gardener would use a rabbit's tail brush to fertilise the blossoms of certain fruits with pollen, and when her own eggs were fertilised he was just left to die. Sam felt justified in " wasting a bit of time," but I don't think I would have persuaded him to do this fishing if a friend of his, Roland Deakin, hadn't come to stay at the laboratory for a few days. Roland was a fellow-student. If I hadn't been so confident that Sam was going to get the job in Malay, and that I was going to join him, this man would have upset me very much ; for he had just got an appointment as assistant entomologist to the Government of British East Africa and was sailing for Mombasa in a fortnight.

Roland was crazy on fishing. He told me in confidence that although he was excited about going to East Africa, he was envious of the job Sam looked like getting, and wished strongly that instead of specialising on insects and botany he had taken marine biology. Sam of course was the ideal man for the job, and yet he wasn't really keen on fishing. I liked him. I thought that next to going to Malaya with Sam there was nothing I would have liked better than going to British East Africa with Roland, even if it meant going far into the interior, miles from the sea. Apparently his job would be to help with investigations concerning a bug that was doing harm to the coffee plantations, but he would have to do a lot of field work which would mean long journeys (" safaris " they were called out there) through the bush and jungle. He had got the job through having a degree of course, and it would have been another grim reminder of my wasted opportunities if I hadn't had the " backstairs route " to Malaya to think about.

I was pleased to be able to promise Roland some good sport, and Sam professed himself quite keen when I told him that this wouldn't mean just standing on the scaurs waiting for bites. They were spring tides, not so heavy as the Easter ones had been, and not quite ideal for the type of fishing I had in ' mind. It meant that they were high in the afternoon and actually ebbing at dusk, which was the best time for fishing. Very rarely could you catch fish on the ebb. We set off just before dusk. Ordinary sea-rods were no use for this job. I had prepared for each of us a long bamboo (thousands of these, thrown overboard as useless dunnage, were washed ashore from passing ships during winter gales), and, as in my early pennock days, I wound a length of line from the butt to the tip, allowing a free length as long as the rod itself. There was no need for a reel or a cast. A single gut-snooded cuddy fly was the bait.

Opposite to Garry Nab and Beck there is a wide indentation in the sweep of the scaurs, forming a secondary bay as the tide recedes. Here is a patch of clean sand, a popular summer bathing spot. But on the north side a scaur runs directly seawards for nearly four

hundred yards, almost like a pier. It would have been a grand spot
for winter cod fishing but for the fact that even with a moderate
swell the waves broke against the edge of the scaur and you had
to keep dodging the spray from them. But to-night the whole Bay
was like a sheet of glass. There was not a breath of wind. And yet
when we reached the scaur we could hear a continuous seething and
rippling sound. We could see by the peculiar light of the sun's
afterglow, and that of the newly-risen moon, that the water was
furrowed by rippling rings, as though a heavy rain was falling. I
knew by the sound alone that the sprats were in, and we hadn't
got our flies tied on before we heard the louder plopping of bigger
fish, which I judged to be billet. I said to Sam and Roland very
confidently :

" Here they are. And I hope you won't get bored with catching
them. All you've got to do is cast your fly where you see the big
ones breaking the water, draw it with a bit of a jerky motion
towards you, and strike when you see its belly flash. Heave them
straight out on to the scaur. We ought to have brought a basket.
Never mind. They'll be all right in a heap with the tide ebbing.
We can put them on a string to carry home."

Being the host, I was not anxious to catch the first fish. In fact
I deliberately fumbled with my tackle while my guests got to work.
There were no technical difficulties to overcome as in cod fishing.
Roland anyway was an expert with a rod, and Sam was throwing
his fly just where he wanted to. And there was no need to aim at
any particular fish. They were darting everywhere into the solid
mass of sprats, and it was as though a miniature bombardment was
going on in the water. This itself was highly phosphorescent. Each
fish left behind it a trail of bluish fire. In addition, the moonlight
caught the silver bellies of the big and little fish whenever they
turned, and flashed brightly. But those big fish would have
nothing to do with the cuddy flies. I had no better luck myself. I
began to feel nervous, particularly about Sam. Fortunately we'd
had something to eat before starting off, and he certainly could not
complain this time about the cold for the air and sea were almost
tropical.

" I don't understand it," I said apologetically. " I've never
known billet not take the fly once they've got on the feed and
after dusk."

"Don't see why they should take a bit of feather when they've got nice live sprats to eat," said Sam. "Damn it. I felt one brush past my line then—but it didn't touch the hook."

"What about trying a live sprat instead of the fly?" said Roland, more practically. "Just shove it on the fly hook. Have a double chance then."

There was no difficulty in doing this for there were plenty of stranded sprats among the weed on the scaur top, some still alive. The big fish however soon showed that they were quite indifferent to this more realistic lure. Sam started whistling, the first dreaded sign that he was getting bored. Roland, again showing himself the true angler, suggested that the moonlight might be making the cuddy fly too conspicuous, and he cut his off the hook leaving only the sprat. Privately I did not think that would make much difference, but I waited the result eagerly. It didn't work, and I was thinking myself of trying a limpet when Sam gave a sudden yell.

"Got one. Got one at last."

He jerked it out on to the scaur, and clasped his hands on it as eagerly as I would have done myself. He held it up still flapping in the moonlight. It was not a billet but a horse mackerel, a lovely looking fish very much like a tunny and a comparatively rare close-in visitor to our coast. But it was foul-hooked near its gills, not caught by the mouth. Sam knew its Latin name of course.

"*Caranx trachurus!*" he shouted. "Horse mackerel. Are they any good to eat? It's a nice sized fish."

I had to tell him no; that in fact the fishermen regarded them as a pest, as they sometimes sank their herring and mackerel and had no commercial value. It was known too that where you found them in large shoals herrings and mackerel were scarce. But I was glad Sam had caught it. He was still quite excited, and he did not demur when I suggested that, as there seemed to be nothing but horse mackerel about and they were not going to give us much sport, we'd best try somewhere else. As the tide was getting very low I thought of a spot just south of the Landing. Here was another sort of temporary cove called Grunwyke, which in certain states of the tide and weather was used as an alternative landing or launching place by the fishermen.

It took us a fair time to reach Grunwyke, and it meant passing in front of the village. I was worried that the sight of the laboratory might remind Sam of some urgent work he had to do, or more dangerous still, of another meal, but he did not appear to notice it. The village looked enchanting in the moonlight. In some peculiar way it increased the height of the ancient buildings which stood on each side of the Slipway so that they almost looked like the battlements of a great castle. The moonlight was so strong that you could see the very colour of the weathered sandstone with its veins of yellow and rich brown, and the red pantiles were lovelier than they were even in the bright sun. Over one's shoulder the moon made a glittering path across the pools and creeks between the scaurs, and across the open Bay to the dark shadowed cliff of High Batts : but north of the village it shone clear on the lesser cliff of Low Batts, and you could actually see the green of the fields above, and the contrasting grey of cut meadows. The Slipway was deserted. All the fishermen were out at their salmon nets. There were few lights in the cottages. The whole scene was beautiful and romantic, and I knew that in spite of my wanting to get away from it, I loved this place and that wherever I travelled I would want to get back to it some day. But the thought of getting back made more alluring still a sudden picture I had of Malaya and Penang and the Java Sea, and I had an impulse to slap Sam on the back and shout to him, " My God, won't Penang look thrilling in the moonlight," which however I repressed, for I could tell that he really was pleased with his success with the horse mackerel and was quite eager to try the new place, and I didn't want to get his mind on to anything else.

The scaurs forming Grunwyke were not very prominent. The important feature was that they converged towards the shore, thus forming a sort of trap for the sprats when driven in by the bigger fish. I had seen them very thick in here before, but I was not prepared for the astonishing sight that met us when we approached it. For at least twenty yards above the end of the creek there lay a solid mass of dead or practically dead sprats, looking in the moonlight exactly like an immense snowdrift : and from the water's edge outwards, the creek was literally boiling with them and bigger fish. We saw one, it was either a billet or a cod, drive into the mass and shoot straight out of the water on to the shallow scaur and lie there stunned for a few seconds before jerking back into the water. But at first Sam and Roland were more impressed with the dead sprats. They picked them up by the handful and let them pour back on to the pile. They looked like quicksilver. Sam, ever practical, said :

" My God ! There's tons of them. Cartloads. Think what you could make if you could can them. Half the so-called sardines you buy in shops are just sprats, and sprats are just the young of herring. What'll happen to 'em ? Suppose with this weather they'll be stinking by to-morrow. In any case the next tide will disperse them. But think of the waste. Damn it, you'd think the farmers would come down and lead 'em away for manure. Think of the waste."

We started fishing from the scaur. Here the water was much shallower than it had been on Garry Beck and the sight of the big fish more tantalising, for they were so near that by bending down you could have touched them with your hand. They were mad. Time after time they were rushing practically ashore with half of their bodies out of the water. And we got slightly mad too before long. These were not horse mackerel. They were much too big. They were billet and cod, and I thought I saw conger and big flatfish, but it was hard to tell in the turmoil of flashing bellies and the phosphorescent flames. But none of them would look either at cuddy fly or sprat-baited hook. I foul-hooked a billet by its tail, but lost it. Roland actually foul-hooked a live sprat. Then Sam did get a billet and landed it, but this too was foul-hooked. Roland was getting furious.

" It's absurd. Never seen so many fish in my life. Can't catch one. Damn it, I'm going in to try with my hands in a minute. What we want is a net. Not angling, I know, but, damn it, this is absurd. Look at that. Almost on dry land again ! "

I remembered suddenly that I had a piece of old salmon net in the laboratory. It wouldn't be angling, I agreed, but we had given the fish every sporting chance of being caught. I ran up for it. By the time I returned Roland had managed to foul-hook a small codling, but he was ready enough to abandon his rod. We were wearing rubber deck boots, but I suggested we'd probably fill them and we'd be better off in our bare feet when we waded in. I was not certain as to the best technique to adopt, but I thought if I waded down the lower scaur and Roland stood on the other I could heave the net over to him, thereby closing the creek. Then we could all go to the shore and wade out towards it making as much disturbance as we could. We did the setting successfully, anchoring each end to a stone. Then we started the driving process.

It was a queer sensation. We were actually wading through living sprats, and they stroked and tickled our bare legs. But the big fish, still feeding on them and unaware of their doom, did not tickle. They bumped, and I'll admit I got a shock when I trod on something that heaved up under my foot, and the next moment felt something that must have been a fair-sized conger glide past my leg. A shout from Sam suggested that something pretty big had hit him, but he did not know what it was and he was certainly not put off by it. Even when Roland asked me if I thought there might be any crabs or lobsters, I had a feeling that if there had been they would not have deterred us from hauling the net, which gradually we were approaching. Angling or not, it was desperately exciting. The big fish at last knew there was something wrong. They were moving net-wards. We saw the gleam of a big one in the net itself. I cried halt when we were within about six feet of it, and almost thigh deep in the water. We splashed the water with our hands and kicked to make as much noise as we could. Then I asked Sam to get on to the bare scaur and seize that end, while Roland and I moved to the other. When all was ready we started to drag it up the creek and ashore.

We could not get it quite to the shore. It contained at least a hundredweight of fish and it would have broken with the strain. I had never seen anything like that haul. There were billets and codling by the dozen, but more exciting still, there were salmon trout (one a beauty of about four pounds) and there were flatfish, a real sole, plaice, dabs, flounders, and one big conger, only this managed to escape. There were crabs too, but finding these did not stop us from making another shot as soon as we had cleared the catch. The second haul was not quite so good. By the time we had shot it once again the tide had started to flow, and I saw that if we were to save what we had caught we'd have to finish. Sam was dead against this. I think he'd have gone on till daylight, he was so excited. But the net was an old one, not designed for dragging along a rough bottom; anyway it was now almost in tatters. While Sam and Roland made the fish into a pile higher

up the scaur clear of the tide, I ran up to the village and ' borrowed'
a couple of fish baskets from a laid-up coble. But even with these
we had to make two journeys.

I'd never seen Sam so excited. I thought it was the luckiest
thing that could have happened so far as our future was concerned.
Although it was getting on for midnight, we lit the cottage fire,
fried some plaice and made tea, and after that we went into the
laboratory. We did not sing as Roland wasn't fond of music. We
smoked and joked about our experience and the fun we'd had, and
Roland said it had been one of the most exciting fishing trips he
had ever made, and that he wished like anything that instead of him
going off to East Africa we were all going to Malaya, for the fishing
out there ought to be wonderful. He felt just green with envy
about that yacht. Sam did not raise any of the arguments he'd used
with me against going. For once he sounded really enthusiastic
about it, and I felt sorry for Roland, although the job he was
going to sounded thrilling enough, and he admitted that he would
probably get some good fishing there in the rivers and lakes if not
in the sea.

He had to leave next day by the morning train. We went up
to the station to see him off. I felt horribly depressed when the
moment came to say good-bye. In daylight one's thoughts are apt
to become more real and practical. I wondered if the time would
ever come when I'd be starting off for a foreign country, on a great
adventure. Penang had seemed so real last night in the moonlight.
It seemed so remote in the light of day. Again, I'd taken a great
liking to Roland. It seemed likely that we should never meet again.

Little did I guess as the train moved out on that sunny morning
in July of the year nineteen hundred and fourteen that in less than
eighteen months I should be lying in the next bed to Roland in a
military hospital in Nairobi, Roland, then a member of the East
African Volunteer Force suffering from dysentery, myself an officer
of the Royal Flying Corps recovering from the effects of my first
crash.

Whether the Malaya appointment was ever made I never knew.
Sam did not take it anyway. Timber ranked as an industry of first-
class national importance from the outbreak of the war. Sam went
into timber. But if my disappointment about Malaya was great, I
was determined to have adventure somehow. The slogan had

already gone up, " Business as Usual." Not for me ! I had, through Sam's influence, got my appointment as Curator of the laboratory, but what would the laboratory be without Sam ? I was still assistant master at the village school, but my job could be ended by a month's notice on either side, and that was the exact length of the summer holidays. I'd enlisted before the end of August— " Two years or duration "—and the only thing that bothered me as I took the oath was that the war would be over before I was in it.

Book Three

I

On the whole the war was very kind to me. The voyage on a first-class passenger liner to Mombasa (calling at Las Palmas, Cape Town and Durban) was a fair substitute for my dreamt-of voyage to Penang and East Africa a fair substitute for Malaya. At Government expense (and with a handsome salary which I could not then spend) I was able to travel by aeroplane, train, motor car, mule, donkey, on foot and occasionally in a sort of sedan chair carried by porters, through a considerable part of what is now known as Kenya : through the whole of German East Africa, from north to south and again from east to west : to see a great deal of Portuguese East Africa, Nyasaland, and a little of Rhodesia. I was able to sail in another passenger liner converted into a hospital ship back from Mombasa to Cape Town for two months' sick leave in a convalescent home : to return overland (first-class sleeper) through Cape Colony and Natal to Durban, thence by liner back via Lindi, Kilwa, Zanzibar, and Dar-es-Salaam to the front. After my two and a half years of active service that ended with my worst crash, I had another voyage on a hospital ship from Dar-es-Salaam via Aden and the Red Sea to Suez, thence overland to Alexandria and Aboukir. I was sent to hospital in Cairo, given a month's sick leave and a free railway pass to Luxor, where I saw all the sights the peacetime tourist would see, but at no expense. Then as a medical board classified me as unfit for further flying duties, I was ordered home, sailing from Alexandria to Taranto, thence by train along the east coast Adriatic route via Bari, Ancona, Bologna, Milan and down to Genoa and the Riviera route to Marseilles, north again by way of Lyons to Cherbourg and Southampton.

Join the Royal Flying Corps and See the World ! was the old recruiting slogan ! I saw a good measure of it. Because our aircraft in East Africa were very low-powered " obsolescents " from the Western Front, and because of difficult atmospheric conditions, our flying had to be confined to early morning and late afternoon, and in the height of the rainy season there was little flying at all. There were no conventional parades or drill for flying officers. Usually we could spend the hot hours of the day as we liked, and I spent them exploring the bush or forest adjacent to our camps and aerodromes. The whole of that country was one vast zoo. Once clear of the camp, you couldn't walk twenty yards in any direction without seeing something interesting. The fauna varied of course. Our first aerodrome was on the Serengetti Plain, a level stretch of fairly open bush extending east from the foothills of the stupendous snow-capped Mount Kilimanjaro. Here, like cattle on a ranch, were great herds of hartebeeste and gazelle, troops of zebra, giraffe, ostriches, and the creatures that preyed on them, lions, leopards, cheetahs, hunting dogs, and the carrion-eating jackals and hyaenas, vultures and maribou storks. But gradually we chased the Germans south across their colony, through the swamps of the Pangani River, into the mountains of Usambara, down to the coast and back again to the Central African Tableland and Lake Nyasa, and the fauna changed according to the type of country. There were elephant and rhinos, buffalo and eland, water-buck, reed-buck, kudu, wild-beeste and, in the rivers and lakes, hippoes, crocodiles and fish. My first fishing trip to the Pangani River was a curious contrast to my last unhappy one to Juggerhowe! Our aerodrome was about four miles from the river in open bush. I had with me my personal boy, a happy-natured, honest, mission-trained but naturally indolent and stupid native of the Wataita tribe of British East, named Maganga. He'd been trained as a house-boy, to launder and cook, and knew nothing about the bush except that it contained lions, snakes and scorpions and other horrible creatures. He fancied himself as an English linguist, but actually his vocabulary was small and his grammar confused. He had a passion for personal cleanliness, and his drill shorts and shirt were always as beautifully ironed as my own, and he wore the smartest of black town boots polished so that they looked like patent leather. Maganga would have much preferred staying in camp in the hot hours of the day, but as you never knew what would turn up, I had to have him to carry my rifle and game and ammunition bag, while I carried a single-barrelled 16-bore shot gun I'd bought in Mombasa.

Maganga was a distinct embarrassment on any sporting trip.

His dread of man-eating lions and snakes was nearly equalled by his fear of tearing his clothes on a camel thorn or getting his boots dirty. Fortunately it was then the dry season, and although we saw a few snakes and the spoor of a lion, there were no dangerously exciting incidents on our outward journey. But there were plenty of things to see, columns of black soldier-ants moving in formation over the sun-baked earth, acacias festooned with the nests of weaver-birds, colonies of chattering parakeets in the occasional baobab trees, long-tailed and brightly-coloured whydah birds, toucans, horn-bills. We encountered a Masai warrior carrying his long steel spear, with a tuft on it showing that he had at least one lion to his credit. He was a magnificent looking fellow, not tall, but with the limbs and torso of a trained athlete. He wore a loin cloth of soft goathide, and a sort of open cape made of the same material. His face was more Egyptian than negroid, and looked aristocratic, sensual and cruel. His hair was plaited into a sort of wig dressed with fat and a reddish brown pigment. The Masai had been treated abominally by the Germans when they settled in this part of the colony. Like the rest of the natives they were obliged to stop and stand stiffly to attention and salute whenever they met a white man, which was what this one did now, but when I smiled at him and greeted him in English he moved off at once, with a loping gait like a leopard. Maganga sniffed in a very superior way.

" *Yum-yum !* " he said contemptuously. " You smell him ? No good. Never wash. No civilise."

" Yum-yum " meant cannibal. The man certainly had carried an aroma with him, but I was sure that the Masai, although they had long been known for their ferocity as fighters, had never been that. Maganga was showing himself a snob, and I wondered what that proud-looking warrior with his beautifully-plaited hair and graceful cloak and shining spear must have thought of us in our shorts and shirts, especially of Maganga's black boots, and whether our smell (or absence of it) was offensive to him.

We pushed on towards the river, whose whereabouts was marked by a belt of tall darkly-foliaged trees rising above the light green of the acacias. Although we were at least eighty miles due south of Kilimanjaro its twin summits rose clear into the sky, the lesser one sharp and serrated, the main one flat-topped and symmetrical, and its snowfields and glaciers lying on it like a moulded cloud. Below the snowline the treeless upper slopes, composed of lava emitted from the long-sealed crater, were of a blue just darker than the sky itself. It was all wildly beautiful whichever way you looked, and although there were no flowers growing on the red sun-baked ground, there were occasional mimosas among the acacias and camel thorns, and the scent of them hung like a vapour until we neared the river, when I smelt a mustiness that took me back instantly to the bogs of Browe Moor and Juggerhowe itself. We found that the banks of the river had a belt of tall papyrus growing on both sides of the narrow belt of trees, that soon we were in what a few weeks ago before the rains ended would have been swamp. This was now bone-dry underfoot, and we could not get as much as a glimpse of the river itself. Maganga was scared at the prospect of forcing our way through the papyrus. There might be a lion in it, there certainly would be snakes, and he pointed dramatically to a patch of dried mud which bore the almost complete impression of the belly and tail of a twelve-foot crocodile.

"Tembe," he said. "What you call crocodile. Very bad thing. Best go back."

But I could hear the water if I could not see it. We moved along the edge of the papyrus belt until shortly we came to a gap that obviously had been made by the passing of several hippoes. I exchanged the shotgun for the rifle, and led the way, Maganga reluctantly following, and treading carefully to avoid the heaps of hippo dung. Suddenly we heard a terrific chattering in the trees near the river, and we saw the branches shaking. They were green monkeys, scores of them, the first I had seen outside of a zoo, and I think they were the first that Maganga had seen too, although he must have seen baboons. They were in a great state of alarm, but they must have felt fairly secure in the tall trees and did not retreat as we neared the river. We saw it at last. The papyrus had been trampled down on each side of the track we were following, leaving the bank fairly clear. There was dried mud and sand underfoot, and I was reminded at once of the Mill Dam, for the river itself, fed by the melted snows from Kilimanjaro, was dirty and sluggish and seemed scarcely to flow at all. And I was possessed by the same excitement as on that occasion when I had first tried out the Squire's fly. Yet how different it was ! Instead of the gnarled oaks of the Mill Wood the trees were almost straight as pines and were immensely tall. Although the river was more than twenty yards from bank to bank, their branches in places almost bridged it ; did so, in fact, for the monkeys, which ran or leapt or swung from side to side. Instead of an undergrowth of hazels and brambles, there was papyrus and graceful raffia palms. Instead of the cooing of the solitary pigeon that had haunted me that day, there was the chattering of the monkeys, the croaking of the toucans and a constant twitter of small birds. And straight opposite to us on a spit of bare sand nearer the opposite bank were three objects which at first looked like stranded logs, but were actually crocodiles, roasting themselves in the shafts of sun that came through the gaps in the canopy of trees. Maganga eyed them nervously. They would have made an easy rifle shot. But I had no wish to disturb their siesta, and my mind now was wholly on fishing. Here indeed was a mystery comparable with that of the sea. What sort and size of fish might be lurking under the surface of that deep murky water ?

I had no real fishing gear beyond a length of stout line and some hooks I had fashioned myself of aeroplane bracing wire in our mobile workshop. I looked about me in the jungle for the equivalent of a Mill Wood hazel and found a growing bamboo, which was even better. I rigged it as I had done our rods for the evasive billet the night I had taken Sam and Roland fishing, and then I looked for bait, making Maganga help me dig into the dry mud for possible worms. But we did not find any, and in fact I never did find an earth-worm in East Africa. There were locusts in the papyrus however, and I soon had my hook baited and thrown in up-stream, so that it would move down with the gentle current. Nothing happened for a long time. There was no sign of fish on the surface of the water. But the presence of the crocodiles, which in spite of popular repute are chiefly fish and not human body eaters, encouraged my belief that the river contained plenty of fish, and this was supported by the sight of a cormorant standing on a tree stump not far from the crocodiles with its wings outstretched to dry in the sun exactly as you would see one on each of the marking posts at Bramblewick Landing.

Although we were in the shade of the trees it was intensely hot. Manganga having assured himself that there were no snakes in the immediate vicinity, and that the crocodiles were not actively interested in him, had found a clean reed-strewn spot on the bank to sit on, and was falling asleep. I sat down too, but I wasn't bored. The monkeys, less terrified now, were still gambolling among the trees. Some of them were daring to come quite close. Some of the females had their very small babies hanging on under their bellies, and I saw three youngsters travel down a branch that came near to the crocodiles, and shriek and pull faces at them just as village boys would plague an old tramp. I saw their parents rush after them and chase them away, but the crocodiles did not stir. I got tired of casting so I weighted the line with a cartridge and let it sink, resting the rod on the bank, but, remembering my experience at Tom Bell Nick, keeping one hand on the butt. Suddenly I noticed something like a piece of waterlogged wood floating down the middle of the river, but moving faster than the current. As it drew nearer I saw that it was the head of a hippopotamus It went under, but emerged again just opposite the crocodiles. The monkeys shouted at it, but the crocodiles took no notice. It went under again, and then to my great joy it came up near the opposite bank and emerged from the water and stood for a full minute on the bank while its calf, which I had not seen at all, emerged miraculously from the river close by and joined it. Then both of them vanished into the jungle. It was soon after this that I felt my rod jerk, and I was still so excited by what I had seen that I half imagined it was a hippo I had hooked. I gave a shout that brought Maganga to his feet in terror. He must have thought that the crocodiles were attacking us, for I had got my fish out of the water before he realised what had happened. It was a good fish, about four pounds, but I was disappointed with it. I had expected something brightly coloured, fantastic in shape, tropical. The thing I had caught looked like a cross between an ordinary eel and a rock fish quite common at home, the bearded rockling. It was stouter, but slimy and coloured like an eel. It had a flattish head with a large mouth full of fine teeth and fringed with longish tentacles. It was, I learnt later, a species of barbel.

Maganga was quite excited about it, especially when I told him that it was probably good to eat, but he didn't like the job of handling it. I baited again with a locust, and soon got another, about the same size. I went on like this until I had got about half a dozen, and by then it was becoming obvious that there was no other sort of fish to catch. I tried baiting with a piece of the fish itself, but caught nothing at all that way, and as I was due back at the aerodrome by four, I thought of packing up. And it was on my final throw-in that I had the most dramatic surprise of my first African fishing trip. I got a sharp bite. I struck, felt the weight of the fish (much less than the previous ones) and whipped it straight out of the water to Maganga's feet. He had by that time overcome his reluctance to handling them, and before I had time to see what it was, he had bent down to seize it. As he touched it he gave a loud yell, and recoiled from it as though it had been a snake. He was wringing his hand.

"Bwana—bwana! He bite me!"

I looked at his hand. There was no wound or sign of a sting. I looked at the fish. It was silvery, with a slender body not unlike a smolt. It had no spines and so far as I could see no sharp teeth. I laughed at Maganga. He had evidently imagined the thing had bitten him. And then I touched it myself, and was startled to receive a sharp galvanic shock, not serious but enough to make me wince. I was never able to identify that fish, for I lost the drawings and detailed notes I made of it. It had lost its galvanic power by the time we got back to camp, for of course it was dead, and none of my fellow-officers would believe it had possessed them, and anyway they were more interested in the barbel, which, if they had a rather muddy taste, made a welcome change to tinned salmon at mess that evening. But I did discover later that " electric " fish are found in many African rivers, including the Nile.

Actually I did not get much river fishing in East Africa. Previous to the war, some English settlers in British East had tried the experiment of introducing trout into the clear mountain streams of the Highlands not far from Nairobi, which contained no crocodiles or ferocious native fish, and I believe the experiment was a success, but I had no chance to see them. Later in the campaign I was to see similar streams in the Highlands of German East Africa, which I am sure would have been suitable for such cultivation. You could not have distinguished them from a Highland or a West Yorkshire burn. There was heather and bracken on the banks, and real Scotch thistles and the sundew, a fly-catching plant that grows on our own moors : that was one of the many things I would have liked to have tried after the war, a glorified version of my boyhood dream of having a trout stream of my own and making a pool in it like the Miller's Dam.

My sea fishing too was limited, but I had enough of it to confirm my conviction that it was more exciting than fresh water. I was stationed for several weeks at Dar-es-Salaam and at the one-time slaving port of Kilwa. As the coast belt was intensely cultivated, chiefly with cocoanuts, by the late German settlers as well as by the native Swahilis and Arabs, there was no hunting and all my spare time was spent on the shore. There were coral reefs, perhaps not so fascinating as the Great Barrier Reef and the coral islands I'd read about as a boy, for there seemed to be only one species of coral polyp engaged in the eternal process of changing the dissolved lime-stone of the sea into rock. His industry was stupendous, but it was stolid and all to a simple unvarying pattern. There were no fantastically shaped clumps or mushrooms or slender plumes such, as you'll see in a museum. The reefs indeed were very much like our scaurs, only more flat and even. In places they spread for nearly half a mile seawards from the cocoanut or mangrove fringed shore when the tide was down. They formed a sort of porous crust which crunched under your feet, and it was only in the pools that you could see the living polyps extending from the rock like masses of tiny flowers. The reefs at low water were haunted by gulls and curlews. I had only to close my eyes and listen to the curlews to put myself back on Bramblewick shore. If the corals were dis-appointing in their monotony, there were plenty of other animals in the pools. There were many gorgeous anemones. There were starfish and brittle stars, bigger and brighter than the ones at home There was no thick weed, no tangles even at low water springs, and I missed our flat " Doto " stones, which meant that I could only find animals capable of withstanding the tidal exposure to the intense light and heat of the tropical sun. In the little caves of the pools however I found sea-cucumbers (the edible beche-de-mer of commerce), many fantastically shaped and coloured rock fish and crabs, and a species of sea-slug with gills and papillæ which would have thrilled the artist author of *British Nudi-branchiata* !

I couldn't fish from the reefs for there was no deep water. I rigged up a scaur-line, and tried a variety of baits, including an anemone which bore a strong resemblance to our Yorkshire scaur-cock, but the gulls pecked them off before the tide flowed and I had no success. At Kilwa I became friendly with an old Swahili fisherman (all the young ones had been "conscripted" by the Germans as "askaris" or porters before our forces had pushed them into the interior) who lived in a hut on the beach with his two elderly wives. His name was Hamza-bin-Nazar, and his wool and beard were quite white. Before the war he'd had a regular job supplying the local German Commissioner with fish, at a flat rate of one rupee a week. It took me some time to overcome his diffidence. The only white men he had met were Germans, and he didn't like them. They had taken all his sons and a daughter and hadn't paid him a single rupee as compensation. But I conveyed to him by signs and my scanty knowledge of Ki-Swahili that I didn't want any saluting or standing to attention when I spoke to him. I gave him and his wives tobacco and sugar and some old shirts, and I found him as genial as old Captain Bunny, with whom he had a great deal in common, even the same twinkling eyes. His boat was a dug-out with outriggers and a crazy sail made of odd pieces of cloth and sacks like a patchwork quilt. But she sailed better than the *Lydia*. The outriggers gave her a grip on the water that took her almost into the eye of the monsoon breeze that blew from the sea all day long, and once we had made our offing from the edge of the coral reefs we bowled along the coast like a yacht. I wished I had included some spinning tackle in my tropical kit for I think we might have had some good sport railing, but I had to be content with hand-line fishing. This certainly fulfilled my expectations of what tropical sea-fishing should be. Bait was a simple matter. As soon as we arrived at the fishing ground (in the lee of a dry coral reef which some day doubtless would become a genuine island) Hamza picked up a wooden buoy, and hauled in a number of large earthenware jars nearly every one of which contained an octopus. He hadn't baited these. An octopus likes a lair in which to lie in wait for its victims, and the jars apparently must have seemed just the right sort of accommodation. He put them in a live bait box which he hung over the side, and cut them up as we needed them.

There was no waiting for the fish to bite. You simply dropped your line and something got on at once. It would have been dull but for the fact that at least every other fish was a different species, or variety. I did not know the correct names of any of them. Some were like bream, some were like wrasse, some like hake, and ling, and gurnard, but nearly all of them were barred or mottled with bright colours. One had curiously twisted lines on it that looked like Arabic writing, and Hamza (who was a Mohammedan) became voluble when the first of these came on board. He pointed to the marks, and kept repeating the word *Koran*, and I discovered later that he was trying to explain that these formed a phrase from the Prophet's writings and that the fish (whose flesh was highly prized) had once been touched and blessed by Him, just as our own haddock with its two dark " fingerprints " had been touched and blessed by Christ in the miracle of the fishes ! We caught a species of fish that was shaped like a Rugby football and covered with sharp spines like a hedgehog, but which in a minute or two collapsed to the shape of a gurnard. We caught some fair-sized sharks, including one " hammer-head " with its eyes fixed on the extremities of long processes jutting laterally from the head. There were skate too, but unlike any that I knew at home. All the time we fished old Hamza chewed betel nut, and his eyes twinkled, and he talked and talked, and although I could not understand a quarter of what he was saying it was just as though I was back in the old *Lydia* with Captain Bunny.

What a contrast flying made with these idyllic excursions ! It was at Kilwa that I had one of my most exciting flights. The place was very unhealthy. We were only a small detachment away from the squadron and with only one serviceable machine, a B.E.2. C. with a single 70 h.p. engine and a full-out speed of sixty miles per hour. Many of the mechanics and all the flying officers except one pilot and myself had gone down with malaria. I think that I had kept fit by going fishing, but the pilot, the Hon. Bernard Howard, had a theory that the only certain way of beating the germ was whisky, which he drank at the rate of well over a bottle a day. He was middle-aged, tall and lanky, with an aristocratic face and bearing. He could talk of nothing but horse racing and casinos and women and wine, and the good times he'd had getting through a fortune he'd inherited. But he was a grand pilot: He'd joined the French Flying Corps at the outbreak of war, had been shot down, taken prisoner, and then escaped. I had never seen him tight, but the only time I had flown with him sober (when there'd been no whisky in the mess for two days) I'd been terrified because I could actually feel the trembling of his hands on the joy-stick and it was just as though an engine bearing had partly seized. But this flight took place on Christmas Day and there was no scarcity of liquor.

The local military situation at that time was not favourable to our troops. A force of infantry had been sent up from the coast with the object of blocking an enemy retreat from his main positions on the Rufiji River. This force had occupied a German stronghold among the densely wooded mountains about forty miles from the coast, but a German force with artillery had moved swiftly down and had virtually laid siege to the stronghold itself. Our men were short of food and were under constant bombardment. The object of our flight was reconnaissance. There was no such thing in those days as dropping stores from aeroplane by parachute, and it was a last minute suggestion that we should take with us a large parcel of cigarettes that had come to our mess from some " Comforts for the Troops " organisation. Bernard was well dosed with his prophylactic, and we left the ground at about half-past four. It was a small awkward aerodrome fringed with cocoanut palms and mango trees, and our landing wheels actually brushed a cocoanut as we took off seawards into the monsoon breeze. The sensation of flying always produced in me a sort of ecstasy that was mingled with apprehension. I did not know much about engines, but by this time I had become so used to the noises made by a Wolseley-Renault that I knew exactly if all the components were working properly, and I could tune myself as it were to the total rhythm and vibration. When it was all right I could forget it and enjoy myself, looking at the view which, at all times, was superb and especially so when it included the sea.

On this occasion the engine was pulling well, and once we were definitely clear of the palms I felt happy. It was a typical fine-weather sky with a few little high floating clouds which appeared static. The air was crystal clear, and with the sun lowering, its light was losing that harsh brilliance which in the noon hours seems to bleach the colours even of the sea. The sea now was a deep blue, and flecked white with the breeze, and with patches of livid purple where the clouds threw a shadow. With this the fringing cocoanuts and dark green mango trees made a lovely pattern. Squat white-walled Arab and Swhaili houses gleamed among the trees. There were white-sailed dhows on the sea itself, getting smaller and smaller as we climbed to our cruising height. We turned landwards, flew over the aerodrome again, and then after another seaward circuit settled to a north-westerly course for the mountains and Kibata.

I have said that the air was crystal clear, but that phrase does not convey its exact optical quality. I have seen something like it at home. You get it in summer occasionally during squally thundery weather in the calms between squalls, when it is as though you are looking at hills and trees through clear water or a lens : when everything stands out with an extraordinary clarity. But at home in such weather, and from the ground there is usually a short limit to the extent of your view. Here the limit was only the curving of the earth, and from our cruising height of 4000 feet, you could actually observe the globular curve of the sea to the dead horizon line. North-westwards, to which the land gradually rose in a series of hills and tablelands and mountains, the earth's curve was neutralised and I could easily recognise the summit of a mountain peak near to which we had been stationed for several weeks, one hundred and fifty miles away. With a powerful telescope I believe I could have picked out every detail of it.

A river, the Matandu, runs into the sea some ten miles north of Kilwa. We passed over the upper reaches of this, but its whole course was visible, with every detail of its sandbanks and seaward mangrove swamps. With my field glasses I could see scores of hippoes. From here onwards there were no human habitations. There was nothing but forest-clad hills beneath us, and owing to the height of the trees and the denseness of their foliage one could not even see the game tracks which are such a feature of the open bush when seen from the air. Not at all a pleasant place for a forced landing, I thought. But the engine was still pulling well and soon, staring ahead, I got the gleam of something white among the hills. It was our first flight to Kibata, but the place had been described to us as a typical German military post enclosed with a wall of masonry. I pointed it out to Bernard, and he nodded his head in confirmation.

All the time the hills were rising, but our ceiling was 4000 feet above sea-level, not the *ground*, and when at last we approached the fort it could not have been more than half that distance beneath us. It was built on the actual summit of a hill. The forest had been cleared for a short distance on the north side. Here, as we got immediately overhead, I saw a couple of shells burst, but I did not see the gun flashes, and possibly because the Germans had spotted us and did not want to give their position away there was no more firing. Bernard waggled the joy-stick to attract my attention. He pointed down at the fort. Even without glasses I could see quite a number of our soldiers, apparently waving to us. Bernard bore off from the fort a little, I undid my safety belt, got hold of the parcel of cigarettes and leaned out to clear the bottom wing. He turned again and then started a fairly steep power dive. The fort lay ahead and soon was not more than five hundred feet beneath us. I kept my face turned to Bernard, for it was for him to judge the range. Suddenly he pulled out of the dive and zoomed, nodding to me to let go. I let go and saw the parcel sail past clear of the tail and rudder. That was the last I did see of it, for the next moment the engine stopped. As we'd been climbing we lost forward speed, stalled, and, it seemed to me, came backwards. Then our head dropped and we started to dive, fortunately on an even keel, but straight for that clearing in front of the fort where we had seen the shells bursting.

I looked round at Bernard. There was only the sound of whistling bracing wires now, and I heard him shout.

"Engine's konked. Going to pancake in that clearing. Jump out and run for the fort as soon as we crash. The bastards will be shelling us. Did you see the parcel drop? Wish to hell we'd put a couple of bottles of whisky with it. Bet *they* haven't a drop!"

It didn't occur to me then how funny it was that Bernard should be worrying about his whisky when we were within a few seconds of crashing on a mountain side, and a no-man's land at that. I had no time to feel worried about myself, or, for that matter, frightened. I instinctively curled up my legs and waited for the crash. I saw the ground not less than two hundred feet below us, saw that it consisted of jagged rocks and thick stumps of trees, and then I heard the engine splutter and roar again, and felt the plane flatten out from its dive and start to climb. The fort was above us and we were surrounded by hills but ahead was a valley; we flew along it, climbing all the time, and soon we were above the highest of the hills and on our homeward course, the engine running perfectly. I turned to look at Bernard, and waved my hand to express my delight and relief, but as I did so the engine stopped again. We did not stall this time. Our head just went down and we began to glide towards the forest. I was frightened now and no mistake. I had more time to think about it. For miles around us there was not a patch of bare or level ground. It was real forest country, not bush. It we safely pancaked on the treetops, there would still be a nasty drop from them to the ground. I looked at Bernard. He did not look particularly alarmed, but he did not speak and just pointed significantly with one finger downwards. He had hardly done this than the engine again spluttered and began to roar full out. We soared up and still flying homewards, reached almost to our normal cruising height before it stopped again and we got into another glide. The awful thought suddenly came to me that it was not the engine that was going wrong but Bernard himself, either through an overdose of whisky, or for the need of another one. I shouted to him.

"What's up?"

He shook his head and answered:

"Don't know. Must be a petrol choke. It may pick up again before we crash."

It did pick up but not until we were so close to the trees that I could see the great trunks of them and the rough ground beneath. We climbed for about three minutes, and then it stopped again, but this time only for a short period. Fortunately the hills were falling towards the coast, so that our height above the ground was increasing, but for the next twenty minutes the process of stopping and picking up again was repeated at least three times so that our course was like that of a switchback railway. We reached the valley of the Matandu. We went into another glide within landing distance of a wide patch of what looked like clear and level ground, and Bernard yelled to me that he would try and make it. Lucky for us the engine picked up before we saw that it was actually swamp. We saw both hippoes and crocodiles at the edge as we roared up from it, the engine behaving once more as though it had just been re-tuned. And this time it did not falter until we had got to a good 3000 feet. The coast line lay beneath us : Kilwa and our aerodrome within easy gliding reach. Bernard made a perfect landing with the engine running again, but of course throttled, and he taxied with it up to the tent hangar, where two mechanics and Maganga and Bernard's own boy were waiting (the latter according to his master's parting instructions) with a glass of neat whisky, and while Bernard drank his I shouted to Maganga to bring one for me too.

There were three interesting sequels to this adventure. First, it was discovered by the mechanics that the trouble had been caused by a leaf that had got into the air duct of the carburettor. The suction of the engine had gradually drawn this against the gauze filter, choking the air flow, and valve-like it had fallen back when the suction ceased, enabling the carburettor to work again. Second, that night Bernard became very ill, with a temperature of 105. He protested violently, but he was too weak to prevent us taking him to hospital, where the doctors diagnosed malaria. He kept all the other patients awake shouting for whisky, which naturally was forbidden, but next morning on the pretext of getting some of his kit, he got his boy to smuggle in two bottles, which apparently he drank. His temperature was down that night. He walked out of hospital next day and was flying again the same afternoon, although for once I was glad that he went alone. Third, many years after the war I was travelling in the night mail from York to Bristol with a single fellow-traveller. We started talking and I discovered that he was an ex-corporal of the Loyal North Lancs, and a member of that very force that had been besieged in Kibata. They'd seen the parcel come down and had at first thought it was a sort of bomb that we had intended for the Germans. They'd had a pleasant surprise when they'd picked it up. There had been no tobacco in the " camp " for over a week.

I was lucky. In spite of my many crashes and forced landings, and that I was nearly burnt alive in the last one, I did not receive any serious injuries. I had plenty of adventure. I learnt a great deal about the geography, the natives and their customs, and the natural history of East Africa. I learnt something of colonial administration, German and Portuguese as well as British, and got first-hand insight into the work of Christian missionaries among the blacks. I saw some bloody battles, and if war in its techniques has become more hideous, its fundamental purpose of slaughtering human beings has not been changed. I met, lived with, and worked with many interesting white men, including the great naturalists Selous and Cherry Kearton, both boyhood heroes of mine, and I was not disillusioned with them. Cherry was attached to our squadron for a time as photographic officer. I think he had been in East Africa at the outbreak of war engaged on making another of his wonderful films of wild life. I was actually flying over a place called Beho-Beho, between Kissaki and the Rufiji, when the action took place in which Selous, who had dined at our mess the previous night, was killed by a German bullet. He was then 66. I met Jan Smuts on several occasions, one of them very pleasant, when he praised a map and a report I had made on a German position he intended to attack ; another not so pleasant, for we had occupied a German light railway in our advance south, and the General had issued orders that in no case had the track to be used for motor transport, for which it was admirably suited. I was not aware of these orders. It was urgent for us to secure a more advanced aerodrome, and having spotted a likely place by air, I was sent off with a tender and driver to make a detailed examination. The road being used by our advancing troops was a mere track through the bush and very rough. For some distance it ran almost parallel to the railway, and on the homeward journey I told the driver to get on to the railway itself. We were doing about 40 when we struck a place where the track actually crossed it, and there, negotiating a particularly bumpy section of the bush track in low gear and raising clouds of red dust was the G.O.C. and all his staff.

The General raised his hand at us. We pulled up, and reversed. He had got out of his car. I got out of mine, stood rigidly to attention and saluted. He cursed me in mixed English and Dutch for a full minute without stopping. Behind him were three cars full of generals and staff officers, all of them begrimed with red dust and all staring at me savagely. I think I must have said " yes, sir " at least a dozen times during that minute, and saluted almost as often, but I just didn't understand what he was cross about, and when he stopped at last and told me to be off, I saluted again, got back into the tender and told the driver to proceed, still on the railway track. Fortunately a staff captain held up his hand then, ran up and said to me, in angry undertones :

" You bloody fool. Don't you know that road is barred ? Get on to the bush road and out of the General's sight before he has you shot."

At another period in the campaign we had attached to us as M.O. the distinguished traveller and naturalist Dr. Wollaston. We often went out collecting together, and we salvaged a magnificent collection of butterflies from a German bungalow which had been partly wrecked by artillery. He was a great friend of the Rothschild family, and after the war was left a fair amount of money and became an Oxford Don, chiefly I believe with the object of continuing his own scientific studies in the peaceful atmosphere of Oxford. It was shortly after this that he was interviewing a student on some disciplinary matter when the youth pulled out a pistol and shot him dead.

Our officers were a mixed crowd. There were several Boers, including a grand fellow named Emmett, a nephew of General Botha, and now I believe of high rank in the R.A.F., a famous white hunter, W. D. M. Bell, reputed to be the best rifle shot in Africa, a fine artist too and our best pilot, only he didn't like having an observer with him as he always carried a repeating rifle with which he tried potting German soldiers at low level. An observer would have interfered with his line of fire. There was a Londoner named Garood (another splendid pilot) who earned fame by crashing in the Rufiji swamps. He was missing for five days, and when found by a patrol was clad only in his vest. He had taken off the rest of his garments to dry them and had fallen asleep. A troop of monkeys had stolen the lot. There was an ex-British East District Commissioner named Brett, one of the quietest and most unassuming, and most intrepid men I have ever met. He had a way with natives that was little short of magical, and they seemed to worship him, and this without any of the German goose-stepping and saluting bally-hoo. There was a fiery little Welshman named Carey Thomas who, if he'd been younger and on the Western front, would undoubtedly have been a fighter ace, for he did not know what fear was, and we had some very exciting flights together. Ironically, Carey Thomas was shot down and killed in an aeroplane during some industrial riots in South Africa after the war. Also there was my last Flight-Commander, Hodgkinson, of a well-known west country yeoman family, a landowner, a master of hounds, an occasional player of cricket for his county and member of the Bath Club. I believe he owned the land on which, after the war, was discovered the famous Wookey Hole and that he made a lot of money out of it. We flew together regularly for many months from aerodromes in Nyasaland and Portuguese East. He was a cool and steady pilot whose judgment never faltered even under the most trying circumstances, when, for example, we ran out of petrol over the Livingstone mountains and had to glide down a ravine between terrific cliffs to pancake without scratching even the plane in a field of maize on the shores of Lake Nyasa.

Most of these men were public school and university. They ragged me unmercifully about my Yorkshire accent. I hated it because I didn't know I'd got one. But I did discover in the end that words like last and mast and fast have a long and not a short *a*, that *one* should be *wun* and not *wan*, that if there are four syllables in " comfortable " they should not be pronounced as four words, and in the end I believe I learnt to speak quite nicely.

E

2

INDEED, the war was to me as they say in Yorkshire, " an education in itself." Unfortunately, although I had bagged a store of experiences as a bee bags nectar, I had also bagged some of Africa's less pleasant fauna, notably the protozoan of malaria, and on top of this my nervous system had gone all wrong. Yet even more virulent than the bug of malaria was the bug of Africa itself, that terrible yearning to be back. It was this yearning, this nostalgia which undoubtedly contributed to the failure of my marriage. Claire wanted me to be a writer. While in hospital in England I had started to write a narrative of my flying adventures and had sent the first instalment to *Blackwood's Magazine*. The editor had written a charming letter about it, asking me for more and suggesting that the series might ultimately be published as a book. As I had read in one of Arnold Bennett's books that a young writer having " landed " *Blackwood's* might well consider himself on the road to literary success, I certainly thought I had found a pleasant career for myself, or rather re-found one, for it was practically the same thing as Sam and I had worked out that night in the laboratory before the war, the only difference being that my subject, my raw material, was not marine biology or popular science. It sounded ideal. To travel and have adventures. To come back and turn them into books which would provide cash for more travel and adventures, and so on until I had made so much money we could just keep on travelling !

Although *Blackwood's* paid me well for the serial use of my story, they could not offer any cash advance on the royalties of the book. Claire had no money. I'd saved something out of my Service pay, and I had also received a gratuity on my discharge from the Air Force, but I'd been helping Mother and Dad (who after a spell of munition working was back at Bramblewick optimistically painting again), and we had precious little capital for our first adventure, which therefore had to be a modest one. We invested in a portable tent, a couple of push bikes, mine equipped with heavy grocer's-boy carriers fore and aft, and set off (it was the second summer after the war) on a cycle-camping tour of Normandy and Brittany, the idea being that we should continue south to the Mediterranean coast, find a fisherman's cottage and lay up there for the winter so that I could write. I had no doubt that Blackwood's would take a whole series of articles on our experiences.

The tour was not a success. From the morning we mounted our bikes in Rouen for the first stage of our journey to Lisieux it rained almost without stop. We had one dreadful night under canvas in a pinewood about twenty miles south of Rouen. It rained so hard that it was impossible to make a fire. The tent was not waterproof and we were too cold and wet to sleep. We made progress, but from that time on our tent was never pitched again and we had to spend our nights in inns, which, although the food was good and the bed-linen clean, were nearly all infested with bugs or fleas. And what a dull monotonous country it was, even when you could see it when the rain mists occasionally lifted. How I longed for Africa, the sunshine, the clear vistas, the sound of drums instead of the eternal lowing of Normandy cattle, for black people instead of the gloomy-looking peasants who seemed more under the weather than we were, although they were kind enough whenever we had to call at a farm for eggs or milk or to ask the way. I had brought my trout rod, but the only possible looking trout stream I saw had more notices along its banks than the Mill Dam. We reached Lisieux (a mediæval architectural museum piece) and cycled (it went on raining) from there to Falaise, where we saw the castle where William the Conqueror was born, which was interesting to an Englishman, and especially to me, as 1066 was one of the few dates in history I did remember. But here, having in a moment of recklessness decided to stay at the best and most expensive hotel, I got a sharp attack of fever and was laid up for a week. We were not enjoying ourselves. Claire wanted to give up the tour and go to Paris. She wanted to see the Latin Quarter and thought it would be a very good thing for me as a writer if we could live there for a while (a garret would do) and meet other writers and artists. I, next to Africa, wanted to get to the Breton coast, to meet the fisher people about whom I'd heard so much, to see the famous marine zoological collecting grounds at Roscoff, where I remembered the University of Paris had a biological station. We compromised on a plan to go to the coast first and then go by train to Paris if we had enough money left, and when I was well enough we set off for Avranches, which is near to Mont St. Michel.

It was the French holiday season. Mont St. Michel was as thick with tourists as Southend on a bank holiday, and still it rained. We pushed on to St. Malo, but this too was full of wet and shivering holiday-makers, English as well as French, and as we could not find accommodation we had to move on before I had a chance of really seeing the fishing port. Finally we got to Roscoff itself. But there was no available accommodation. The place was full of French university students, ostensibly " working " at the biological station but actually out to enjoy a seaside holiday as well as the weather permitted, very much in the same way the laboratory students had done at Bramblewick. Lying about half a mile off the mainland however was a small island with rocky cliffs called the Ile de Batz, reached by sail ferry. Our guide book told us that this island was famous for its ancient church and for its warm climate due to its proximity to the Gulf Stream which enabled its inhabitants, who were farmers as well as fishers, to grow early market garden produce. Also that it was a quiet seaside resort with one good *pension*. We found the *pension* rather primitive but clean and also cheap. As our funds were getting low we decided to settle there while I wrote the first of my articles and got some money for it. The sea-fishing promised to be good. I was excited at the prospect of exploring a new sea shore which had such a reputation for the richness and variety of its fauna. But it was evident that the Gulf Stream was not working that summer! If the rain stopped for a spell then we got a freezing wind from the sea, or worse still dense fog, which soon changed to rain again. The fishing was not good. All that one could catch was wrasse, which were pretty enough to look at but were not good to eat and gave no sport whatever. I discovered that my interest in marine biology which had been reawakened on the African coral reefs had waned. Even the wonderfully equipped biological station at Roscoff did not interest me as it would have done in the pre-war days, although Claire was excited by the work of a young French student (" art " and not directly " biology ".) who was making drawings of fish and other marine animals and adapting these for decorative purposes for wallpapers and tiles.

The station owned an old steam trawler which was used for deep-sea investigations. We were invited to make a trip on her but Claire, although a good sailor, was shrewd enough to refuse. The vessel was crowded with students, and before we sailed they were like a lot of school children going off on a treat. They ran up and down the decks, climbed the rigging, posed on the bridge (one of them wearing baggy velvet trousers and a beret with the skipper's telescope under his arm, and smoking a cigar) and yelled and sang wildly. Their enthusiasm was maintained until we left the lee of the Ile de Batz and steamed head on into a heavy north-westerly swell. From that moment they started going down like ninepins and I felt really sorry for them, for used though I was to boats and ships I had never experienced anything comparable with the pitching and rolling of that ancient trawler. The wind brought the smoke down on to her decks. Though the student with the velvet bags had long since lost interest in his cigar all the sailors and officers appeared to be smoking something of an equally pungent brand. And this was nothing compared with what followed, for having steamed seawards for about an hour the engines were stopped and a huge wooden beam weighted with iron and with several bundles of old herring net tied to it, was lowered overboard amidships. The ship swung broadside to the swell and was allowed to drift to windward, this giving her just sufficient way to drag the contraption along the bottom. She rolled from rail to rail. The decks on which the poor students were lying like corpses were continually awash. There was a freezing N.W. wind and I think I came nearer to being seasick than ever in my life before or since. And all that the " trawl " caught at the end of an hour's fishing was a quantity of ordinary star-fish, one or two crabs and smaller crustacea and some jellyfish. Two of the students required stretchers to take them to their lodgings when we got back to harbour.

I don't think we should have had such a bad time on the island if the weather had been normal. The farmer-fishermen were grand fellows. They had all the qualities of courage and seamanship of our Yorkshire fishers, without their dourness. Several of them could speak English, for their chief agricultural crop was onions, and before the war they had come over to England every year to hawk them (tied in strings). One old fellow, Pierre, wore gold ear-rings and he had sailed regularly on the St. Malo fishing schooners to

Newfoundland and the Banks. He had been wrecked several times and the last time at St. Malo itself after a six months' voyage. He had been the only survivor. There were about a score of guests at the *pension*. They were mostly middle-class business men and their wives from Paris. They seemed to spend all their time eating or sleeping. Only two of them ever went out in the rain. One was an ex-airman who had been shot down in the second year of the war and had spent the rest of it in a prison camp. He was thin and nervy and could scarcely sit down indoors even to a meal. But he could sit for hours on the end of the little pier with a fishing line catching useless wrasse which he brought home and showed triumphantly to his dark enormously fat wife, who was as placid as a sleepy cat. The other was a middle-aged Parisian shop-keeper, with white podgy face and hands. He wore city clothes with a mackintosh over them when he went out. He had a small calibre repeating rifle. With this he used to wander round the coast of the island, potting sitting seagulls and cormorants. He never bothered to pick them up when he had shot them: he just liked to kill them; and when I dared to complain he just smiled blandly and said " it was the sport." Apparently he came to the island every year just to enjoy it.

But the most remarkable of our fellow-guests were two tall English ladies, who always sat together at the opposite end of the long table d'hôte to us. They had made a polite greeting to us on our arrival, but apart from that had maintained a stony silence towards us and the rest, and only spoke in low tones to one another. One of them, a very handsome woman, intrigued me very much for her face seemed vaguely familiar. I wondered if I had seen it in the newspapers connected with some case. It never occurred to me to find out her name from the *patron*. Then an astonishing thing happened. I knew that my Blackwood book had been published, and we were expecting any day to receive our presentation copies from the publisher : but the mails were erratic, and in fact we had not seen an English newspaper since leaving Rouen. It would be indelicate to describe exactly how the thing happened, but I have said that the *pension* was rather primitive in some respects. Enough that I happened to notice a piece of newspaper lying about and recognised it as *The Times*. I picked it up. It was torn top to bottom straight down a column with the right-hand side of the column missing. With a start I saw my own name under a heading BOOKS OF—and under my name part of the title of the book. It was indeed a review, and it came first in the column which obviously was headed BOOKS OF THE WEEK. It was my first review, and in the world's most famous newspaper, yet it was quite impossible from what it said on the left-hand side to tell whether it was a favourable one or not, and the circumstances in which I had found it forbade me to inquire about the other half which must have been the property of one of those prim and proper-seeming English ladies. It kept us guessing for days, and we tried all sorts of favourable and unfavourable suggestions for the missing words. Then at last the mail did come. It happened that we met the postman at the entrance of the *pension* and watched him give the letters to the *patron*. There were two parcels with my publisher's name on them. The *patron* handed the bigger one to me and I claimed the other but he shook his head, and pointed to the address on it and said it was for one of the English ladies. I was bewildered. I saw that the name was Wollaston, and yet it looked very much as if it contained my own book. And at that moment the lady herself appeared, and at once I knew why her face was familiar. I told her that I had just discovered her name, that a Dr. Wollaston had been attached to my squadron in East Africa. Was she any relation? She was his sister. It was my book, and it was he who had had it sent to her.

It so happened that she and her friend were leaving the next day. They un-froze, and it was from Miss Wollaston that I learnt about Dr. Wollaston's early career as an explorer and naturalist and that he was the author of several distinguished travel books. Little did either of us guess how tragically his career was to end. Despite that the ice was broken however, I hadn't the courage to refer to *The Times* review, and we didn't get a chance to read it for a long time. It was favourable, but reading the book with detachment years later, I thought that the reviewer had been kind to me for it was not very good. Its subject was fresh and a contrast to that of fighting and flying on the Western front. I had managed to convey some sort of a picture on that so-called " side-show," of the country itself and its natural history, and of the special thrills of tropical aviation, but it was written in a colloquial style, full of cliches and purple patches and with a vein of facetiousness running through it, which the reviewer had been kind enough to call humour. But we got a kick in seeing my first published book, with a coloured picture of a Kilimanjaro sunset on the jacket, and many of my snapshots reproduced inside, including one of my faithful Maganga. And our next mail brought a letter from a well-known agent saying that he had read the book with very great interest and that he would like to know if I intended to take up literary career. He had in fact received an inquiry from a well-established publisher asking him if I would consider writing a boy's adventure book based on my East African experiences. The agent pointed out that unknown authors did not as a rule get more than £50 outright for this type of book, but this publisher was willing to pay £100. If I would wire my acceptance he would have a contract made at once.

I gaily sent that wire. We left for Paris by train the next day. Paul, the marine biological art student, had given us the address of his studio in the Latin Quarter, with a pressing invitation to call on him if we came to town. We did so and stepped straight into the authentic atmosphere of La Boheme. Claire was really happy. Paul fixed us up at a cheap pub. He introduced us to all his pals, painters, sculptors, writers, composers. All of them were "modern": most of them were genuine, their poverty and unconventionality not a sham. We went from studio to studio. We saw the most amazing pictures and sculptures. I didn't know much about modern art or art cults. Cezanne, Gauguin, Piccaso, Matisse, Epstein, Mestrovic, James Joyce, Wyndham Lewis, Ezra Pound hadn't meant a thing to me, although they had done to Claire. I don't suppose that many of the " futurist " pictures we saw were great art or works of genius. But I did feel there was something behind it all, a genuine revolt and perhaps the beginning of a renaissance. I was bewildered. When I recognised however that a picture or a piece of sculpture need not be representational, the spit and image of the " subject," I began to get at least the glimmerings of understanding, and I saw things that thrilled me without my being able to know why. We joined in studio parties, and drank beer and vodka and absinthe in the open-air cafés. We went to music halls and opera and ballets. Claire was in her element. She could speak French like a native, and I am sure she would have been content if we'd found some sort of apartment and settled down for at least that winter. But our money was nearly gone. The life we were leading was too distracting for work. I was at a disadvantage in having only my Scarborough school knowledge of French'(how I cursed again my wasted opportunities) and often at a party when every one was talking or arguing excitedly about art, and the tobacco smoke mingled with the fumes of alcohol was so thick that you could hardly see across the particular studio we were in, that terrible nausea for Africa would come over me, and I'd have a fierce longing to be off.

3

I'D TAKEN Claire to Bramblewick soon after we'd been married. She hadn't liked it very much. As an alternative to Paris she suggested we might find a small flat in Chelsea or Bloomsbury and spend the winter there. But next to Africa I felt I must live somewhere near the sea while I wrote my boy's book, and we ended up by taking a small furnished house on the outskirts of Ilfracombe. It was one of a terrace of semi-detached brick villas of the Victorian period, and furnished in the same tradition complete with aspidistras. Poor Claire ! I didn't like it myself, although there was good cod fishing from the rocks, and the coast scenery was grand. When the book was finished however and I got the money, less the agent's ten per cent, we moved to London and took a small furnished maisonette on the Chelsea side of Fulham. The publishers were pleased with the book. They wanted me to write another, but the agent agreed with me that unless the price was at least doubled, or I could rattle them off at the rate of half a dozen a year, there wasn't a future in writing for the young. This agent specialised in the handling of travel and natural history books. He was in fact the agent for the Kearton brothers, Sir Ernest Shackleton, and Radclyffe Dugmore, and Captain Knight, and part of the activities of his firm was arranging lectures. He painted a glowing picture of the profits made in books and lecture fees made by these men, and said it was a pity that my experiences were only those I'd gained in the war, for there was a slump in war-books as evidenced by the sales of my own, which had been round about 500 copies. I could use a camera. Why didn't I go off to the wilds again and get the material for a new book. It was a feather in my cap landing Blackwood's for a start. But there were plenty of other publishers eagerly looking round for the sort of book he had in mind, willing to pay thumping advances, even up to a thousand pounds, for a likely winner. Had I any ideas ?

I had. I'd already read all the books on African exploration and natural history I could lay hands on. I'd seen all the films (including the first of Cherry Kearton's) of African big game. Some of them had been grandly exciting, but the makers of them, even Cherry, had been out for the sensational ; close-ups of lions and elephants and charging rhinos. They suffered from the same fault as most early (and many later) documentaries. They lacked form, and above all *story*. They were simply pictorial statements of fact, and the makers prided themselves on this. These were *real* lions and *real* elephants, taken in the *real* bush or jungle and how clever and patient the photographer was to make them. This, especially in Kearton's case, I knew. He had worked with primitive apparatus and equipment under the most difficult pioneering conditions. His films were a technical triumph. But the fact remained that they were just a series of moving portraits, and that apart from the genuine location, you could photograph lions and elephants and zebras and giraffe to much better advantage in a zoo. My idea was not so much to show the animals in their native haunts, but to give a complete picture of tropical Africa, to show how all the creatures that lived in it were subject to one great law, the law of the survival of the fittest.

It would be an epic of Evolution ! Here in the parts of Africa I'd seen you got just the same relentless struggle for existence which (thanks to Sam's teaching) I'd observed going on among sea-shore animals, but on a grander and pictorially more dramatic scale. I'd dramatise these animals. If I got a shot of a herd of Grant's gazelle, or hartebeeste (on the Serengetti Plain that would be as easy as filming dairy cows on a farm) I'd link them to a shot of a prowling lion, pausing and sniffing their scent. I wouldn't waste days in an uncomfortable " hide," plagued by tsetse flies and mosquitoes, if I could use a captive or even a tamed lion for this short linking shot. I'd fence a small area of bush or jungle, aim the camera at a given spot, and with concealed beaters drive the lion to this spot, and control its " action " there with other beaters. A fake ? What was all acting but a fake, the creating of the illusion of reality ? And provided my lion was not a placid old circus performer it would look as natural in that genuine setting as any wild one. Anyway my concern was to tell a story, not to impress an audience with my prowess as a photographic hunter of big game. The detail would not matter if the total illusion conveyed reality. And most of the detail would be authentic for I would not be out just for the sensational and dangerous animals. In that fishing trip of mine to the Pangani River, the sleeping crocodiles, the monkeys, the mother hippo and her calf, and that proud Masai warrior was the easily obtained material for a thrilling sequence of action all fitting into the main theme. And just as dramatic in their photographic possibilities were the smaller creatures of the bush and jungle : the wood-eating and mound-building termites, the carnivorous red ants which would strip every particle of flesh from a dead antelope in a matter of hours and leave the skeleton to bleach in the sun, the big black soldier ants moving in regular columns across the veldt to attack and destroy a colony of termites, the trap-door spiders, the ichneumon wasps which caught huge beetles, anaes-thetised them with their sting, impregnated them with eggs, and sealed them up in clay to become a living larder for their own young. I'd once heard a little bird called the honey guide twittering in a forest and moving from tree to tree, and, unobserved, an animal something like a small badger following it on the ground. The bird reached a tree that swarmed with bees. Its twittering became more excited. The animal promptly swarmed the tree, and started pulling out the comb from the hive in a hole of its trunk. He wanted honey. The grubs fell on the ground and the honey guide claimed its reward in the grubs. Such an incident if filmed surely would hold any audience. With clever sub-titling (I'd not dreamt of sound films then) it could be made quite funny and very human, and yet it would fit into the story just as well as a shot of a leopard pulling down a gazelle, and the hyenas and jackals and vultures and marabou storks joining in the feast. I would bring in the human habitants of the bush and jungle too, and show the part they played in the struggle for existence. Show them hunting, fighting among themselves, how one tribe triumphed over another, not necessarily by force of arms, but by skill in adapting themselves to their environment, for the " fittest " of the tribes I had seen were agriculturists and not fighters at all.

The agent seemed impressed. He said cautiously that it would cost a great deal of money, into tens of thousands of pounds. But it wasn't beyond the realms of possibility that the money could be found. An expedition like that would make a fine book. Why didn't I put the whole scheme in writing, then he would submit it to various wealthy people he knew who might be tempted. In the meantime though, he advised me to go on writing so as to keep my name before the public. Why not have a shot at a thriller for grown-ups in the Edgar Wallace or Victor Bridges style ?

I put my scheme in writing : in the shape of a prospectus. Not only that, I bought a book on scenario-writing and wrote a detailed shooting script of the film, including sub-titles. Claire was thrilled about it. She wondered which steamer route we should take when we went out to East Africa, via the Cape, or Suez. She did so much wish it would be the Suez route and that we should have a chance to see Egypt, and the wonderful sculptures. I felt uneasy about Claire. I thought that the best base for operations would be the valley of the Pangani River about half-way between the coast and Mount Kilimanjaro. It was an unhealthy place. It was supposed that the Germans had deliberately retired down that route in order to subject our unseasoned European troops to malaria, which indeed caused far more casualties than battle. Mosquitoes and tsetse flies abounded. Clearly it was not the country for a white woman to camp in. But then probably Claire would be content to go to some place like Nairobi in the Highlands which was healthy and wait while the film was being made. She was interested in primitive art, and she would find plenty among the Highland tribes, and of course the main thing first was to secure the financial backing.

I hadn't guessed how difficult this was going to be. I had supposed that the chief desire of all rich people was to make themselves richer. I thought that no one could possibly read my prospectus and fail to be convinced of its feasibility, and that the profits of such a film would be more than treble its cost. Week after week passed without the agent reporting progress, although he kept on asking me if I was getting on with my thriller, which I had actually started. I thought he was just slow and stupid, and I made more copies of the prospectus and sent it off to various wealthy people whose names were prominent in the public eye, including Lord Northcliffe and Lady Houston. I read in the papers that Lord Rothschild, whose hobby was natural history, had financed a zoological collecting expedition to West Africa. He had a sort of honorary appointment in the South Kensington Natural Science Museum. I called on him there. He was charming and genial, and

he asked me to give him a copy of my prospectus and also to lend
him a copy of my book. But I didn't hear from him again. Nor did
he return the book. I read too in the papers that Mr. Bernard Shaw
had been speaking at some function in London about the future of
films, and that he had said how valuable they could be education-
ally, especially in revealing the wonders of natural science. As I had
read all his plays and seen many of them acted, and thought he was
the one great genius of our time, I wrote to him enclosing the
prospectus. I got one of his famous postcards back, but it was not
signed by him but by his almost equally famous lady secretary. It
said, " Mr. Shaw asks me to tell you that his job is plays not films."
I tore it up in disgust and swore I would never read or see one of
his damned plays again, a vow I did not keep, for my admiration
for him as a man and an artist remained (and remains) little short
of idolatry.

Spring came. We remained in Fulham. Claire liked town and
was happy. She'd got some sort of job in a small West-end picture
gallery specialising on modern art and she was meeting a lot of
interesting people. She was also attending courses in art and art
criticism at University College, and going to the School of Oriental
Studies. We went to all the shows we could afford, especially the
Old Vic, and concerts at the Albert and Queen's Hall and at the
smaller halls in the West-end, and of course we went to the movies.
I learnt to appreciate the music of Beethoven and Bach and Schubert
and the sculpture of Epstein, whom we often met in a little
Bohemian Club in Beak Street together with his famous model
Dolores. He was a fascinating man, short but with the physique
of a navvy. There was no pose about him. He seemed to be quite
indifferent to the criticism some of his sculptures had aroused,
particularly his alleged cult of " ugliness," but you couldn't be in
his presence five minutes and not be convinced of his absolute
sincerity and that he was a very great artist. I was becoming quite
a highbrow myself, but I used to go to another " club " which was
in complete contrast with this, and was a constant stimulus to the
life of adventure I yearned for. This was in an old-fashioned coffee
house called Groom's at the Strand end of Fleet Street, where a room
was reserved every week day for the managers of the combined
literary and lecture agency, and the men for whom the agency
acted. Some were stay-at-home people like Will Owen the

cartoonist, and Hamilton Fyffe, who later became editor of the *Daily Herald*. But often famous explorers came in, and it was there that I met Sir Ernest Shackleton, Captain Worsley, Evans of the *Broke*, Frederick Villiers, the famous war correspondent, and H. W. Nevinson. Shackleton had a most fascinating personality. He impressed you first with the extraordinary breadth of his shoulders, but you forgot this when you heard him talk in his bluff sailor's voice. He belonged to the true tradition of British sailor adventurers, a dreamer and artist as well as a fighter. I felt very shy of him, and I don't think I ever had the courage to speak more than a dozen words to him, but I know that if he had asked me to sail with him on the new voyage of Antarctic exploration (for which he was then raising money by writing and lecturing), I'd have gone like a shot and thought no more about my African proposition. In fact the words I did speak to him were an inquiry as to whether he was taking a naturalist with him on his new voyage. He was, but the post was already fixed.

I had to go on writing my thriller and doing newspaper articles throughout the whole summer. I hated being in town when the weather was fine. We had occasional outings to Richmond or Hampton Court and hired a boat. There were always plenty of men and boys fishing in the river, and I think if I'd been by myself I could have found some consolation in just watching them, for the technique was like rock fishing and seemed to consist chiefly of watching and waiting. I hadn't lost hope about my expedition to Africa. I went on writing to people, and every day I rang up or called on the agent to see if he had any news. I'd kept up a dilatory correspondence with Sam throughout the war and after. The firm had done well out of timber. It had expanded and had bought a large estate in Norfolk, chiefly for its timber. The manor house and several farms had gone in with the deal, and Sam was managing the estate and a new sawmill the firm had built. I hadn't had a chance of seeing him until he came to town one day. He hadn't changed much. He was still bossy and outwardly full of self-confidence, but I soon found out that he was not satisfied with his life. (He was loyal to his father, yet it was clear that the old man's strong personality had not softened with success, and that he'd have his unbending way in everything.) Science was calling him once more. It had its close application to timber of course; for example, an immense amount of damage was done both to trees and timber by various insects. The death-watch beetle was very much in the news because of its attacks on the roof timbers of churches and historic buildings, but that damage was nothing comparable with that of the powder-post beetle, *Lyctus*. Sam had thought of taking a refresher course in the London College of Science, and then carrying out a research on this particular pest. It would be like the work he had done on *Doto*, but of course it would be of direct economic value, and there might be a fortune in it if he could discover a way of rendering timber immune; he was really enthusiastic about this proposition. But he was not enthusiastic about my own when I explained it in detail.

He didn't know much about films of course. Hadn't time to go regularly to the pictures, but it seemed that the ones that made the money were the comics and the westerns and society dramas. It was clearly a risky business anyway, and I couldn't expect these rich men to gamble their brass on it when they could see a safer return in industry. Besides I was married now. Surely I'd had all the adventure I wanted in the war. I'd made a good start at writing. It was time I'd settled down. Ought to have a family too. What was the point of getting married, if I was just going to go on roving round the world. A rolling stone gathered no moss.

Winter came. I still hadn't completely lost hope. I tried all the film producing companies in Wardour Street, American as well as British. I even saw the manager of the great German film company UFA, who had just opened an office in London, and although it was rather embarrassing explaining that I was proposing to make the film in what had lately been German territory, I got more encouragement from him than from any of the other film people I had seen although he was doubtful whether under the very special circumstances his firm could take it up. I tried a new approach. I had written an article on air surveying for the *Royal Geographical Journal*, and I had been proposed and accepted as a Fellow of the Society. The President then was Sir Francis Younghusband of Thibetan fame. He didn't look a bit like an explorer. He was short, and very much like the pictures of Lord Roberts that were on cigarette cards when I was a boy. He had clear blue eyes, and a most engaging manner. He read my prospectus, and he talked about it with me for nearly an hour, and he was really enthusiastic about it until we came to the subject of finance. He said, like my agent, that it would cost a great deal of money, £40,000 at the least. I dropped a hint that the Society might contribute some of it, but he shook his head. It was not strictly a geographical expedition. It was to a country already explored and mapped. Still he knew of one or two people who might be interested. He thought the whole thing a splendid idea, and it certainly would have his personal recommendation and blessing. I heard nothing from Sir Francis for a very long time. It was not indeed until early in the New Year that I got a letter from him asking me to go and see him at the Society in Kensington. He was just as affable as he had been before, and said he was terribly sorry that he had been unable to interest any one in the scheme in a practical way. But he hadn't asked me to see him just to hear that. Was I still keen on going on an expedition to tropical Africa? A new company had been formed in which some of his friends were taking a financial interest. Its object was to send expeditions to various parts of the world with a view to making natural history collections and photo and cinema records of geographical and general scientific interest. It was a commercial undertaking and as such could not be sponsored by the Society. But if I liked he would recommend me privately.

I saw the managing director of the new company by appointment next day. He was an extraordinary looking man, for he had only one eye, in which he wore a monocle, and only one hand. The other hand had a silver clip on it, with which however he was very adroit. I learnt later that he was an inventor and an engineer and that he had been employed in a government explosives research laboratory during the war and had received his injuries from an accidental explosion. He staggered me first of all by asking me if had I any capital to invest in the new company. When I said very hastily " no," he just laughed and signed to me to help myself to a Turkish cigarette from a large box on the table. He took one himself with his clip and put it between his lips.

" My own invention this," he said, indicating the clip. " Damn sight more useful than a cork hand."

He went on to say that he had asked me that question because he and his directors had studied my prospectus with great interest. In fact they had been considering seriously the possibility of taking it up. It had been decided however that it was too big an undertaking for a first venture. If the one at present contemplated proved a financial success, then undoubtedly mine would be given a more favourable consideration. This one had already been planned for sometime by a well-known young sporting gentleman, who had served with an armoured car unit in Egypt and the Senussi campaign. He had got one or two other gentlemen to put up some money, but not quite enough for what was planned, an expedition across the heart of Africa from West to East, to collect animals and make a film. The new company had decided to supply the extra finance and take over the scheme lock, stock and barrel. A famous "white" hunter had already been engaged, so had a skilled cameraman. But it was felt that a good field naturalist was essential and my name had been suggested privately by Sir Francis Younghusband. The salary offered would be £20 a week, with all travelling and maintenance expenses. At the end of the expedition, and provided the film was a success, I might be asked to lecture with it in this country and America at a salary not less than £20 a week but probably more with a small percentage on takings. I would be free to write about the expedition, articles or books, but of course the company would require a percentage on my profits, this to be a matter for arrangement. All being well the expedition was leaving within the next few days, passages to Dakar in French West Africa having been provisionally booked. Did it appeal to me as a counter-suggestion to my own scheme, which the company might very well take up eventually.

My heart was beating so fast I could scarcely say " yes." The director gave me a keen look with his one good eye, and said :

" Good," and went on. " Well, I'm expecting the leader of the expedition any minute now. Very pleasant sort of chap. Hope you'll like each other. . . ." Shortly the telephone buzzed. He picked up the receiver, and I heard him say :

" Right. Bring him in at once."

The door opened and in came a short, thick-set youngish man in well cut dark town clothes and overcoat and a bowler hat, and carrying a gold-banded umbrella. He did not look much a soldier or explorer, but neither had Sir Francis, and I liked him instantly. As we were introduced he shook hands with me as though I had been a life-long friend. He addressed me by my Christian name and told me to call him "George," then he said that he had read my articles in *Blackwood's* and had been particularly interested in them because he'd been serving in North Africa. It was his experiences there that had given him a great longing and ambition to go back, only to a part of the Continent he did not know. What did I think of the proposition? The director told him that I had accepted the post.

George shook my hand again.

"Splendid," he said, "absolutely splendid. Look here, I've got my wife waiting below. I'd like you to meet her. Let's go round to the Cafe Royal and have a drink on it. There's a lot of things I'd like to discuss."

The director declined George's invitation to join us, but indicated that he had a word or two to say to him in private before he went out, and I had to wait a minute or so outside the room. George joined me again smiling.

"By jove," he said, as we moved to the lift, "I can't tell you how pleased I am you've taken the job. I'm frightfully keen on natural history but don't know a darned thing about it. The director gave me that film thing of yours to read some days ago. I thought it was wonderful, only perhaps just a little too scientific to be popular. But I'd like to get as much natural history as possible into this one. That honey guide business, for example. Positively grand."

George's wife was waiting in a taxi below. She was quite young and charming, and again George asked me to forget the surname. Every one just knew her as Paddy. We were in Suffolk Place not more than three minutes' walk from the Cafe Royal, but we taxied there, and in the meantime Paddy had asked me if I was married and said she would like to meet my wife. So I rang up Claire, told her the exciting news and asked her to come to the Cafe Royal as quickly as she could.

It was all like a dream. I could hardly believe that it was really settled that I was going to Africa again. The cocktail which George immediately pressed on me increased my delirious joy. He produced a pocket map of Africa and spread it on the table. He pointed to Dakar, and traced the route that he proposed to follow. We were to go first to Timbuctoo, then strike slightly south-east for Lake Chad, and from there into the upper basin of the Congo through the very heart of Africa to Uganda, and finally British East and Mombasa. No filming expedition had yet tackled anything quite so ambitious as this. Probably it would mean travelling through country where no white man had previously set foot. New animals might be found, perhaps new tribes. The film record should be quite sensational and the best thing about it was that it was not to be confined to big game. It would include everything and give a real picture of the Dark Continent. We were drinking our second cocktail then and I was far too elated to think how like this scheme was to my own, so much like it that indeed George might have been quoting from my prospectus. But if I had thought that I would not have been critical for I liked him too much. Claire had joined us when we got to the third round of cocktails. She and Paddy seemed to take an instant liking to one another. I heard them (just as one sees out of the tail of one's eye) talking about Paris and Florence and art, while George and I went on talking about the expedition. He got more and more enthusiastic as I told him about the methods I had thought out of getting shots of various animals, including fish. My idea for this was to have a large portable aquarium with a plate-glass front, arrange water weeds in it so it looked quite natural then pop the fish in alive. If we got some very small crocodiles we could even do the same with them and no one would be able to tell them from big ones when they saw the film. George thought that I must certainly get such a tank. The company of course would pay for it, but I'd have to be quick for it was practically certain we were sailing in less than a week.

I don't know how many drinks we had. When we parted George gave me a letter to a well-known firm of tropical outfitters and told me to get anything I wanted within reason in the way of kit. I should need at least three suits of white drill, as we were going to a French Colony first and it was important to impress the high officials we should meet; and I mustn't forget the aquarium. Claire thought that George was delightful, and Paddy simply sweet. Did I hear what she had said about Hyères? Claire told me as we bowled along in a taxi for the outfitters' shop that Paddy had said that her mother had a large villa at Hyères and wanted her to go and live there while George was in Africa. That Paddy would like Claire to go too, and that she knew her mother would be delighted.

I thought that things could not possibly have turned out luckier even if it had been my own expedition I was going on. Everything had happened just right.

4

I AM SURE that Sir Francis Drake or Sir Walter Raleigh, or Scott or Shackleton, never set off on an expedition with greater ambitions or higher hopes of achievement than I did on my second voyage to Africa. We sailed from Bordeaux (having travelled overland from Boulogne via Paris) on a cargo passenger ship of the Chargeur Reünis Line which maintained a fortnightly service to West Africa calling at all the French Colonial ports as far south as the Congo. George had been very apologetic when telling me that I was booked second class: it was just because the provisional bookings had been made sometime ago, and he'd had no hope then that the film company would allow him a naturalist. He gave me no hint that the company's purse strings were tight. He himself of course was obliged to travel first. So were the other two gentlemen who had put money into his original proposition and were coming along mostly with the idea of sport. Curiously enough both of these were doctors. One of them (I'll call him Miller) was an ex-Surgeon R.N. He was short and powerfully built with a pleasant clean-shaven face, very much the naval type and not very talkative. The other, Dr. Hilton, was tall, more than middle-aged, also reticent in his speech, and generally enigmatic. He walked with a pronounced limp and yet it was not until long after that I discovered he had a cork leg ! I learnt that both of them had answered an advertisement George had put in the Personal Column of The Times asking for a limited number of ex-officers to join a sporting and scientific expedition through tropical Africa on a profit-sharing basis. As these were the only two to answer, the thing would have fallen through but for the providential action of the film company.

Actually I was much happier second class with the salaried members of the expedition : Pereira, the cameraman ; Harry, his youthful Cockney assistant ; and the white hunter, Jock. Pereira was more than a cameraman: he was an inventor, and he looked like one with his long hair, pale face and rather wild eyes, and his thin nervous hands whose fingers were stained with tobacco and photographic chemicals. He had invented all sorts of gadgets connected with ordinary cinema photography. He told me that he had invented the moving picture machines that one used to see on piers and seaside promenades before the coming of the American Amusement Fairs with their complicated devices for parting the holiday maker from his money. The principle of the machine was a book of photographs, each a " still," but with the figures in it moved between each shot so that when the leaves were turned quickly you got the illusion of action. The pictures were short and the subjects innocent, but the titles were provocative to the lower instincts of the British male on holiday, " What the Butler Saw," " A Night in Paris," " The Artist's Model " being typical. That was no reflection on the inventor of the mechanics of the apparatus. Pereira's cabin, which he shared with his assistant, looked like an inventor's laboratory from the first day out at sea. He had fixed a little vice on the edge of the " pull-down " washing basin, and a small grindstone. He had several kits of tools open on the bunks or on the cabin floor. There were several ordinary cameras and tripods, cases of chemicals, a blow lamp, all mixed up with camp kit, and it was a job to sit down anywhere. But he fascinated me.

This was not his first filming expedition to tropical Africa. He had in fact, only a few months before, returned from one in the Soudan with an American sportsman who wished him to take moving pictures of himself shooting big game. But it hadn't appealed to him very much as a cameraman. His ambition was to get close-ups of the animals themselves in their natural surroundings, and that was why he'd welcomed the chance of coming with George. He didn't believe you could do this successfully by using Kearton's " hide " methods. The animals could not help smelling you and becoming nervous. So with George's consent he had bought a camera that had been invented chiefly for use in aircraft. It was called the " Aeroscope." It could be worked by hand and also it worked by means of compressed air and a tiny engine. His idea was to hide this near a water hole or a river drinking place, and have a long thin wire from its release to the distant place where he was hiding. There'd be less chance then of the animals getting your scent.

Unfortunately the model he had got was second-hand and slightly out of order, and he'd had no time to have it repaired. This was his main job now, and another snag was that he'd forgotten to bring the air pump which was a necessary part of the equipment. It required a powerful one. As a substitute he had managed to buy an ordinary bicycle pump in Paris, and every now and again in the process of putting the running gear right, Pereira connected up this pump to the valve and made his assistant work furiously at it. But after twenty minutes' pumping the engine would only run for about ten seconds, which of course wouldn't take a very long picture.

There was more room in my cabin, which I shared with Jock. He was a West Highland Scot with a brogue and a gift of the gab that you'd have guessed was Irish. He was lean with a deeply lined sun-tanned face, longish black hair which was always untidy. He had a real gift for yarning, and he seemed to have had as many astounding adventures in the bush and jungle as Trader Horn, and I think that most of them were true. He'd done everything, gold and diamond prospecting in the Transvaal, trading in the Congo and Portuguese East, cattle-dealing, storekeeping, running a newspaper, ivory hunting and, of course, "white-hunting," which is the name given in East Africa to the professional running of big game expeditions. His last expedition however had been in the very country for which we were bound.

It seemed that he had held a roving commission to collect live animals for a big American zoo. Through an agent in the interior he had heard of the capture of two half-grown giraffe in the district north-east of Timbuctoo. They were not ordinary giraffe. They had very special markings, and cabling the zoo from Dakar, he received an offer of £500 each if he got them alive on to an American-bound ship. The price asked by the agent was twenty pounds apiece, and Jock saw himself making at least eight hundred clear profit out of the deal, although of course everything depended on their being alive at the moment of shipment.

By rail, car, marching, and by native boat too when he reached the upper waters of the River Niger, he got to Timbuctoo, and finally to the settlement in what used to be called the French Soudan

where the giraffe were in captivity. They were just as the agent
had described them, about half-grown, perfectly healthy and toler-
ably tame. They had been captured as tiny calves, and reared on
goat's milk. The deal was done, and Jock began the coastwards
journey of something like a thousand miles. He had to hire natives
to help him on the first section of marching to the river. He had
to go very slowly so as not to tire the beasts. One was a colt, the
other a filly. He called them Paddy and Kathleen, and despite that
they'd both get panicky if they encountered even the week-old
scent of a lion, they were well behaved and he soon got very fond
of them. They would feed out of his hand. It took him a month
to reach the river at Kabara near Timbuctoo. He had to spend
sometime rigging up a pontoon with two native dug-outs braced
together with beams and a sort of pen on the deck thus formed.
It took him a whole day to coax them into this contraption. The
thing he had to avoid above everything was making them " nervy "
for they would have gone off their feed and died. The first part
of the river trip was made with a motor launch as tug. This broke
down and he had to hire more natives to scull and pole the raft up
river. This, by the way, was the upper Niger which rises in French
Guinea, not very far from the coast and flows north and east in a
great irregular curve before turning south into Nigeria and to the
Gulf of Guinea. The river trip took him three weeks. Paddy and
Kathleen were quite happy on the fodder that was cut for them
at every stopping place, but what had begun to frighten Jock was
their rate of growth, which was terrific. However he got them
safely to the railway terminus near Bamako, still about six hundred
miles from the coast but with a railway covering all but about forty
miles of this near the River Senegal. No horse boxes were available
on this railway of course. He had to hire a truck and construct
another pen on it. While he was doing this Paddy and Kathleen
were in a small paddock in the village, where they aroused a great
deal of interest especially among the younger generation, for this
was not giraffe country, and besides Paddy and Kathleen were tame
and would eat almost anything that was offered. Returning from
his labours on the truck Jock found Paddy lying on the ground
and Kathleen standing watching him with pathetic interest. He was
dead before nightfall, clearly having accepted something from the
village boys that did not suit his digestion. Kathleen however must

have had more sense. Jock mounted two sentries over the paddock and a day or so later safely entrained for the coast. He reached Dakar all right, but no ship was expected for several days. He had to make another paddock for Kathleen and was careful to see that no one interfered with her, for the five hundred pounds was nearly in his pocket although his expense outlay was eating heavily into it. Two transit " cages " had by this time arrived from the American zoo, one of them alas redundant. The ship came in. There was an agonising delay while she discharged a part of her cargo : then at last all was ready to lead Kathleen to the quay side. Once she was ship-borne, the shipping agent and the ship's officers would be able to give their testimony that at least one-half of the contract was fulfilled, and Jock also comforted himself that he would get at least twenty pounds from Paddy's pelt which he had removed carefully and preserved with arsenical soap. Unfortunately between the paddock and the quay were several streets and across one of them was the naked main of Dakar's electricity supply well above the height of ordinary traffic, but within fatal reach of Kathleen's head. She was killed within a stone's throw of the ship and the reward of five hundred pounds, and all poor Jock got out of his trip was the price of two pelts.

I liked Jock. He got excited when he told his yarns and moved his hands like a Frenchman. He had a trick too of closing his eyes as he was approaching the climax of a story, and then opening them wide very suddenly with great dramatic effectiveness. If I was a little doubtful about him at times, it was just, I think, because the yarn to him was more important than strict accuracy. The giraffe story anyway was authentic. And again one felt that he would be a useful man to have around in a fix, and we'd get plenty of those, I thought, before we completed our crossing of the Dark Continent.

I thought I was lucky in every way. It was a joy to be on a ship again, although this one was anything but a crack liner. She was old, and slow, and steamed with a permanent list to starboard so that when she really rolled her starboard rails were almost awash, and you felt she'd never swing back. We heard that a sister ship had been wrecked sometime before with a considerable loss of life, and I noticed that her lifeboats were unpainted and badly cracked with exposure to the sun, and that some of the falls on which their

successful launching would depend were completely rotten. Apart
from one day of heavy weather in the Bay however we had nothing
but steady following winds all the way down the west coast of
Africa, which we sighted on the fourth day. It was the coast of
Spanish Morocco, Rio de Oro, flat and low-lying and practically
desert. It was the very country Defoe describes in the early part
of the adventures of Robinson Crusoe when his hero escaped from
the Moorish pirate in a small boat together with a boy called Xury.
This part of the narrative was usually left out of the juvenile versions
of the classic, but to me it was a powerful appetiser for the island
adventure and just as miraculously authentic in its detail. Monotonous though that coastline was and completely unlike that of East
Africa (with its fringing mangrove swamps and belts of cocoanut
palms and mangoes, and always hills and mountains in the distance)
I could watch it through my glasses by the hour, with profound
excitement. The main thing was that it was Africa, and that soon
I should set foot on it again.

Nearly all the other passengers were French : colonial officers
and n.c.o.s returning from European furlough : civil officials,
business men. I was reminded of the podgy Parisian shopkeeper
of the Ile de Batz *pension* when some of these amused themselves
shooting the gulls that followed the ship with rifles and pistols. As
the ship's purser seemed to regard this as a conventional pastime
for the passengers, like shuffle board and deck quoits, one could do
nothing about it, but I was glad there were no albatrosses to be
slaughtered and invoke an ancient mariner's curse upon our ship,
with its already embarrassing list to starboard. I did like the French
but there was no doubt that they looked at life from a very different
angle to what we did. Travelling steerage was a party of about
twelve girls. There was nothing striking about their appearance or
behaviour. Their clothes were only moderately smart, they were
not extravagantly made up, not one was pretty. They were all
about twenty to twenty-four. They looked like shop assistants, and
if I had been told they were going out to take commercial jobs or
even to be teachers in mission schools I would have believed it. In
fact the middle-aged lady who had charge of them (she travelled
second class) might have been a school marm or a missionary. She
was dressed in severe black, with a rather hard but certainly not a
vicious or cruel face, and the only jewellery she wore was a gold

chain and crucifix. Actually the girls were bound for what was politely termed a Casino in one of the ship's ports of call beyond Dakar. It was the cabin steward (who had once been a waiter in a Soho restaurant and could speak English well) who told me this. He was amused when I said that they must be the victims of a white-slave racket. No. It was quite voluntary. They knew what they were doing. They were practical. The French girl of that class wanted above everything to be married, a good husband, a nice little house, children. But the man desired beauty, a good figure, or then he must have a good *dot*. Those girls had no beauty. Figures perhaps, but nothing special. Money was not easy to earn in France after the war. There was much unemployment. These girls were practical. The contracts offered by the "casino" agencies were generous. Only two years. The climate in any case made that necessary. There was a regular salary, plus commissions on drinks ; opportunities for gratuities, a bonus and second-class passage home at the end. By then they would have saved a good *dot*. If they were sick of men they might be able to set up a little milliner's shop or cafe or some other business. Some it was true might die of the climate, but was that worse than dying of starvation at home ?

We lost sight of the coast for a day or two and our next landfall was Cape Verde, which hides the roads and the port of Dakar from the north. It was early morning when we sighted it. George came along to the second-class promenade deck in pyjamas and dressing-gown. He was rather bleary-eyed and after drawing my attention to the strip of land just visible on the port bow, he suddenly touched my arm and made an extraordinary speech.

"Pretty thick night last night. Drank far too much whisky. Lost a deuce of a lot of money playing poker in the smokeroom. Double weakness of mine, whisky and cards, I don't mind telling you. Look here, will you do me a favour ? I want to knock off drink. Completely knock it off."

I felt embarrassed, for in spite of George's easy manners I had regarded him with a respect due to the leader of the expedition and the source of my salary. He smelt of liquor but he wasn't tight. Before I could think of anything to say he gripped my arm again and looked at me very earnestly.

"Listen, old boy," he said. "I want you to bear witness that

I knock off drink from now on. That I'm absolutely on the water wagon. I want you to remind me if you see me trying to touch a drop of whisky. Don't hesitate. Just say, Don't forget your promise, George."

It was clear that he wasn't joking. I said of course that I would do what he said. But I was relieved when he looked again at the land, and said in quite matter-of-fact tones :

" Good to see Africa again, isn't it ? We ought to be in this afternoon. By the way, it's rather important that we make a good impression when we disembark. I didn't tell you, but we had a lot of difficulty in getting permission from the French Colonial Office to travel through French territory. Had to give assurances that the objects of our expedition were as stated. You know. Personal characters of all members good. That we weren't communists or anarchists or mineral prospectors or engaged in any illicit commercial enterprises. Also that we were sound financially. Not likely to go broke and become a charge on the authorities."

I could not help laughing at the idea of that, and George laughed too and said :

" Only formalities of course. But we've got to remember it's a foreign country, in spite of our being allies in the war. I don't suppose there'll be any sort of official reception waiting for us, but we ought to be wearing white drill, the usual dress for European civilians. You've got a suit of course, and pipeclayed shoes and white topee. You might tell Jock and Pereira about this. I'll have to hurry along for my bath now. Don't forget about my promise, will you ? "

He left me feeling bewildered, but as I went down to my cabin I decided that I could not attach much importance to what he had said. Obviously he had been drinking fairly heavily the previous night and was suffering from a bad hangover. When he'd bathed and breakfasted he'd be quite normal again and probably have quite forgotten the extraordinary request he had made. White drill trousers and tunic and white shoes and topee were among the items of kit I had bought at the firm's expense. I gave George's message to Jock, who was still in his bunk, but he laughed.

" Och—no. That'll be all right for the first-class passengers, but I've too many friends and acquaintances at Dakar and I'll not have them laughing at me stepping down the gangway dressed in such fashion, even if I had the wherewithal. It'll be khaki shirt and shorts for me. From what I know of the officials ashore there'll be none of them take the slightest interest in who's on the ship unless, be damned, it's the party of females, and I understand they're not going to dispense their favours here at all."

I found Pereira and his assistant also in pyjamas. Their cabin was stifling and full of the vapours of methylated spirits and of blow-lamp fumes and flux. Pereira was doing something to the engine of the Aeroscope camera. He didn't know that we had sighted land, and looked very harassed when I told him that we might be disembarking in a few hours, and then he cursed, and turned the blow-lamp off. The sweat was streaming from his forehead.

"We'll have to give the damned thing up then. It's an engineer's job anyway. Perhaps we'll find an engine shop ashore. It'll take us at least three hours to pack up. And fancy having to dress in white drill. Well, I suppose he knows what he's talking about. . . . Come on, Harry. Start clearing the tools from the bunks. . . ."

I was disappointed in Dakar. I'd expected something like Mombasa, cocoanut palms, whitewashed Arab houses, native huts and fishing craft. The land was flat and low lying. The town was modern and French at that. There were ugly warehouses along the harbour front. There were rows of villas reaching out along the shores. There were a few stunted palms, but the predominant trees were blue gums, which I learnt later had been introduced from Australia, and they were all in line like the poplars on a typical French highway. There was no delicious smell of spices in the air, and the air itself lacked that crystal optical brilliance which had been such a feature of East Africa, where fog or haze was unknown except over a swamp or river, at very early dawn. The sun was intensely hot, but the northerly wind that had followed us throughout the voyage was strong as ever and became more apparent as we crept slowly in to the quayside and it chilled like the draught of a ventilator in a heated stokehold. I was disappointed too to observe that the natives who made up most of the people who were waiting on the quay were dressed in conventional khaki drill shirts and trousers or dungarees. They were dockers and labourers. They were black and negroid but they had not the happy broad grinning faces of the Swahilis I had recalled with such a strong nostalgia since I had left East Africa.

For the first time I had a sense of foreboding about our expedition. How completely different this was to our disembarkation at Mombasa, when, despite that I'd been wearing officer's uniform with Sam Browne belt, I'd felt less formal than in the present rigout. George, the two doctors, Pereira, Harry, were all wearing the same absurd kit, which but for the topees seemed more suitable for the operating theatre of a hospital. George himself, except that his eyes were a trifle bloodshot, showed little sign of hangover, but I thought he looked rather nervous and self-conscious as he stared at the few Europeans on the quay. The expression on the face of Dr. Hilton was as usual completely enigmatic. Dr. Miller looked, as I felt, disappointed, Pereira worried and preoccupied, evidently with his Aeroscope, and only Harry, who had never been out of England before, and Jock, who had evidently recognised some friends on the quay and was grinning at them, seemed happy. It seemed clear soon, and I didn't know if George was relieved or not, that there was no official reception waiting for us. The Europeans were the port officials, shipping agents and chandlers. They came aboard as soon as the gangway was lowered, but no one went ashore, and shortly all the passengers for disembarkation were summoned to the first-class saloon for passport and customs examination. Actually an hour passed before even the French passengers started to go down the gangway and at least another half-hour before George, looking really bothered now, joined us from the saloon on the deck. He spoke to the doctors, and I heard him say :

"They're a lot of half-wits. Given us personal O.K. for disembarkation, but all our equipment's got to go into bond, including all the whisky and the raw film. It's got to stay there till the papers arrive from Paris. May be weeks. I'll have to go and see the British Consul at once. Where's Jock ?"

I don't know how he'd managed it but Jock was already on the quay, chatting to his friends. We started down the gangway, George leading, and again I couldn't help thinking that we looked like a party of hospital attendants in our gleaming white clothes. But not for long. Abaft the gangway, and to windward, the bunker hatches were open. A derrick was just hoisting the first load of coal from a truck on the quayside, and the container was tipped just as George reached the quay. The dust swept down on us like a black sandstorm. The effect was astounding. We now looked like a party of nigger minstrels half made up for a show.

Our personal luggage was already on the quay, so there was no immediate chance of changing. Luckily however a couple of rather decrepit-looking taxis were waiting on the quay road, and we were soon on our way to Dakar's chief hotel, where George had booked accommodation by radio from the ship as he had anticipated that there would be at least a few days' delay before we left by rail for the interior.

5

I WAS NOT a party to the discussions that took place between George
and the doctors during the day of our arrival on African soil, and
on many following ones. That something was seriously wrong I
gathered from George's continued harassed look, and from the fact
that at least some of the discussions were heated, with the enigmatic
Dr. Hilton showing definite signs of anger towards our leader. The
first hint of the cause of the trouble came when I was obliged to ask
George for a few hundred francs on account of my salary. He
asked me amiably if I would mind accepting just half of the
suggested sum, as there had been some sort of muddle about the
amount of cash the Company had agreed to send to the expedition's
credit at the Dakar Bank. He had cabled the managing director
about this, and of course it would be put right in a few days, but
he had been obliged to pay Pereira and his assistant and Jock their
full salaries, and this had left him rather short of funds. I was not
unduly alarmed. George said that the muddle probably had arisen
because the money had to be transferred in the first instance to the
head office of the Bank in Paris, and there were all sorts of difficulties
about the rates of exchange. On top of that I must realise that the
Company itself was only newly formed, and the staff inexperi-
enced : and again that we were in a foreign colony, French at that,
with the French nursing a sort of grievance against the British
because of what had happened at the Peace Conference. In spite
of the expedition having been O.K.d by the Colonial Office in
Paris, the Dakar " Customs " were refusing stolidly to release the
stores, especially the raw film and whisky. Speaking personally
(and I had noted that since we had come to the hotel George had
drunk nothing but grenadine, a sort of lemon squash) he would
not mind if the whisky stayed in bond for ever. But both the
doctors insisted that it was an absolute indispensable requisite on a
tropical expedition, that it had been purchased partly at any rate
with their money, and that they did not intend to start without it.
The devil was that the British Consul was away from the port for
a few days. With his influence, doubtless the whole trouble would
be cleared up at once.

I was worried but not really alarmed. George's explanation was plausible. I felt that it was not my business, and anyway, now that I was in Africa again, I wanted to enjoy it, and above everything get on with the job of making the film, or at least start finding subjects for Pereira as soon as he had got his camera in working order. He and Harry had been busy on it from the moment they had unpacked, and Jock had directed them to a garage where they had found a more efficient pump and facilities for doing the repairs. Jock himself was staying with some of his friends in the town so that we saw very little of him, but I did not need his guidance for my explorations. The town itself did not belie my first impressions. It was ugly and dull. Even the segregated native quarter was laid out in regular blocks, and the huts were like those of a mining village, mostly with corrugated iron roofs. The natives were nearly all dressed in European clothes, and they were rather sophisticated and almost truculent in their manner. There was no colour bar officially in French West Africa. Adult male natives had a vote in the election of the urban councillors (who themselves might be natives) and I believe that at least one native senator had a seat in the French home parliament. I had observed however that no natives entered the hotels or European cafes as customers.

There were groves of blue gums on the inland outskirts of the town, evidently planted as a barrier against the prevalent eroding winds, for even underneath them the earth was composed chiefly of sand. Clear of these the only vegetation was a few stunted thorns and the very familiar baobab tree, with its monstrously fat trunk and domed canopy of short branches and dark green leaves, which made it look like a giant beetroot. But here there were no colonies of gaily coloured chattering parakeets such as one found in almost every boabab on the Serengetti Plain. The only birds I saw were vultures and crows hovering close to the town. The north wind still blew, salty from the sea and gritty and cold except in the lee of the baobabs, where the sun was roasting hot in the very sparse shade. A thin grey haze veiled any distant view of a landscape which I found as depressing as a view of a Yorkshire coal-field. I found several living things of interest however. One stunted bush swarmed with largish ants, and I discovered that almost every leaf was folded on its central vein as you'd fold the flap of an envelope, and that the edges were sewn together with fibre.

F

Each leaf packet contained either eggs or larvæ. They were tailor ants, and I thought that here was a grand subject for a film shot, and carefully took bearings of the bush so that I could bring Pereira to it. In a patch of sand too I found many small conical pits which I suspected were the traps of ant lion insects. They were about four inches across and about three deep, just like miniature volcanic craters. There were plenty of ordinary small ants scurrying about the ground and it was not long before I saw one of these come to the edge of a pit. The dry particles of sand at once gave way, and the ant rolled to the bottom of the pit from which emerged a pair of scimitar-like claws, like those on the tail of an earwig. The little ant was seized and dragged out of sight. I made a sudden scoop with my hand and pulled out the ant lion (it was about the size of an ordinary house spider) with its victim still held in its jaws.

I felt really excited by these two discoveries. I thought that if only George would give me a free hand with the natural history side of the " production " we'd be able to make a film at least almost as good as the one I had planned. Doubtless we should find plenty of even more interesting subjects when we got into the interior and away from European habitations. I soon decided we shouldn't have to wait till then, for making a wide circuit past the outskirts of the town I reached the seashore and found a real native fishing village on the edge of a sandy cove. It was not much more than a mile from Dakar itself. Yet it was almost completely primitive, the huts built of adobe with thatched roofs, and standing among a group of oil palms, and plantains. I was seeing everything now as a film producer, and here indeed was a perfect location : and it so chanced that as I came upon the place, the fishermen themselves were preparing for " action."

There were about a score of men altogether. They did not look like the sophisticated Senegalese of the town. They wore only loin clothes and turbans on their heads, and standing watching them were several women with naked breasts, and dozens of naked happy looking children. A large native dug-out was just aground on the sandy beach on which a considerable ground-swell was breaking. Into the stern of this boat the men were stowing a large net, one end of which appeared to be fixed to a stake on the beach. They were all talking excitedly to each other, paying no attention whatever to me, and it made me think of my boyhood days at Bramble-wick when all the boats were being launched after a spell of bad weather, and fishing prospects had suddenly turned good, or more exciting still when the lifeboat was going out to a wreck. It seemed that fishermen all the world over had something in common: they got excited and quarrelled with each other, but that never seemed to stop them doing their job efficiently.

I was completely fascinated, but all the time I was seeing it as a scene in a film. When the net was stowed, all hands mustered round the boat and started to push and heave it towards the surf. Some of them sprang aboard as its head floated. The rest pushed, then more got in and seized their paddles, with two men staying in the stern and paying out the net. The boat reared almost on end and soon it was clear of the breaking seas, moving straight out, the corked net visible in its wake. The technique soon became clear. About fifty yards from the shore the boat began to slew round. Soon it was broadside to the swell and moving parallel to the beach. Some members of the shore party had remained at the mooring stake. Some moved on along the beach, keeping pace with the boat, then halted when it started to come shoreward. The crew handled it superbly. They were using their paddles now as a check to the run of the surf, although the net itself was acting as a drogue. One sea did break over its stern, but the next moment the boat touched ground, the crew leapt out, all hands seized hold and it was dragged up the beach. Each end of the net was now manned, and the task of hauling it ashore began. The fishers started a sort of working chanty, and I would have given a lot to have understood the words. The women also sang, beating time with their hands and feet, and the children ran to a spot on the beach midway between the two groups of heaving men. Gradually as the net came in and shortened the men moved towards each other. The climax of the haul was approaching, and I could not help but think of that summer's night at Grunwyke, when Sam and Roland and I had hauled in our old salmon net, so heavy with fish we dare not lift it.

This beat Grunwyke. The men stopped hauling when the purse of the net was a boat length from the beach, and even then I could see the glitter of fish in it. Some of them armed with gaffs waded in up to their armpits. One hooked a tunny about five feet long but it required two others to help him fetch it to the shore,

where it lay kicking just like an immense mackerel. They waded
back to help with another big fish, this time a shark, and several
more tunny and moderately sized sharks were brought in before
the net was hauled in again and dragged up the beach. It was a
prodigious catch, and more varied than anything I had seen in East
Africa, although there were several species, including the sea
porcupine, that I'd caught with Hamzar-bin-Nazar. I recognised
a remora, that small shark-like fish which has a sucker on the top
of its head with which it adheres to the belly of a shark close to its
mouth and takes a share of its host's meals. There were sabre fish,
shaped like the blade of a broadsword and burnished like silver,
with a mouth full of wicked fangs. There were parrot fish with
rainbow colours. And what thrilled me almost as much was to see
our ordinary cod and haddock, lemon soles and conger eels, plaice
and flounders. But again my overriding excitement was the filming
possibilities of what I was witnessing. Surely a scene like this
would move any audience. Men, women and children were soon
busy gutting the fish. Gulls, crows and vultures were fighting for
the entrails and even attempting to seize the fish. The big fish
were filleted. There were posts and rails above highwater mark.
On these the fish were hung to dry and cure in the sun. I
noticed an astonishing thing happening on the ground close by
where a large fish, evidently an inedible species, had been flung. It
was being devoured by scores of large land crabs that had emerged
from burrows. But at the same time the carcase seemed to be
shaking and gradually sinking into the ground, and poking at it,
I saw that under it were swarms of large beetles digging away and
excavating the sandy soil. They were sexton beetles. They were
trying to get the carcase buried before the crabs stripped it clean.
Once buried they would lay their eggs in it so that the larvæ when
hatched would have a handy larder.

Hurrying back I found George and the two doctors in the lounge
of the hotel. The doctors were drinking vermouth. George had
a bottle of iced Vichy water in front of him, all three seemed
more cheerful: and talked almost amicably. George asked me to
have a drink. I told him excitedly about my discoveries, and he
at least seemed enthusiastic, but he had his own good news to
impart. The Consul had returned, and he'd had a good long talk
with him. He was going to do his best to get things moving with

the Customs people. Not only that, he'd invited us all to dinner, and it looked as though he was going to take a great personal interest in the expedition. He knew a lot of the country we were going to travel through. His advice would be invaluable. He was, by the way, a brother of Somerset Maugham, the famous novelist and playright. Actually I was less impressed by this than by learning that the Consul had been a great friend of Sir Harry Johnston, the African explorer, whose books, especially the one describing his ascent of Mount Kilimanjaro, had enthralled me. The dinner promised to be very interesting and it was not until George mentioned that we must wear dinner jackets that I felt bothered, for I had not dreamt of including dress clothes among my kit. But George had a spare suit which he insisted on loaning to me for the occasion. It was very important indeed that we should make a good impression on the Consul and his wife. With luck our gear and stores would be released from bond the next day, and we might make an immediate start with the film.

I had never been to a formal dinner party. It was unfortunate that George's figure was larger than mine in every dimension except the length of leg where I beat him by several inches and which meant that I had to keep my braces so slack that I felt all the time the trousers were going to fall down. The Consulate was an impressive building standing in its own beautifully kept grounds some distance from the town. There was an *askari* sentry at the gates, a uniformed black servant to receive us at the entrance door from our taxi (the best that George could hire) and to announce us formally to our host and hostess. My first impression of the Consul was that he looked very much like the photos I had seen of his brother, only more elderly. And my first impression of his wife, which was not dispelled throughout the evening, was of a very elegantly dressed aristocratic English lady whose perfect manners and apparent friendliness were a mask to a strong feeling of disapproval of her guests. It may have been my imagination, but I felt that instead of looking at my face when we met she looked at my over-size wing collar, and the too-broad shoulders of my borrowed dinner jacket, and even saw how my braces were too slack; yet she smiled in a most charming way. There were only the four of us, for Pereira had no dress clothes and had pleaded the urgency of his work. I don't think that Jock had even been asked. We were given cocktails (George accepting one, but toying with it only), then a splendidly uniformed servant announced that dinner was served and we moved into the dining-room, I walking with my hands in my trousers pockets and pressing down on them to maintain the tension of my braces. I did not enjoy that meal, although I had never tasted such delicious food. We had lots to drink too, or at least I had, and the cocktail had been a powerful one, but instead of making me feel happy as drink usually did it just made everything seem more unreal, and it was just as though we were all characters in a stage play and not ourselves at all. I could not rid myself of the feeling that Mrs. Maugham had guessed from the first moment that I was wearing George's clothes and that I was an impostor. Again, I felt that the two doctors while taking part in the general conversation were still bothered about what was happening between them and George, and that George was trying to pretend to every one that everything about the expedition was all right, and in particular to impress the Consul with this fact. I must have got a bit dazed before the meal was ended, but in the early stages of it, I remembered the black servant starting to fill George's glass with claret, and George glancing at me, and then refusing the drink and asking for water. I can't remember anything interesting that was said at dinner. But later when we went on to a sort of veranda to have coffee, Mr. Maugham told us a few of his big game hunting experiences and referred several times to Sir Harry Johnston, and also mentioned several places in East Africa I knew, but whenever I was tempted to speak I thought of my clothes and kept quiet.

George listened with great interest. Then he asked the Consul several questions about the country that we were to travel through after leaving Timbuctoo, and he started to go into various details about the film we were going to make, how it would be an epic of life in a primitive country, showing the connection between the various sorts of wild life and the human inhabitants, and how the struggle for existence went on and on, just as I had put it all in the prospectus of my film. He did not mention that it was my idea although he did mention that I was the naturalist to the expedition. The Consul did not appear to be very interested. Indeed it seemed almost as though every one was getting rather bored and that Mrs. Maugham was hoping that we would soon go, when George remarked that in addition to getting pictures of wild animals and insects and native life he wished to show something of the civilised side of Africa, white colonisation, missionaries, and that it had just occurred to him that it would make an interesting introduction to the film if he got a few shots of the British Consulate here at Dakar. It would be short of course, but give an indication of how the interests of Great Britain were looked after in a foreign colony. For instance, we might have a scene showing a British shipwrecked sailor being landed at the port, and being directed to the Consulate for advice and help. We might have a shot showing the Consulate with the Union Jack flying over it, and another with the Consul himself (with Mrs. Maugham), standing in the garden, or perhaps coming through the drive in a car, with the sentry saluting. I noticed that both Mr. and Mrs. Maugham looked really interested when George said this. Mrs. Maugham tried to persuade George to have a liqueur. She said that although they had a car they usually drove in a carriage with a very lovely English mare, and that it would make an attractive picture with the sentry, although she wouldn't wish to be in it. She hardly felt that she had what was called a film face. We all protested at this remark and George said what I believed was true, that she and her husband looked the typical English gentlewoman and gentleman, and that provided the Customs would release the raw film from bond he'd like to make the shot to-morrow.

We parted on excellent terms, the Consul promising that he would certainly do his best about the Customs, and his wife actually saying that we must come and dine with them again before we left for the interior and that she was really quite excited at the idea of making her debut as a film star.

6

THE FILM was released, and so was all our other gear and stores except the whisky, about which the Customs remained adamant. I did not witness the making of the British Consulate sequence. Neither did the two doctors, who stayed drinking vermouth in the hotel while George did the " directing." I could not help thinking it was a waste of time which might have been spent at my fishing village, and getting those tailor ants. But George pointed out that we shouldn't have had the film out of bond so quickly if he hadn't suggested doing it, that it was always a good thing to keep in with the officials, and that anyway the sequence would probably be cut completely when the film was edited. We would make a start on the fishing scene the next day. The next morning however George received a cable and announced its contents with great satisfaction. The Company had arranged for a further sum to be put to our credit immediately at the Dakar bank. We could start for the interior without further delay. This was a general announcement. Then George and the doctors went into private council. I assumed that the subject they discussed was still the thorny one of the whisky. Later, Jock was called into the council. Later still George told me that a solution to the impasse had been suggested by Jock himself, and while it had its drawbacks and risks, and meant depriving the expedition of its white hunter for the early stages of our journey, it seemed about the only way of overcoming the doctor's obstinacy. Jock would take charge of the stuff and tranship it to a small port lower down the coast where the officials happened to be friends of his, and would not mind lending themselves to what, after all, was only a technical evasion of Customs regulations. He knew the country very well, having hunted in it, and he was confident in being able to porterage the stuff by various roads and native tracks, so as to rejoin the expedition long before we reached the unhealthy malarious districts of the Upper Niger.

George saw the railway officials that night. There was only one train a week to the interior, and only one passenger coach. Unfortunately the whole accommodation in it had been booked for a party of military officers, so we must either wait till next week's train or travel in an ordinary covered truck. There was another heated discussion between George and the doctors. It seemed that by their contract they had been guaranteed first-class accommodation by sea and rail, and that they considered a truck anything but that. I really felt sorry for George for the way they kept holding out against him when he was clearly trying to do his best in difficult circumstances. They agreed to the truck in the end. Jock came to the station to superintend the loading of our stores, for which we had another large truck. He seemed to be more than usually high-spirited and kept on saying to the doctors, who looked just the opposite :

"Now don't you be worrying about the whisky. I'll be there with it long before you're ready to start away down the river where you'll need the stuff. Don't let it worry you at all."

But to me he said privately, with a sudden burst of confidence :

"Ah—what a fuss they're making about the damned stuff. Any one might think it was a great load of treasure. It's a pity now you're not accompanying me on the journey I'm making. It's a fine and exciting country after you leave the coast, with some elephants in the hills and maybe a bull or two worth shooting. It would have better if the whole expedition had gone that way instead of this, but there'd have been trouble with the elder doctor and his gammy leg. Now whatever persuaded a gentleman like that to make a safari across the Dark Continent ? I've doubts whether he'll ever go the whole way."

Jock was grinning as the train began to pull out, and it seemed to me that his last gesture was a wink, directed at myself, but it may have been just that involuntary shutting and opening of his eyes which I'd noticed when he was telling one of his yarns. I felt sorry we were leaving him behind. I was assailed again with a sense of foreboding. We had now been more than a fortnight in Africa, and apart from the "shooting" of the Consulate, had not taken a foot of film. I felt sick when I thought of the fishing village. We'd never get another chance like that. But I soon cheered up. The train was gathering way. We passed through the outskirts of the town, through the last belt of blue gums and soon there was nothing on either side of the line but uninhabited bush, fairly open at first with sandy glades and many baobabs, but gradually becoming more dense until it was an almost continuous thicket of thorn, tall enough to hide any sort of view of the country itself. Many districts of East Africa I had travelled through had been like this. Just when you were getting bored you'd come to a stream or a swamp and find a complete change in the vegetation, or the bush would suddenly end in an open plain swarming with game ; even here in the thick bush there was a chance of seeing something novel, for the train was not travelling more than thirty miles an hour.

George and the other members of the expedition did not share my hopeful interest. We had acquired two native servants. They were travelling in the other truck with the baggage, but under Jock's orders they had unpacked some of our camp gear before we had left Dakar, beds, Beira chairs and a table, and more or less made our own truck habitable. George had unpacked his type-writer and was sitting at the table writing letters. The doctors—we were all (except Dr. Hilton who had full length trousers) wearing the conventional khaki drill shorts and polo shirts—were sitting in Beira chairs drinking lager beer, a case of which they'd brought from the hotel. Pereira and Harry were working at the Aeroscope again. It had behaved all right at the Consulate, using the ordinary handle, but there was still something to be done with its engine. The double sliding doors of the truck were wide open. I sat on the floor with my legs dangling over the track, and although I saw no living thing and not even a different tree or bush to relieve the sameness of the vegetation, I was happy and hopeful for a long time. One thing however had changed: there was no wind. The sky, while not of that lovely clear blue of East Africa, was cloudless, and the heat was fiercer than anything I had ever known, even at Mombasa which is practically on the Equator. The air itself was *hot*. Actually I was no cooler sitting in the draught of it than my companions were inside, but then I was wise enough to resist the temptation to cool myself by drinking, even water. Before we were an hour out of Dakar both the doctors were comatose in their chairs from the combined effect of the beer and the heat, the sweat pouring from their faces on to their shirts, which were literally steaming. It was then, for the first time and because I was on the floor, that I noticed Dr. Hilton's artificial leg. George had aban-doned his typing and was staring glassily at the empty beer bottles wobbling on the floor at the doctors' feet, and Pereira and Harry were stretched out on their camp beds among their tools and the half dissected entrails of the Aeroscope. It was a fantastic sight. They looked almost as though they had been gassed. The heat, which rapidly became more intense, and the sheer monotony of that wall of thorn which had no break, so that it was as though we were moving along a roofless tunnel, defeated me in the end. I lay down on my camp bed and thinking regretfully of how different my first journey on the Mombasa Uganda Railway had been, yet not without hope that this would improve later on, sank into a stupor that finally became sleep. . . .

Our destination was Bamako, half-way from Dakar to Tim-buctoo, but the railway that now joins Dakar and Bamako was not then complete. There was a gap of some forty miles between the temporary terminus of the coast section and the township of Kayes on the east bank of the River Senegal. The gap was bridged with a fleet of motor cars provided by the railway. We reached the terminus after dark. There was no town here, but there was a buffet at the " station " where we got a good meal, red wine included. Darkness had brought little diminution in the temper-ture. The buffet was merely an open shed on the platform, without any walls. Not a breath of air stirred within it and the very effort of eating caused the sweat to pour from our faces and limbs. We were all limp, and while the doctors, especially Hilton, looked cross, there was no arguing. They didn't like the wine, but as they had drunk all their beer, and the water the natives brought was almost hot, they had to follow George's example and drink grenadine, which they could not have liked as it was sweet and had to be mixed with the same nearly-boil water. The cars, which were waiting for us, were Fords (Model T) with trucks for baggage. They had native drivers. The road was a mere track, full of pot-holes, as rough as anything I remembered from East Africa. The drivers seemed to regard the throttle as something to be opened to go and shut to stop, and they charged ahead regardless of potholes or odd stones on the road : but for the fact that we were packed into our seats as tightly as sardines in a tin, we'd have been thrown out many times. I felt almost sorry for Dr. Hilton, the more so as I had discovered the cause of his limp. He kept on being ill, and the one good thing about this was that the convoy had to halt, which gave us a chance to get out and stretch our limbs. On one of these occasions I forgot about the discomforts and disappointments of the journey. The sky was starry, the air still. I heard the sound of native drums, low and distant, and, rising above them, the wail of a hyena. The drums, though distant, were ahead of us ; they made my heart beat quickly with excitement and promise and I felt really happy until I was back in the car with George and the doctors and the dumping started again.

I have only a vague memory of the rest of that journey. We reached the River Senegal about midnight, and I believe crossed it by a pontoon ferry, but the river itself, which was at dry-season level, was hidden in a mist through which came only the faintest glimmer of starshine. We saw nothing of the township of Kayes for the station must have been close to the river bank. Here, however, a memorable surprise awaited us. The train was in. It consisted entirely of modern corridor coaches with first and second-class compartments, including a dining-car and bar. The dining-car was closed but the bar was open, a fact which Dr. Hilton, in spite of his having been so ill, was the first to discover. There was a podgy, perspiring little Frenchman in charge of it. He didn't look a bit surprised when the Doctor asked him if he had any beer : but *we* were surprised when he produced a bottle from under the counter, and then dropped a big chunk of real ice into a glass and poured the beer on top of it. I was more surprised still when Dr. Hilton immediately called for similar drinks for all of us as we gathered round. Only George refused, and took instead his usual grenadine, with ice of course. Every one, and especially Dr. Hilton, seemed good-tempered again. The train started, and he called for another round of drinks, and we all watched the bar-tender dropping the pieces of ice into our glasses as though he was a conjurer. Even when the train gathered way, and a draught came through the open windows, the air was like that from a furnace. The ice itself had melted completely long before we reached the bottoms of our glasses. The Doctor became almost loquacious. He kept on saying it was a miracle finding iced beer on a train in Central Africa, and at this time of night, and he insisted on us having more of it at his expense. He said it was the best thing that had happened since we had arrived in the country, and that he felt at last that the expedition was going to be a great success. He actually smiled when he looked at George, as though he really liked him, and George looked quite embarrassed and apologised for having to ask for another grenadine. I think that with the exception of George, we must have all got tipsy in the end, for the next thing I remembered was waking up on the seat of a first-class compartment, in broad daylight, the train stopped, and a babble of French and native voices outside. I was dripping with sweat, and had a splitting headache and a terrible thirst. We had arrived at Bamako.

7

MY FIRST impression of Bamako was that it was going to be just as civilised as Dakar. George had booked rooms for us at the station hotel. Abutting the station buildings it was a modest affair, little more than a bungalow, and the restaurant an extension of the station platform, with a galvanised roof and open sides. Close to the station however were rows of European houses and shops lining a busy road, and the predominant sound was that of motor cars and trucks and strident klaxon horns. I hoped that we were not going to stay here long, that there would be no more arguments or rows or financial difficulties and that we should soon be travelling through real country and getting on with the making of the film. Actually there were no arguments between George and the doctors the day of our arrival, or in the evening. The food at the hotel was first rate. There were unlimited supplies of beer and ice (there was an ice factory in the town and it was distributed in blocks insulated with sawdust) and the doctors seemed perfectly content to remain in the restaurant eating or drinking. Before evening however, my first impressions of Bamako had changed very favourably. The European quarter centering on the station was only a small part of the town itself. The rest, and it was very expansive, was native. Some of this had been re-planned and re-built by the French authorities. The streets were wide and straight, and many of the huts had galvanised roofs. Farther from the station there was little planning. The streets were narrow and winding. There were houses built Arab fashion of whitewashed adobe or cement with flat roofs, there were thatched huts, and through the streets moved a continuous stream of natives, most of the men wearing long white cotton gowns with embroidered " pork-pie " caps, the women wrapped in gaily-coloured cotton sheets which formed skirt and bodice by dexterous knotting. It was a real native town. Almost every house or hut was a shop. There were no windows to the shops. They were merely the ground floor rooms open to the street, or in some cases projecting into it under a cloth or thatched awning. The majority of them dealt in textiles, displaying rolls of coloured and patterned cotton cloth or made-up native garments. Others were full of earthenware, domestic utensils, jars and bowls and cooking pots, of all them beautifully shaped and decorated. There were bread and fruit and vegetable and spice shops, but most interesting of all, and I was seeing everything from a filming point of view, were the shops of the craftsmen where the shopkeepers were actually at work in full view of the passers-by.

I never learnt the exact ethnological identity of the inhabitants of Bamako, but they were less Negroid than the Senegalese, and clearly had a Semitic strain in their blood. Certainly they were highly intelligent and their craftsmanship was superb. They were artists as well as artisans. There were potters and weavers, and gold and silversmiths, basket makers, and workers in iron and leather and wood, all busy as bees, all deeply concentrated on their tasks and apparently unconcerned as to whether they sold anything or not. There was one man squatting on the floor of his shop in front of a low bench, drilling minute holes into ebony beads, and plugging these holes with silver wire. When the wire was nipped off it left a silver spot on the bead, and with these spots he was making an intricate geometrical pattern. There was another making conventional butterflies and beetles out of soft gold in exquisite filigree. I guessed that they were for clasps on native robes. Most of the baskets that were being made were of tough grass, and urn-shaped, evidently for storing grain, for they were large and had lids. They were all patterned with differently coloured grasses, chiefly reds and yellows, but unlike any tints you would see in the artistic products of an industrial country, and the patterns again were unique. The predominant basic *motif* in pottery and weaving and basketwork seemed to be the V and diamond, and I wondered if this had been inspired originally by the " camouflage " markings and colouration of the skin of certain snakes. This would be an intriguing idea to work out in the film : a shot of a python writhing through grass in which because of its markings it would be almost invisible : then a close-up of its skin, showing the pattern in detail ; flashing from this to a native artist, weaving it into a cloth or basket, or scratching it on to the unbaked clay of a pot. . . .

Again George seemed impressed with the account I gave him of my discoveries, and as Dr. Hilton continued to be in a good mood and pleased with the food and drink he was getting at the hotel, I began to think that things were going to turn out better than I had ever imagined. Before we went to bed that night it was agreed we should all go to the native quarter next morning and decide which would be the best shots to make as soon as the camera was ready. There was only one tiny gadget in the " engine " to be adjusted, Pereira had explained, and the apparatus would be in perfect working order for automatic as well as hand turning. But next morning George said apologetically that he had to call on certain officials in the town before doing anything else, and also on the bank. The doctors found it too hot to leave the shade and the iced drinks of the restaurant. Pereira said that he simply must get the camera fixed. So again I went out alone, with that sense of foreboding once more a weight on my spirits.

And that weight did not completely lift as I extended my explorations of the previous afternoon and found subject after subject of enthralling interest. I found one street, about a quarter of a mile long, made up of adobe and thatched huts, in front of almost every one of which was a native working a pedal American sewing machine making cotton " native " gowns, all, seemingly, of identical cut. Later I learnt that the machines were owned by a French merchant who traded the mass-produced garments " up-country " in return for agricultural produce, principally ground and palm oil nuts, and hides. In strange contrast to this banal scene, I saw in a sort of courtyard a whole family of natives spinning wool from fleece into yarn, and weaving this into narrow strips of blanket with a coloured design of perfect beauty. The loom was hand-made of wood, and might have been identical with those used in ancient Egypt for weaving the robes of kings and queens : the scene itself with two lovely and almost naked girls walking gracefully up and down the courtyard spinning the yarn, and a man and a woman working the loom might have come to life from an Egyptian fresco. I watched a blacksmith forging a mattock. His bellows was a sewn-up goat skin which a bright-eyed and smiling boy (probably his son) worked with a pedal : and not far away was the man's wife with a baby slung on her back, thumping corn in a huge wooden mortar, making a sound like a drum and moving all the time from side to side as though dancing to its rhythm.

I discovered that beyond the streets I had first explored, there was a wide open space, the town's chief market. In all my travels in East Africa I had never seen anything to compare with it. In many ways, however, it was like that of an English country town. On the boundaries there were inns and native eating-houses for the use of the " farmers " coming in from the outlying districts to sell their produce and shop. As in any market, you could tell these countrymen from the townsmen by their un-sophisticated manner, the way they stared at the various things that were for sale, especially the rolls of cloth : and, apart from this, many of them clearly belonged to other tribes of the Bamako stock, while some were real desert tribesmen, Berbers, and Moors and Tuaregs. There were no stalls : the sellers had their goods dis-played on the ground, and some of them had brightly-coloured awnings to shade them from the fierce sun. As well as the food and textiles and pots and pans and baskets and leather goods on sale in the street shops, there were sheep and goats and cattle and camels and ponies and donkeys for sale, not by auction but by personal bargaining. I felt, as I wandered through the market, as an angler might feel, watching trout rising in a pool and having no gear with him, or as a gunless sportsman with pheasants or hares getting up and offering perfect shots. Everywhere I looked there was some-thing to film : a Touareg warrior, with his face almost hidden in a gleaming white head-cloth rode down one of the aisles of the market on a jet black Arab stallion, glancing disdainfully at the goods that were for sale as though the whole world was his : a stout and elderly Moorish sheik turbanned and bejewelled, mounted on a very inadequate ass so that his sandalled feet nearly touched the ground, rode away from the market at the head of a convoy con-sisting of two other asses heavily laden with sacks, two male negroes empty-handed, and finally three yashmaked ladies, two old and one very young, each carrying on her head one of those huge urn-shaped baskets evidently full of food.

There was a mosque on the north boundary of the market place. It was a long squat building with a flat crenellated roof but no minaret. In front of its doorway were several hideous beggars, two of them afflicted with elephantiasis of the legs, one with a huge neck tumour. Another was apparently insane. He had wildly staring eyes, and he was doing a sort of dance with his muscles, making them contract and expand to a definite rhythm without moving his limbs, which streamed with sweat. There was a constant stream of worshippers entering or leaving the mosque. Those that went in had to change their street shoes or sandals for mosque slippers and change back again as they came out: but though the beggars moaned for alms no one seemed to take the slightest notice of them, even of the mad dancer. At the far end of the mosque wall a powerfully built elderly native sat on a wooden chair shaded by an awning. He was of the Bamako type, more Semitic than Negroid, and had a pointed beard. He wore a black camel-hair *burnous* over the conventional white gown with a gold clasp to it and had gold rings on his fingers. At first I thought he was some sort of mosque official, but shortly I observed a native policeman coming towards him holding by the arm an almost naked and very frightened looking youth. The policeman saluted, the youth went down on his knees in front of the chair with his head lowered humbly. The policeman started to talk, gesticulating with his hands and repeatedly pointing to his charge. It became clear that the man in the chair was a magistrate. His face indeed had all the dignity and impassivity of an English judge. He asked the youth a few questions, in a voice as deep and smooth as Paul Robeson's, which were answered almost inaudibly. Then he signed to him to stand up and approach nearer. His right hand flashed out twice, like a whip, smack on the youth's right and left cheek. The youth winced, but he made no sound. He salaamed, the policeman saluted, as they withdrew, and the magistrate was alone again, calm and dignified as though nothing had happened.

I could have spent days in that market, just watching the various native types, looking at their clothes, listening to them talking, or haggling over their purchases. One man was selling fish, not fresh fish which, in the intense heat, would have decomposed in less than an hour, but the sun and salt water cured fillets of the sharks I had seen caught at Dakar, wrapped in leaves like mummies, smelling strong but not really bad : his customers were a villainous looking Berber accompanied by two of the loveliest girls I have ever seen, with dazzling teeth, and liquid eyes with long black lashes, their smooth cheeks dusted with a pale blue powder which I thought might have inspired a new vogue in the beauty parlours of the civilised world. I thought that if we could only get the movie camera into a camouflaged truck or cart and go slowly up and down the aisles we could get thousands of feet of film which, even if the expedition went no farther into Africa, would pay for all its cost. Again I returned to the hotel full of enthusiasm, but again it was squashed, for I found George sitting with the doctors in a restaurant and engaged in still another argument.

It was not until after lunch when I screwed up courage to ask George for a little more money, that he unburdened himself of some of his new worries. He had received a telegram from Jock to say that he had sailed with the whisky, and that he hoped to rejoin the expedition within a fortnight, but at a point some thirty miles down the Niger. George had been discussing the matter of river transport with a French agent in the town, and had learnt that at present the water was too low for the big native dug-outs that were used for this purpose. Road transport as far as Timbuctoo was impossible. We should have to wait for the rains. Dr. Hilton had taken up his usual unreasonable attitude, blaming George for not having known about the state of the river, and saying that Jock, if no one else, must have known it. He had even suggested that there was some sort of conspiracy between Jock and himself (which of course was absurd). Another annoying thing was that the agent of the Colonial Bank and had received no money either from Dakar or Paris, although George had cabled the film company that we had left Dakar. What they had sent to Dakar had, after all, been only enough to cover hotel expenses and our railway fares. In that case I wouldn't mind accepting just a small advance, would I ? It would be adjusted later, and of course there would be no hotel bill to meet. I felt sympathetic. I did not mind much about the cash, which I only wanted for buying some of the lovely things I had seen in the shops and market, but I told him that I was worried because we weren't getting on with the film, especially as I had seen so many wonderful things on my morning's exploration. He said I needn't worry about that. Pereira (I had noticed his absence at lunch) had taken the camera to a garage not far from the station to get something welded : only a small job, as he had explained, and when it was done there should be no more trouble, so we'd start filming at once. That weaving I had seen sounded a grand subject to start on . . .

We did indeed make a start on the weavers next day. The doctors were sufficiently interested to hire a taxi to drive them to the place and to watch the proceedings. I was to discover that there is a vast difference between seeing a subject with your eyes and making a film record of it. The weavers had taken little notice of me as a single spectator. The arrival of our entire company with camera and tripod produced as much consternation as a fox in a chicken run. Not only did the weavers stop work but the news of what was happening must have spread instantly to the neighbourhood. We were almost mobbed. George had hired an interpreter for the occasion. He was a shifty looking half-caste, unctuous towards George, superior and almost contemptuous towards the natives whom he tried to shout back from the courtyard. The sun was fiercely hot. There was no wind, and I did not envy Pereira and Harry fixing up the gear in all the din and excitement, for they and their camera were the centre of interest. The mob was goodnatured however, and kept within bounds. George, who was directing, explained in French to the interpreter that he wanted the weavers to carry on with their work just in the ordinary way, that they must not pay attention to the crowd, and in particular that they must not look at the camera when the film was being taken as that would spoil everything. The interpreter said that he understood and he drew the eldest of the weavers aside and spoke to him in rapid undertones. The weaver himself addressed his fellowworkers. The two girls who had been spinning giggled selfconsciously and there was quite a discussion among them all. One might have guessed the real nature of that discussion, that the interpreter had bettered his instructions and was out to make a twoway profit from the occasion. He told George in French that the people were willing to perform, but that they were very poor, so would the great monsieur pay them something, for example, a hundred francs ? It was not, I thought, an excessive fee to ask as fees went in the film world, but it happened to be the maximum sum (about one pound at the prevailing rate of exchange) that George had been able to advance me on my weekly salary of twenty pounds, and he looked a bit bothered. He agreed however, and told the interpreter to tell the weavers to carry on just as they would do if nothing else was happening, and to Pereira he said :

"Okay, as soon as they start. Take what you can get."

My admiration and respect for Cherry Kearton and Martin Johnson, and for other pioneers of cinemaphotography of native life went up from that moment. The weavers certainly obeyed the first part of their instructions. They began to work the loom. The girls started pacing up and down the courtyard with their spindles. But it was not the idyllic picture of native industry that I had seen first. As soon as the camera started clicking they looked towards it as apprehensively as a wild animal startled by the sudden sound of footsteps. George snapped at the interpreter :

"Tell them not to look at the camera ! "

The interpreter, who was looking at the camera himself, translated his instructions. The weavers, now genuinely scared, turned their faces completely away like children in a game told not to look, and the effect was fantastic, for one of the girls tripped and nearly fell, and there was a roar of laughter from the crowd. Pereira had to stop turning the handle, to mop the sweat from his eyes. George, who was looking hot and worried, asked the interpreter to explain to the girl again that she must not look either at the people or the camera, just do her job in the usual way : to speak to her gently, and not frighten her. But the interpreter, possibly fearing he was going to miss some of his rake-off if the great monsieur didn't get what he wanted, unfortunately misunderstood George's caution or he had his own too strong ideas on how women should be managed. He went up to the girl, shouting and cursing at her, and the girl, with perhaps more excuse than most temperamental film actresses, burst into tears and ran into the shelter of the nearest hut. The crowd laughed again, and for the first time I saw George really angry. He snapped at Pereira :

"Never mind the damned women. Take a few feet of the loom working and then pack up. This is absurd."

That night I was to get a further insight into the difficulties of filming in the tropics. Pereira wanted to make sure that the camera had been working all right, and that he had used the correct lens stop, by developing a strip of the film. He had no tank but he had a dark-room lamp and blacked out his bedroom for the job. Before starting he thought he'd better take the temperature of the water he was going to use. It was only a little less than the temperature of the room which was 105° Fah. The highest day shade temperature I had known in East Africa had been 98°. He managed to get a block of ice from the hotel kitchen and put this in a bucket half filled with water. In a few minutes the block had completely melted and the temperature was below eighty. He used this for mixing his developer and fixing bath. He told me that he was putting a special hardening chemical in the developer to neutralise the effect of warmth on the gelatine of the film : and making the developer weak to avoid too speedy development.

This side of photography had always excited me, but it called for a special discipline that I had found hard to practise. There's a sort of magic in it. You watch the plate or film in the dim ruby light of the dark-room lantern. The weaker the light the safer it is, but the harder it is to see the magic ! Also the slower the process the better your chance of success. There is always the doubt, especially if your subject has been an exceptional one, whether your shutter worked or not, whether your exposure was right or the lens dead in focus. The first doubt is relieved when along the edges of the film or plate a dark even margin appears, proving at least that exposure has taken place. Then very slowly comes a slight differentiation in the body of the negative, the emergence of the image. But whether it is sharp in focus, or correctly exposed you can't tell for certain, and the temptation to settle the first doubt by holding the negative up to the light is very strong. Even when development is complete, there must follow a quarter of an hour's immersion in the fixing solution before the emulsion becomes definitely safe in strong light. And then if your negative is good, the final proof of success is not forthcoming until you have got your positive print after hours of washing and drying, although these processes are speeded up to the point of elimination for press work.

Pereira, in spite of his inventor's temperament and his anxiety to see results, was painstaking and calm. Cine-film is supersensitive and cannot be exposed to any sort of light until fixed. He covered the lamp completely, and did the developing by touch and we waited a full half-hour before he uncovered the lamp and took the film out of the hypo bath. He washed it in the bucket that had contained the ice. Then he held it up to the full light, and gave a cry of disappointment and vexation. The "pictures" or frames, negative and positive, of a cine-film are very small. You cannot examine them for detail without a magnifying lens: though you can form a good estimate as to exposure and sharpness of focus. All you could tell of this strip, which contained about a dozen "frames," was that it had been exposed and that it did bear a resemblance to the scene we had shot. But the whole film was blurred, almost like a frosted window. The gelatine had melted, and when Pereira touched a bit of it with a finger-tip, it ran like wet paint.

I did not appreciate the significance of what had happened or understood why Pereira was so upset until we got out of that stifling bedroom, when he told me that on his expedition with the American big-game hunter to the Soudan he had found the same snag. It did not mean that the actual film was spoilt. It was the development that had caused the trouble, the high temperature of the solutions, which the ice had failed to lower effectively. On the Soudan expedition (the heat had not been as excessive as this) they had abandoned the idea of developing the entire film on the spot but had packed it carefully for development at home. It had, however, deteriorated, and Pereira had decided that on this trip he would develop at suitable intervals. For doing this he had designed a special portable apparatus which was capable of handling a five hundred foot spool. If it proved successful he intended to take out a patent on it. But he had been relying on the chemical hardener for solving the temperature problem. Even with ice it had not worked. What would happen when we got into the real jungle, where it might be hotter even than here?

It might have been one more thing for poor George to worry about during the following days, but if it was he did not mention it. His over-riding worry, and he made no secret of it to me at any rate, was finance. He told me that he had sent several cables to the managing director of the film company asking for a further draft but no answer had come. He could not understand it. Surely they must realise that the expenses of an expedition such as ours were bound to be pretty heavy, and he himself could not see how they could be cut down. We certainly hadn't been extravagant with film, although that was an item we should have to be very careful about. We must not forget that the really sensational stuff lay ahead of us in the more or less unexplored regions. That weaving subject and the other subjects I had told him about were interesting of course, but then Bamako was practically civilised. We must always bear in mind that a film in order to make big money must appeal to the big public, and sad though it might be, the public did seem to put drama and sensation first. George was so charming, and he was so genuinely worried that I could not feel vexed with him. The doctors were badgering him again about the whisky, and criticising him because he had let Jock arrange to take it to a place where we could not join him until the river came in flood. No one seemed to know exactly when that would be. I wasn't vexed with George, but my foreboding was deepening to a conviction that the whole business was going to be a flop, particularly when Pereira told me that George had given him definite instructions that our stock of cine-film was to be reserved for when our real journey began, unless we happened to come across something really sensational.

I found out what George meant by that. He had made the acquaintance of several white men in the town, and one of them named Arnold, the agent for a big European firm of palm oil importers, had told him of an extraordinary thing he had witnessed lower down the Niger towards Timbuctoo. The natives there were very primitive, living entirely by hunting and fishing. They were also expert swimmers, and at regular intervals they practised a ceremonial crocodile hunt. One of the reptiles would be hedged into a certain part of the river, and then a man armed only with a knife held between his teeth would dive in and swim under the crocodile's belly and knife its throat. The whole thing was a sort of religious ritual, an initiation. Often the participants were mauled or even slain, but it always ended with at least one dead crocodile, and the hauling of its carcase ashore would be followed by a feast and dancing. I felt as enthusiastic as George himself about this. I thought it would probably be a rather difficult thing to film if the most exciting part of it took place under water, but then I had my tank and if we could catch a baby crocodile we might fake a good impression of it.

I'd been so fascinated with Bamako's native streets and market that it was not until George mentioned this crocodile business that I thought of visiting the river a mile or so from the town. I started from the open end of the market along a rough road which shortly became a native path wandering between gardens and small maize fields. There was an uncultivated space on my left like a common, and I observed on this a number of shallow mounds, with little earthenware pots lying near them. Two natives were digging a trench. I did not realise that the place was a cemetery, and that the trench was a grave until I noticed approaching across the common from the town a small procession headed by six men carrying a corpse. There was no coffin. The corpse was just bandaged up like a mummy, but of course it was stiff. There were women in the procession and a few children. They were chanting as they walked, but quite cheerfully, and the children were laughing. High in the air above like an escort of aeroplanes moved a flock of vultures. But the most extraordinary thing about the procession was that it wasn't moving in a straight line for the grave but zigzagging, about twenty paces one way, then a half turn, and the same number another, like ships in a war-time convoy avoiding torpedo attack, and at each turn the bearers shook the corpse so that it looked almost animated . . . I vaguely remembered having read somewhere that certain African natives zigzag their dead to the burial ground so as to elude the evil spirits which, not content with having produced death, would haunt and torture their victim in his second life. I wondered, ironically, if George would have thought this sensational enough for his big public !

I did not watch the actual interment. I felt almost as though one of those frustrated evil spirits had fixed on me. I could not shake off the feeling I had of impending misfortune. The River Niger disappointed me. I had hoped that it would be something like the Pangani, only on a grander scale. All that the Niger had in common with the river of such happy memory was the muddiness of its water. There was no papyrus, no luxuriant tropical forest, no monkeys. True that in the wet season its width must have been considerable. Now it was little more than that of the Thames at Hampton Court. Its banks made perpendicular cliffs from the flat land either side. In several places wicked looking rocks stood out of the water and obviously it was not navigable for anything of greater draught than a canoe. There were no birds and the water was too dirty for me to see if there were any fish. The only thing I did see in the water was a dead sheep or goat, its carcase distended, floating feet up and stiff like the legs of an overturned and damaged table. The heat was appalling and I could find no shade. But again, although the sky was cloudless, there was that curious dimness in the landscape. The only hills that were visible, on the town side of the river, were not blue as they would have been in East Africa but greeny-grey and their contours were muzzy. I had a sudden nausea against the place, and then a great longing, not for East Africa but for England. It was a longing that persisted throughout my hot walk back to the town, and was not cured by sight of the market with its tantalising subjects for film photography. Yet I had not guessed what news was waiting for me at the hotel.

I found George sitting alone in the restaurant drinking grenadine and looking very dejected. He asked me to sit down and join him in a drink. Then he told me he'd had some bad news. The film company was broke. It was going into voluntary liquidation. No further funds were forthcoming for the expenses of the expedition. He didn't know exactly what had happened but it was clear they hadn't been able to secure the capital needed for the other expeditions they had planned. Ours up till now had really been financed by what he and the two doctors had put into it. They had merely exchanged their investments for shares in the company. Naturally he had had a disagreeable discussion with the doctors about the matter. They maintained that he was responsible, and morally he supposed he was, but that of course had nothing to do with me: and I must believe that he was really worried about my position. He felt that he had let me down badly. He was certain that if the financial side had been all right my enthusiasm and knowledge of natural history would have gone a long way to making the expedition a huge success.

I was shocked. I knew instinctively what George was leading up to, but more than anything I was shocked and distressed because of his disappointment and I knew at the same time he was absolutely sincere in his sympathy towards me. He suddenly shook my hand.

" Look here," he went on, and for a moment I thought he was

on the verge of tears. " We've been very good friends, haven't we ? We've pretty well agreed about everything. And you've been a very good friend to me. I can't tell you what I owe to you for keeping me straight about the drink business. With all this worry I've been tempted time after time to let myself go. But I've pulled myself up by thinking of that promise I made on board ship. I'm frightfully sorry I've let you down."

I felt uncomfortable. At the same time I couldn't help thinking it was funny he should credit me with such an effective moral influence for I'd said nothing to stop him drinking, and I certainly had not been teetotal myself. I wondered if this last shock had been too much for him and he *had* started drinking. The grenadine belied that thought.

He went on lugubriously :

" Yes, I've had it out with the doctors. They insist that we carry on with the expedition, at least until we join up with Jock. We've got to make a film of some sort, and they like the idea of that crocodile ceremony. Also they insist that we shall go at least as far as Timbuctoo. It's put me in a devil of a jam : means I've got to stand the financial racket myself. That means realising securities, and cabling and writing to my own bank. Weeks of delay most likely. So there's nothing for it but to trim our sails. How do you stand for ready cash, by the way ? "

I had to tell George that I was down to less than one hundred francs. He looked bothered, and for a while remained silent. Suddenly he signed to the native waiter who was hovering by, and he said to me :

" Look here. I'm going to have a brandy. Feel I've just got to. Don't worry about my promise now. I just need it, like a medicine. Will you have one ? "

I did not want an alcoholic drink, but I did not feel moved to protest at George having one. He ordered a large cognac with ice but he was silent while he waited for it, and deliberately I did not look at him in case he thought I was trying to exert my moral influence. I could tell he was feeling a bit guilty about it however, and when it came he remarked self-consciously :

" Medicine, you know. I'll swear I've got a touch of fever or something." And he drank it like medicine, at one draught, and without water.

I had no doubt now as to what he had to tell me, and I tried to help him out.

"I'm terribly sorry about it all," I said. "I suppose it means you want me to go back."

"Not *want* you," he said quickly. "My God, no. I was absolutely relying on you with the film, and personally I wish you'd stay and see the thing through. It's just a matter of finance. If you could carry on without salary, on a profit-sharing basis, I can't tell you how pleased I'd be. But it wouldn't be fair. You're a married men. And you told me from the first you had no capital. No, I'll not ask you to risk it. I advise you strongly to clear off home. You'll meet Paddy, and you'll be able to explain things to her, better than I can do in a letter. Tell her I'm on the water wagon, by the way. I'll cable them when you're leaving. But the devil is your railway fare and your passage from Dakar. Quite frankly, old boy, at the present moment I'm almosy completely without funds. It's a damn good job the hotel people here are trusting us. I think I'll have another cognac. Have one with me this time, will you? There's nothing like brandy when you're feeling below par. I think I must have been poisoning myself with this blasted grenadine . . ." He signed to the waiter again. His manner was becoming more confident, almost courageous. "Look here," he went on when he had ordered another double. "Don't you worry. I've been in plenty of tight fixes in my life, and I've always pulled out. You pack up to-night, old boy. Believe there's a train in the morning. I'll get your fare somehow, and your passage. First-class this time too. I never let my best pals down. Sure you won't have a cognac? Damn good stuff. You couldn't get this in England. Remember that man Arnold who told me about the crocodile? Asked me to dine with him to night, but he's such a damned boozer I refused. Fancies himself at poker too . . . I'm going to see him now, soon as I've had another cognac. Don't you worry about your fare home. Only I'll be terribly sorry to lose you."

It was about three o'clock next morning that I was awakened from a rather fitful sleep by someone sitting down heavily at the foot of my bed. The electric light had been switched on. It was George. He had an empty whisky bottle in one hand, a wad of banknotes in the other. I gathered that he'd had a hell of a night with Mr. Arnold. They'd drunk whisky and played poker for very high stakes ; and George evidently had won in two senses, for he'd left his host under the table. He pressed the wad of notes into my hand and with tears streaming down his red and perspiring cheeks assured me that I was the best friend he had ever had, that it broke his heart to have me go, that he hoped I would have a pleasant voyage home, and that some day we would make another expedition to Africa, a really successful one.

I left Bamako for Dakar on the morning train.

Book Four

I

CLAIRE who was in London on my return had been having quite a good time while I was in Africa. The company had faithfully paid her one-half of my agreed salary up to the time of its liquidation and she and Paddy had been to Florence and Rome to see the art galleries and museums. They had met a lot of very interesting people, mostly painters and sculptors, and Claire thought that it would be a good thing if we went to live in Italy as food and board was so cheap and the whole atmosphere was so inspiring for writers as well as painters. I thought it was a good idea, but our funds were now too low even to pay single third-class railway fare for such a distance. We therefore took a furnished room in Bayswater, and I started work again on my still incomplete thriller for which I had been vaguely promised an advance in royalties of twenty-five pounds. But it was now spring. The trees in Kensington Gardens were bursting into leaf and I found it hard to concentrate on writing, especially as the occupant of the room above us was a professional pianist who spent hours of the day practising scales. Again, I did not feel that the book was a good one, or indeed that I had any ability for writing fiction. One day I picked up a copy of the *Wide World Magazine*. This was the journal which had published the adventures of de Rougemont and by doing so produced a furore of criticism, as the avowed editorial policy was truth and nothing but the truth, and his descriptions of wombats and natives riding on giant turtles seemed inspired by those of Baron Munchausen. The furore had done the magazine no harm of course, and subsequently it had been able to publish an almost complete vindication of the famous narrative. It was now well got up, profusely illustrated with photographs, and a particularly interesting feature was a diagrammatic map of the world with the location of each story or article marked on it.

I thought what a pity it was that our expedition had been such a failure for several of the yarns were just personal narratives of travel and were being serialised. The literary standard was not so high as *Blackwood's*, but it was clear that this magazine (because of its illustrations if nothing else) would appeal to a wider public, and very likely the rates paid would be much higher. I knew that I had not enough material for even one article about our expedition, but I wrote to the editor telling him about my war experiences and my *Blackwood* serial and book, and about the scheme I had for a great African film (although I had now completely abandoned hope about this); I got a letter by return asking me to call at the office in Southampton Street, just off the Strand. The editor's name was Captain Pitt-Keithley. He was most friendly. He told me that he had read my yarn in *Blackwood's* and had been very interested and felt it was a great pity that the public was now sick of anything to do with the war, otherwise he was certain I had material in my experiences worth writing up for the *Wide World*. He made me talk about myself and was sympathetic about what had happened in West Africa, then he asked me about my future. Did I intend to set out on another expedition? Had I ever thought of making, say, a journey by canoe or barge across Europe, or doing something like Frazer's wonderful round-the-world on a bicycle. I thought I had better not mention films, or Africa for that matter, but I said there was nothing I wanted more than to travel to out-of-the-way places and have adventures to write about but that it was just a matter of finance. I'd be willing to go anywhere for my bare expenses, and a reasonable rate of payment for what I wrote. He said guardedly that the magazine was always prepared to consider any proposition, and provided that it was original and attractive enough, to give a reasonable amount of financial assistance. What he had particularly liked about my *Blackwood* yarn was its humour. If I could think out any sort of stunt that would provide material for the same treatment, he would give it careful consideration. The rates paid by his magazine were high, and there were additional fees for all photos published.

It was Claire's suggestion that we should buy a caravan and, starting on the Atlantic side of southern France, travel to the Mediterranean, thence along the Corniche Road to Italy. Or if a caravan was too expensive, emulate Robert Louis Stevenson, and travel with a donkey (or donkeys) which would carry our tent and baggage. She was full then of the writings of Alfonse

Daudet, and became enthusiastic at the thought of travelling through Provence, the land of the troubadours. We might even be troubadours ourselves and earn our living as we travelled by singing to the inhabitants. We could buy a piano accordion or some sort of guitar which she as an accomplished pianist could quickly play. It was not easy for me to pretend that I thought the idea a very good one. The only singing I had ever done was with Sam and the two Bramblewick girls. Our best line had been hymns and it seemed doubtful whether such music, even to the accompaniment of a piano accordion or a guitar, would appeal to the inhabitants of France, less still of Italy. The memory of our cycling tour in Normandy and Brittany was fresh in my mind. I was not yearning for Africa but I suspected that Claire was thinking more of Italy than of the journey itself; and anyway I was doubtful whether the idea would appeal to the editor.

I was wrong. Captain Pitt-Keithley thought it a first-class proposition, only he dismissed the idea of a caravan as being too conventional. The donkey was original and far more likely to be funny. If it was a success he'd start the series in his Christmas number. He would pay me fifty pounds down and take a series of at least six articles at twenty guineas each plus half a guinea for every photo used. He did not (which any one would think rather important) ask me if I knew anything about donkeys, but perhaps he thought the venture would be more likely to yield fun if I did not. I made a great spurt and finished my thriller, and just before Easter we left for France.

As we had to go via Paris it was natural that we should call on Paul, and I could hardly protest against Claire's wishes to linger a few days to make the round of the studios and art shows. The rate of exchange made our capital feel impressive. We met several artists who knew the south of France and we were advised to begin our journey at Bayonne, where undoubtedly we'd be able to pick up a donkey for about thirty shillings. The Basques, we were told, were a delightful people. The Gascons even more so. We attended one wild studio party at which an American girl student played a ukulele and sang jazz, and before we left Paris Claire bought one of these instruments, brand new in a case, complete with a book of instructions.

It was evening when we arrived at Bayonne. We got a room

at a good hotel. It was a gay little town. There were open-air cafes, and in the *place* a band was playing and people were dancing on the pavement. How different, we thought, was this from an English provincial town where at this time of night all the shops would be closed, and all gaiety would be hidden behind the blinded windows of pubs. We started to look for a donkey next day. We discovered that as a means of transport the donkey was not as popular in this part of France as we'd been led to believe by our Paris advisers. That even in the mountainous districts we proposed to travel through there was an excellent bus service. But we found one by the end of the week, owned by an obese innkeeper (half Basque, half Portuguese) on the outskirts of the town. It was female, white, much larger than the ordinary English donkey, and it was almost as obese as its master, due he informed us to its being fed almost exclusively on maize, one of the main crops of the country. She was also, we guessed, fairly aged, but Alphonse assured us that she was only eight, that she was strong and had a most amiable disposition ; she was, he said, accustomed to working in a market trap, and we could have her (her name was Blanchette) with harness and trap for the equivalent of twenty-five pounds. It was Hobson's choice. I had contracted to make the trip with a donkey. The trap (it was a good one) if not so romantic as Robert Louis' panniers offered many advantages, and after some argument the deal was closed for eighteen pounds with a sack of maize and a bottle of wine thrown in for luck. Next day we drove Blanchette down to our hotel and loaded the trap with our baggage, which included Claire's so far untried ukulele. Then we set out on the first stage of our journey towards the foothills of the Pyrenees, which would have been visible from Bayonne but for the fact that they were blanketed in heavy cloud.

We enjoyed our first day on the road. Alphonse had not exaggerated either Blanchette's strength or her amiability. She trotted steadily along with only the mildest sign of disagreement with the signal of the reins when I steered into the left side of the road instead of the right. Although the mountains were still enveloped in cloud we had sunshine all the way, and indeed we had to seek the shade of some trees when we halted for lunch. The country was pleasant to look at. It was all intensely cultivated.

There were fields of barley and oats and wheat as well as maize. The hay harvest was in full swing, and we saw an even more primitive beast of burden than an ass, for most of the hay wagons were drawn by teams of oxen. The oxen were almost entirely swathed with blankets and wore masks. Later we learnt why !

The fields were small, as in Brittany. Farms and farm cottages were numerous. The buildings were all gleaming white but they were roofed with red semi-tubular pantiles, and most of the dwelling-houses had vines trained up their walls with their leaves stained greeny-blue with copper sulphate solution against the ravages of pests and blight. The peasants were dark and handsome with flashing eyes and very white teeth. All those we passed smiled and wished us good day, and from the hay fields we heard the men singing ; Claire said it had been just like that in parts of rural Italy which she and Paddy had visited, only there the men usually sang songs from opera, while here they seemed to be singing traditional folk songs. She wondered how long it would take her to become expert on the ukulele and whether she would have the nerve to play it to these people who obviously were so instinctively musical ; and I thought of Sam and me and the Captain's two daughters singing " Abide With Me " and " Greenland's Icy Mountains " and " Sweet and Low," and I thought I'd want a lot of practice before I'd started being a troubadour. Actually we were never to put ourselves to the test, for when late in the evening we reached a likely camping ground and started to unload our things, we discovered that the ukulele was missing, and I remembered that soon after we had left the outskirts of Bayonne I had heard a noise as of something falling behind us, but I had been so concerned with driving Blanchette I hadn't turned round.

It was a bad start for our first night in the Pyrenees. Many worse things were to follow. We had halted where the road crossed a little stream bordered with alder and sallows, but with a fairly dry patch of grass on one side. We unharnessed Blanchette, let her drink and then tethered her to a tree with a bucket of maize in front of her. We now realised why all the draught oxen we had seen had been masked and covered with blankets. We were assailed by swarms of cattle flies which stung viciously and caused Blanchette to kick and jerk at her tether. In addition there were swarms

G

of ordinary flies, and as the evening drew on midges and gnats, and the fire we lit made little difference to them. Moreover the flames seemed to attract many enormous stag beetles, which, harmless enough, made a most sinister noise and were heavy enough to hurt when they collided with one's face. It was the same tent we had taken (and pitched once) on our ill-fated cycle camping tour of Normandy and Brittany. After supper that consisted of Alphonse's wine and an omelette (in which Claire discovered a portion of a stag beetle) we were glad enough to get into the tent, and had no sooner done so than we heard the ominous patter of rain. We had no light except an electric torch whose battery I wished to conserve. It was pitch dark in the tent until there came suddenly a vivid flash, a ghastly green because the tent itself was made of green canvas : and this was followed very quickly by a loud clap of thunder. It was the prelude to one of the most violent thunderstorms I had ever known. The flashes soon became almost continuous, and we must have looked like corpses to each other in that horrid canvas-filtered light. The tent stayed erect, but if it was rot-proof it certainly was not waterproof against the deluge of rain : and anyway I'd had no time to dig a trench round it, and even our sleeping bags were soon soaked with the surface water which streamed under the tent walls. Unlike most violent thunderstorms I had experienced, this went on and on all through the night. It was not until daybreak that it eased off and we had the courage to go out, to find Blanchette dejectedly surveying her bucket that was now filled to the brim with water; and the deluge had given way to a drizzle falling from a leaden sky. We bundled our sopping things, tent and all, into the trap, harnessed up, and plodded along the road for several miles (with the cattle and ordinary flies as energetic as they had been in the sunshine) until we came to a village with an inn. We got a meal and were shown a bed which looked as though it would have bugs in it (as indeed it had, but they were no worse than cattle flies) and we stayed in that inn for three days of practically continuous rain. When on the fourth day we set off again in blazing sunshine, the mountains for which we were aiming were still enveloped in cloud and we got another thunderstorm before evening, only this time we saw it coming, and were able to reach another inn before the rain started to fall.

I believe that there are many great joys to be found in the simple life, that a man may gain immense physical and spiritual satisfaction in living hard, in making his bed the ground and his roof the starry heavens, or, concession to his innate dislike of direct cold and wet, a tent or bivouac. But if you are used to living in a house and sleeping in a bed, and having meals cooked for you and eating them at a table at a convenient level, you've got to get used to the rough sort of life before you can really enjoy it, and in our case we did not get a chance to do so, for the weather was to prove at least as bad as it had been in Brittany. Certainly it was not so cold, but there were times when, wrapped in our raincoats, we would have welcomed an Atlantic wind. Also we did get some sunny days, but never once did those heavy clouds retreat from the mountains whose beauty our guide book described in superlative terms.

If we did not see them we did reach them after many days of plodding along through a countryside that was quite lovely when the sun came out but dull and monotonous in the rain. We got to a little town called Mauleon built on the banks of a roaring mountain river, the Saison. We had four days' continuous rain here, but there was a hotel without bugs, and I began the writing of the narrative, for our funds were nearly exhausted. I had read many of P. G. Wodehouse's books and short stories and, consciously or unconsciously, I adopted his style, remembering of course the magazine's policy of publishing nothing but the truth. There was no need however to invent facts or to elaborate them. We had had no striking adventures, no real thrills or hairbreadth escapes from death such as seemed to happen to most contributors to the *Wide World*. We had seen nothing of very great geographical interest. But the editor wanted humour, and already some of the things that had happened seemed humorous in perspective. It was only the character of Blanchette that bothered me. I had to make her a little more the donkey of tradition. Her amiability would have seemed too perfect to be true. Actually I thought I had made a good job of the first instalment, that it was quite funny, as funny as Wodehouse or Jacobs or Jerome, almost as funny as Mark Twain ; it was not until long after that I recoiled from it with disgust as I did from my war book.

From Mauleon we travelled (from inn to inn, for it rained

every night) to Oloron, a town of similar character, only bigger
and built on the confluence of two mountain-born rivers, the
Ossau and the Aspe. Here we waited in a good hotel for news
of my first instalment which I had sent express to London with
an urgent appeal for funds. The Editor telegraphed a money
order with a message to say my story was satisfactory. I wrote
the next instalment, and on a morning that began with bright
sunshine we set off up the valley of the Ossau for our first real
assault on the mountains. The road we took was one described
in a special folder issued by a French omnibus de luxe touring company which in the summer ran a weekly service over it. I wish I
had that folder now to quote the glowing descriptions of its scenic
beauty, especially of the breath-taking panorama seen from the
highest point of the road near the summit of the Col d'Aubisque,
from which it descended into another valley parallel to that of the
Ossau, and called Gave de Arrens. That point was over five thous-
and feet above sea-level, but the road was described as well graded,
and we had no doubt that the amiable and indefatigable Blanchette
could make it. The nightly rain storm found us at a picturesque
village on the banks of the Ossau called Izeste. There was
a small hotel run by a lady from Paris, and she was very proud
of the fact that all her bedsteads were iron and therefore bug
proof.

Again we set out in sunshine. The road climbed. The
mountains were closing in on us, but a dense cloud reached
from what we judged to be about half their height to well above
their summits and soon it started raining again. We were in a
tourist county but we saw no tourists although a few cars passed
us going up to or coming down from a spa high up the valley
called Eaux Bonnes. This place, which we reached late in the day,
was actually in the cloud bank which had gradually lowered as the
rain set in in grim earnest. It consisted almost entirely of hotels and
boarding houses surrounding the medicinal springs which, according to our guide book, were chiefly of a sulphurous character and
highly efficacious in the treatment of throat and bronchial com-
plaints. I thought myself that if I had a sore throat or bronchitis the
last thing I'd want would be to drink sulphur water and stay in a wet
place like this ; indeed, the town authorities or the owners or share-
holders of the hotels and springs must have realised that the cure

might be more disagreeable than the complaint and had accordingly provided certain social attractions. There was a park where an orchestra played and an open-air cinema, neither of them functioning because of the weather. There was also a casino which we visited expecting to see some high life, but the stakes were small and all the players seemed to be suffering from very bad colds and looked bored and depressed. I'd often thought that this spa business was simply a money-making racket, that if cures were made they were chiefly the result of faith and the general discipline in diet and rest that was cleverly incorporated in the treatment, and my conviction was strengthened when I got our hotel bill next morning. Even the water in our baths had been charged for as though it had been full of radium salts. If there was one element that ought to have been cheap in the French Pyrenees it was water. It was raining again when we started for the Col d'Aubisque and visibility was not more than twenty yards in any direction, and what was visible was only pine trees and rocks and occasionally a swollen stream gushing down to join the main river we could hear roaring below us. I felt depressed and Claire did not cheer me up by talking about Italy and how once we got on the Corniche Road it would be sunshine and blue sea all the way, for without daring to measure it on the map, I guessed we were over three hundred miles from the nearest point on the Mediterranean coast and more than twice that from Italy.

The road was serpentine. It was well graded, but although Blanchette would have taken us in the trap without complaint we could not take advantage of her good nature, and anyway it was less uncomfortable to walk. On and on, and up and up we went, the rain continuing in a steady downpour. We crossed and re-crossed the river several times, and it was obvious that the bus company's folder had not exaggerated the wild beauty of this mountain gorge with its roaring torrent and many waterfalls, but we were not in the mood to appreciate anything connected with water, and again, visibility was still limited by the fog. At last the road made a sharp bend from the river gorge, and its gradient increased. The pines gave way to bare hillside with only short mountain grass and heath growing between the outcrops of naked rock. We felt a wind and the rain began to drive, but it could not have made us any wetter, and it had the advantage of giving us

relief from the flies. We lunched on biscuits and wine as we
walked. There were no habitations. There was no traffic whatever on the road, and I wondered why it had been built for
already we had come through many huge cuttings in the
mountain side and the bridges we had crossed were very substantial. It did not occur to me that it was a military road and of
strategic importance to the relatively near boundary between
France and Spain.

We were mountaineering, but we had only our aching limbs,
the colder temperature and our map to prove that by late in the
afternoon we were approaching the highest point of our climb. It
was still raining, and although there was more light, showing that
we were no longer hemmed in by mountain walls, the fog if anything was denser than ever. At last we reached level ground, and
there was a guide post to confirm that we were actually at the top.
At the foot of the guide post and scattered on the ground close by
were many broken wine bottles, sardine tins, food and cigarette
cartons, bits of old newspaper, banana skins, cigar stubs, evidence
again that we were at a tourist's beauty spot, that this was where the
omnibus de luxe parties halted to admire the view. It was about
six o'clock. We were cold, tired and hungry. The nearest inn was
at Arrens, some ten miles away. It would be downhill and it seemed
the logical thing to go on. My conscience however was heavy
about my articles. We were supposed to be travelling over the
Pyrenees and we still hadn't seen anything that could be called a
mountain, and because of the weather I had taken scarcely any
photographs. I felt it was up to us to have at least one night on a
mountain top. If by a miracle the clouds did lift in the morning I
would be able to get a picture of this famous view the guide book
and the folder raved about, with Blanchette in the foreground ;
and besides we wanted to see the view for its own sake. We set
about the job of making camp very much in the same spirit as you'd
take a cold bath on a winter morning, thinking how noble you'd
feel when you'd got out and were warm again. We found a rocky
hummock that gave us some protection from the now almost
freezing wind. We pitched the tent and arranged the trap in front
of it as an extra wind and rain break, and got our primus stove going
with great difficulty. And then as we were about to start cooking,
a miracle happened. The wind had shifted a point or two. It

stopped raining and a curious light suffused the gloom of the fog. Almost immediately the pall of cloud above us was torn open and we had a glimpse of blue sky. The rift expanded swiftly. The fog started to roll away from the road, first in wraiths and then completely dissolving. We saw green around us and suddenly a mountain peak appeared on the opposite side of the valley we had climbed from, and in less than five minutes the view the guide book and the folder had described was before us and below us with scarcely a wisp of cloud or mist in sight. The lowering sun blazed on us hotly.

It was indeed a grand view and the wine bottles and other debris of the tourists in the foreground did not spoil it. There were some magnificent peaks east, south and westwards of us, the Pic de Ger, the Pic du Midi d'Ossau, the Pic de Vignemale and dozens more, some of them with traces of unmelted snow near their summits. We looked down into the valley we had climbed from and the hotels and boarding houses of Eaux Bonne with their gleaming white walls showing among the pines seemed really lovely. The foam on its boiling river caught the light and you could trace its course into the Ossau to Oloron, and southwards of that was an immense sweep of almost level verdant country, veined with other rivers and roads and dotted with villages, and all of it lit with evening sunshine. And to the east we saw our road winding down the side of another mountain into the Gave de Arrens, whose river, running almost parallel with the Ossau, led to the holy town of Lourdes some twenty miles from Arrens. The effect on our spirits was remarkable. With the air clear and the sun shining, even the Mediterranean and Italy seemed feasible. But in less than twenty minutes the mists began to gather on the high peaks and creep down towards us. The sun disappeared long before its setting. Soon we were completely enveloped in fog and if it did not rain immediately it was darker and gloomier than before. But I had got my snapshots.

We had a hell of a night, worse than our first one in the thunderstorm. The wind got up about midnight. It rained in torrents and it was intensely cold. To add to our discomfort Blanchette (who probably had never been so cold in her life before) kept trying to get inside the tent, backside first, and although we did not discover this till dawn, she put her hoofs on our aluminium kettle and, greater

calamity, smashed the pump of our primus stove so that we had
to start our journey through the continuing fog and rain to Arrens
without breakfast. But I comforted myself with the thought that
we had at least seen the Pyrenees and had an adventure which (again
in retrospect) had its humorous significance. Actually I got a
complete article out of it, and the snapshot showing Blanchette in
the foreground of what the bus folder called " un vue immense et
superbe " was perfect. This article and two more leading up to it
I wrote at Arrens, where we found a reasonably clean and relatively
bugless inn and stayed for a week in the hope that the weather
would relent and give us at least one more view of the mountains.
That hope was not realised and at last we set off down the Gave de
Arrens for Lourdes where at the *poste restante* I expected to find
another remittance from the editor, and also our forwarded home
mail. The settlement of the inn bill, modest though it was, had
left us practically broke again. The road was downhill most of the
way but it was still foggy and raining and we could neither confirm
nor dispute the folder's claim that the scenery was among the most
ravishing in Europe.

It was a good job that we did not come to Lourdes in the height
of the pilgrimage season, that is, from August to September. We
found it crowded enough. All the small inns were full and we had
to go to the Hotel d'Angleterre, the most swagger of them all.
The uniformed commissionaire looked rather disdainfully at
Blanchette and our cart. Obviously he was accustomed to guests
arriving in Rolls-Royces or luxurious continental cars. The hotel
had a garage of course but no stables. However he told us where
we could find stabling, and we got a room with telephone and
water h. and c. for a pound a night, meals extra. I felt that we had
earned a little luxury and also a bottle of hock with our dinner, and
anyway there was plenty of money waiting for us at the post office.
Actually there was nothing at the post office when we called after
dinner. I was alarmed and wished we had found a less expensive
place to stay at but it was too late to change now even if we had
been able to find anything cheaper. The town was simply packed
with people, the majority of them obviously pilgrims or holiday-
makers. We were in time to see the torchlight procession to the
Grotto. It had stopped raining. But the rain clouds hung heavily
on the mountains producing a premature dusk. On the hill that

rises above the Grotto an enormous crucifix was already lit up with electric lamps, a symbolic sky sign and advertisement for what was going on below. The procession was long and moved at a funeral pace. It was headed by a bishop and various lesser clergy and a surpliced choir. Each pilgrim carried in his hand a long thick candle with a paper shield on it so that it looked like a lily, and as it moved along what was called the Boulevard de la Grotto the whole procession chanted, the pilgrims raising their candles high above their heads at the recurrent phrase of the chant, " Ave Mar—i—a."

My views on Church religion had not changed much since I had read Charles Darwin and Haeckel's *Riddle of the Universe* as a boy at Bramblewick. Yet there was certainly something moving about this ceremony. The chant if monotonous had a curious infectious lilt like a savage dance. The effect of those myriad moving candles each reflected on the gleaming wet pavement, and all under the dark canopy of the mountain rainclouds, was deeply exciting. But I should have had to have been a very hard-boiled Roman Catholic not to have been at least mildly revolted at some of the things we saw at Lourdes, whose chief lay industry appeared to be taking from the religious pilgrim what he had left from his gifts to Our Lady. He was apparently rooked for his board and lodgings. Everything in the shops was at least 25 per cent dearer than prices in Paris or provincial towns. Most of the things offered for sale were tawdry ; and the biggest business and the biggest swindle was in objects of religious significance, wood and plaster crucifixes, models of the Grotto, of Christ, and the Virgin Mary, and all manners of utensils for carrying away specimens of water from the Grotto's Miraculous Spring.

The religious fame of Lourdes is comparatively modern. It was in 1858 that a fourteen year old peasant girl, Bernadette Soubirous, alleged that the Virgin had appeared to her several times in the cave at the foot of the hill and ordered that a shrine should be erected at the spot. It was quickly discovered that the spring had miraculous healing properties (only miraculous—for the water was not even sulphurous like Eaux Bonne's) and its fame spread. Rome took notice, and so did the railways and hotel speculators. The Grotto was railed off, a shrine was built with a statue of the Virgin placed on the cave wall as Bernadette had described, in a white robe with

a blue scarf. The spring was canalised into taps and basins in which
the sick could wash. Churches and convents and real hospitals were
built in the town. The annual pilgrimage became internationally
famous so that in 1903 (our guide book informed us) no less than
80,000 pilgrims visited Lourdes in the months of August and
September. The number of cures was not stated but the walls of
the grotto were hung with crutches and other surgical devices, the
gifts and relics of the healed, and of course these symbolised only
orthopædic cures of the lame and paralytic. It was alleged that
many blind persons had regained their sight after praying at the
shrine and drinking or bathing in the holy water.

We saw the ceremony at the Grotto itself next day. It was a
grim spectacle. Scores of sick people were gathered in front of the
Grotto rails, some on crutches, some with the most terrible tumours
and skin diseases, many blind, and several lying on hospital wagons
completely paralytic. We noticed prone on one of these wagons
a little girl about ten years of age. With her in addition to a nun
were her parents and two other elder children, a boy and a girl,
obviously brother and sister. The sick child had a lovely but very
wan face. She was paralysed but kept trying to raise her head to
see the Grotto and the statue of the Virgin. The parents' eyes were
closed while they prayed and chanted with the priest, but every
now and again we saw the boy and girl glancing at their sister,
expecting, you could tell, that a miracle was going to happen any
second, and in spite of Charles Darwin and Mr. Haeckel I joined
in that prayer myself, staring at Our Lady of Lourdes whose
beautifully carved and painted face seemed almost to live and move
in the glow of the innumerable motive candles surrounding her.
But there was no miracles that day and we saw the lame and the
sick moving back to their hospitals or lodgings or perhaps to the
trains that were to take them to their distant homes from which
they must have set out with high faith and hope. And we noticed
the little girl, smiling up at her parents and brother and sister, who
were all crying although the nun who was with them looked quite
calm as though she at any rate hadn't expected much. . . .

We went to the post office and the mail was in at last. There
was another telegraphed money order from the *Wide World*, and
again a message to say that the instalments were satisfactory. But
the most exciting item in my general mail was a long letter from

my literary agent. It announced the acceptance of my thriller by the publisher who had vaguely commissioned it. It also announced the sale of the first short story I had ever written to the *Red Magazine* for twenty guineas. This was the one about a shore-crab I had written at the laboratory before the war and had been rejected by almost every British magazine (including the *Red*) and I had only let my agent have it as a sample of my work. It was not just the sale that was so exciting. The editor had told the agent that he was most impressed with my work. That he was anxious to meet me and discuss further and regular contributions for which payment on an increasing scale would be made. To this the agent added that the *Red* was owned by the Amalgamated Press, one of the biggest publishing houses in the country. The *London Magazine* was one of its better known journals, a difficult one to land but rates were even higher. Things were looking up in the publishing world. It looked as though we were in for a boom. Every week new journals were being brought out, and writers were being sought after. The supply of short stories was likely soon to be short of demand. It would be a very good thing, the agent's letter concluded, if when I had finished the *Wide World* series, I returned to London, not only to meet the editor of the *Red* but several other editors he had been discussing my work with recently. Fiction really was a much better paying proposition than travel stuff. I had a chance for some really big money if I caught the flowing tide.

Claire was not altogether pleased at the idea of going back to London. She felt that we had now enough money to have at least a short spell in Italy. After all, we were nearly half-way there and that would mean much less railway fare. She did not say so, but I believe that she thought the *Red Magazine* was a slight come-down after *Blackwood's* and even the *Wide World*, for it had made its reputation chiefly by serialising the novels of Miss Ethel M. Dell (which frankly at one time I had enjoyed, especially *The Way of an Eagle*). But I did not think so much about the literary quality of the magazine as the money. I saw at last a chance of becoming really rich, and if that happened anything would be possible, even Africa again and my great epic film. Anyway we were both sick of the Pyrenees and its weather. We had grown fond of Blanchette, but I'd already got material enough to conclude my series and there seemed no object in going any further. We found a market gardener who bore a remarkable resemblance to Alphonse. He estimated Blanchette's age as double that stated by her original master and her value (with the trap thrown in) as considerably less than half of what that amiable rascal had charged us. But the man looked kind, and we felt she had paid us a good dividend so we let her go and caught the night train for Paris where, seeing that we were in funds again, I agreed we might spend a few days before returning to London and its pavements of gold.

2

THE AGENT had not been over-optimistic in his statement that we were in for a literary boom, and in my first interview with him he told me that if I could go on producing short stories of the same quality as the one he had sold to the *Red* my future was assured. He advised me to stick to nature stories for the time being and to stick to the *Red* so long as the editor continued to pay good rates, which should increase as my work became known. It was important that he was buying only the First British Serial rights. Many young writers working without an experienced agent did not realise how valuable other rights might be. The agency had representatives in America and on the Continent and in the Colonies. The last two were not so important, and the American market was very difficult to land by an unknown British author. But once I had got a footing there, there was no telling how far I might climb, especially if later on I could start producing straight fiction stories with human characters instead of animals. Rates in America were much higher than at home. The *Saturday Evening Post*, for example, would pay as much as two hundred and fifty pounds for a single short story. Not only that. The circulation and prestige of the *Post* was so high that a story appearing in it stood a good chance of being bought by a Hollywood film company at a fantastic price. Such a sale, if the film was a success, would rebound to the magazine's and the author's credit, and really there was no limit to what a successful short-story writer might earn except that imposed by the American and British Income Tax authorities.

I found the editor of the *Red* equally encouraging although he naturally only spoke about his own magazine. I gathered that he felt that he had made a " discovery," that he expected me to give him at least an option on all my future work, which swelled my pride in spite of the fact that I was secretly wishing that the *Red* was more of a quality magazine like *Nash's* and the *London* and the *Strand*, for it was printed on very cheap paper, with an unattractive cover, and its price was only sixpence. He said that what had impressed him most about my story was its originality, and the way

in which I had made such a repulsive creature as a crab really
attractive, and almost human. He was not quite certain that his
readers would agree. The public taste in literature was a difficult
thing to assess. But undoubtedly I had plenty of other animals to
write about, especially African animals, for St. Mars and Bensusan,
and of late years Mortimer Batten, had pretty well rung the changes
on British natural history. Again, although he could take as many
nature stories as I could write (for shortly the *Red* was to change
from a monthly into a tri-monthly under the titles of *Green* and
Yellow) he would very much like to see a straight fiction story, love
or adventure, from my pen. I could not think of any such love or
adventure story straight away, for obviously they needed a plot ;
but I listed several African animals which I knew would make grand
" nature " stories, the very animals I had planned to include in my
film, and I suggested that all would have the same underlying theme
of the struggle for existence. The editor seemed delighted, only
he warned me not to make the stories too scientific or educational.
Eighty per cent of his readers were women. Women liked having
their emotions stirred. The sort of nature story they liked best was
one that illustrated, as romantically as possible, the universal
instincts of mating and motherhood. The story of any sort of
animal making a nest or lair, having young, hunting food for them,
protecting them against enemies, was certain to please.

I felt as I stepped out of the sumptuous new offices of the
Amalgamated Press in Farringdon Street and walked down to
Ludgate Circus and the beginning of Fleet Street and sniffed the
flavour of paper and printer's ink exuding from the basements of
the great newspaper offices, that I had indeed got a footing on the
ladder of success. How different all this looked from the early days
of Peace when newspapers still consisted of a single sheet and the
newboys had to chalk their contents on the pavement. The boom
had started. Immense rolls of paper were being hoisted by derricks
from trucks into the storerooms or lowered down to the presses of
the newspaper offices. Fast vans were dashing off with early racing
editions of the London evening papers, the *Standard* and *Star* and
Evening News, which before six o'clock would consist of almost as
many pages as the popular " nationals." These, the *Mail* and *Express*
and *Daily News* and *Chronicle*, *Sketch* and *Mirror* (soon to be joined
by the *Daily Herald*) seemed to be getting thicker every day,

although murders, divorces and "stunts" occupied the feature pages which had once given news only of battles. The rest of the space was chiefly advertisement, a good deal of it advertisement of the paper itself and its growing circulation.

I wandered into a newsagent's shop which had a big counter display of weekly and monthly magazines and journals. I had some difficulty in finding the *Red*, in spite of its conspicuous colour. It was at the back of the counter along with several other cheaper fiction magazines. In front was *Nash's; The Strand; The Windsor; The London; Pearson's; The Wide World* and *The Royal* along with the high-class weeklies, the *Sphere* and *Illustrated News* and *Punch*. *Blackwood's* and the *Cornhill* and *Chambers's* lay farther back among the highbrow and political weeklies. But most conspicuous of all, for copies of the current number were suspended with clips on a wire stretched above the counter, and down both sides, was *Nash's;* still with a coloured portrait of a pretty girl in the Harrison Fisher manner on its cover. I picked one up from the pile in front. Its heavy glossy paper had a lovely feel, and as I opened it and turned the pages it gave off a peculiar fragrance that may have come from the paper itself or some volatile oil or essence used in the making of the ink. It was beautifully printed and illustrated. I was attracted by a brush drawing showing an Arctic fox, with pines and snow, and saw that it was an illustration to a nature story, only by an American author. *Nash's* I knew was really the English edition of the *American Cosmopolitan*; whose rates my agent had mentioned were nearly as high as the *Post*. I thought enviously, fancy landing *Nash's* and the *Cosmopolitan* with one and the same story ! If the *Red* paid me twenty guineas for my first, then these two should each pay at least twice as much. Perhaps they would pay fifty each, a hundred pounds. The first few paragraphs of the yarn did not seem much better than I could do myself. If I wrote only one story a week and it was accepted, I might earn as much as five thousand pounds in a year !

I wrote my first "commissioned" story for the *Red* that night. It was about a lioness whose mate had been killed in a trap while raiding the flocks of a Masai village. The whereabouts of her own lair (where she has two suckling cubs) is discovered by the natives. One of the cubs is a weakling and dies. All her fierce maternal instinct is centred on the other. The natives set fire to the jungle grass and advance with spears upon her. But she outwits them and with her cub in her mouth escapes through the ring of fire and steel to freedom. I made the setting of this story the Serrengetti Plain, and while I was writing it I felt myself actually there, within sight of Kilimanjaro, and I could even smell the sun-baked red earth of the veldt and the scent of mimosa. I called it *The Last Born*. The editor gave me his decision within three days. He liked it better than the one about the crab, and although it was shorter, said he would give me twenty-five guineas for it. It *was* good. It was written from actual observation, at white heat and with complete sincerity, and (while I was writing it) without a conscious thought of the financial reward. Nearly a year later I had a letter from an English lady in South Africa, the wife of a settler, who said *The Last Born* had thrilled her more than any story she had read for years, chiefly, she thought, because she was rearing a cub of her own. I took this remark literally and in my letter of thanks expressed interest in her cub and wondered whether she would sell it to a zoo when it got really big and perhaps dangerous. My letter had been posted days before I realised that by cub she meant her own baby !

It was now summer and the weather was fine and warm. I should not have thought it possible for me to be content and happy to stay in London, and not be longing for the country and the sea. It was Claire who had wanderlust. She wanted us to go to Italy before the really hot weather came, or failing that to the south of France near to Marseilles, where Paul had told us there were several fishing villages which had become almost artist colonies. But I was smitten with the double fever of literary creation and money-making. If we left England now, if we even left London it would mean losing touch. I was still doing all the business arrangements through my agent, and was lunching with him regularly at Groome's. But he himself agreed that personal contacts with editors were invaluable and he introduced me to many that he knew and left me to do the talking. Not that we were thinking of going outside our gentleman's agreement with the *Red*. For the present at any rate there was no question of offering my short stories anywhere else. But the more my name appeared before the public the better all round. They were nearly all newspaper and weekly journal editors I met, and with the idea of writing articles for them. At that time the *Daily Mail* was running what was called a magazine page of six short articles on special subjects. As its circulation was now advertised as being over a million the publicity value of such an article sounded enormous. I wrote one on the animals that any seaside holiday-maker could find in a rock pool (I thought of that day with Adeline while I wrote it), and another on the running of a salt-water aquarium. Both were accepted, and the fee for each was four guineas. But the editor's policy with regard to this page was variety, in author as well as subject, and although I placed several more articles with him, he turned down many more, which however I placed with other papers at a lesser fee. I met the editor of *Country Life* with the result that I sold several articles to him. There was a big interest now in commercial flying and the inauguration of world air routes. I wrote articles on tropical aviation for the *Illustrated News* and *Sphere* and had one accepted by *The Times*. But my most regular market for short natural history articles became the newly started *John O' London's Weekly*, for which I did a weekly column.

I was working hard, and earning quite a lot of money, but somehow or other we were managing to spend practically all I earned. We had to have a home somewhere. Claire fancied a studio flat in Chelsea, but the nearest we could find was one in a superior part of South Kensington, the top floor of a mansion which had been converted into maisonettes. The rent was enormous, but so were most rents in London then. Furnishing it even on the instalment plan was expensive. But the address was impressive, there was a telephone, and out of my expected income of thousands a year it did not seem so extravagant. But very much to Claire's disappointment Chelsea had very little in common with the Latin Quarter of Paris. There were no open-air cafes or restaurants where you could just talk with any one. If there were studio parties we didn't find them, and the people Claire had met at her art gallery were away on their holidays, most of them, ironically enough, in France or Spain or Italy.

Even the editors and my agent went off for their holidays in August. We went to Devon for a fortnight, staying on a farm near Chagford. The weather again betrayed us however with rain and fog and we were glad to get back to London where early in September life started to be normal again. I had by then written about a score of nature stories for the *Red*. All had been accepted and paid for at what the editor politely but firmly said was his ceiling price for a nature story, twenty-five guineas. I was beginning to see that there was another ceiling too in this kind of literature. You could change your animal and your scene but the theme must always be essentially the same one of mating, and home-making and hunting and being hunted. I got stuck with one yarn about a leopard, for it was just going the same way as *The Last Born*. I was even using the same phrases, and they no longer sounded fresh and sincere. And then suddenly I began to think of my leading character not as a leopard but as a woman, white and civilised but simple and primitive in obeying what the editor had called the universal instincts of mating and motherhood, and Shaw, in *Man and Superman*, had called the Life Force. It may have been Shaw's Ann Whitefield who was re-created in my mind, but she was in the guise of a woman I had seen in a travel film of Sweden or Finland, tall, fair-haired, broad-faced and with high cheek bones : stolid, impassive, but potentially volcanic. With her was invoked a portrait of Jock, the white hunter of our ill-fated expedition to Timbuctoo, only bigger and even more virile and yet undeniably a Shavian John Tanner, a hardened bachelor fighting against his destiny. Jock in one of his yarns had given me a picture of his way of life in a Portuguese colony. I had my own vivid memories of Portuguese East to draw on, and I remembered at some port or settlement in that country an hotel and store owned by a Swede, and very popular among the Portuguese officers of the nearest military post. It was easy to make Jock an Irishman in perpetual trouble with the Portuguese authorities through ivory poaching, but feared by them individually when on the spree : easy to make the girl (Olga) the daughter or niece of the old Swedish trader just out from Europe, serving at the bar of the hotel which becomes a new and more powerful centre of interest to the amorous Portuguese officers. But to them Olga is a carven image.

Unaware of her existence for he has been up-country on a poaching expedition, Doyle, the woman hater, comes into the hotel one night to break a drought which normally would have turned into a three days' spree. He goes to the bar. His eyes meet Olga's for a second and then wilt to the sudden flame that burns in hers. He takes a bottle of whisky and a tumbler from her, pays for it, moves to a chair and sits down. The room is full of officers, one of them, the commander of the post, Doyle's particular foe. There is a coin-in-the-slot pianola with a repertory of two tangoes and two excerpts from opera. The gaudy uniforms and medals of the officers contrast with the dingy furniture of the room, which is lit by a single oil lamp hanging over Olga's head so that her hair is like a halo of gold. She serves the officers, but all the time her eyes are on Doyle, who drinks, and compelled by an irresistible attraction stares back. The commanding officer himself, inflamed by Olga's beauty, observes her interest in Doyle. Emboldened by drink he dares to make an insulting comment on it to her and the company. Doyle gets up and strides towards him, takes him by the scruff of the neck, drags him to the bar and orders him to ask for Olga's pardon. The officer wriggles loose and draws a pistol. Doyle strikes him with his fist, knocks him out. But two of the officer's companions come behind Doyle and smash him on the head with wine bottles. He goes down, and like hounds on a cornered fox, the whole company crowd round him kicking and beating him. Olga, like an enraged tigress, leaps over the bar and lays into them with a wine bottle, screaming to them to get out. She routs them. They leave their officer where he fell. She bends over Doyle. She dresses his wounds with cloth torn from her dress. He regains consciousness. She helps him to his feet. He looks at the officer. Grasps the situation. The soldiers will be returning with reinforcements. He will be arrested and charged perhaps with attempted murder. He understands this too. He tells her he will go back to his hunting camp, over the border. Once there he will be safe. He *does* escape the consequences of his provoked assault. But he does not escape Olga and the Life Force. She goes with him, for he is too groggy to walk unassisted, and as I saw the thing as a story within a story, recounted by a doctor in the smoke room of a ship homeward bound from West Africa, the climax was easily invented. The narrator, medical officer to an English mining company, was a friend of Doyle, and knew of his disappearance with the Swedish girl. A year after a native brings him an urgent summons and leads him miles into the jungle. And there he finds a humble and anxious and otherwise metamorphosed Doyle, clean-shaven, hair short, clothes beautifully clean : a little bungalow with a trim garden, and inside it, Olga about to produce her first born.

Again I wrote at white heat, and despite that it was in its sub-conscious origin a hotch-potch of Shaw and Conrad and of the *Blue Lagoon* with a bit of Edgar Wallace and Somerset Maugham thrown in, it was a good magazine story. I got a shock when the editor of the *Red* told me candidly he did not like it. It was well written, he said, and the characters all stood out, but the whole idea was un-suitable for his readers. They would regard it as immoral. I had not even got my hero and heroine married. If he published it he would be getting letters of protest from half the old spinsters and clergymen of Great Britain. I pointed out that I had written it to the very same formula he had given me for my nature stories. He agreed, but said that you could print quite a lot of things about an animal that you simply daren't print about human beings. No, he was glad I had had a try at straight fiction for he had been feeling that in some of my later nature stories I was repeating myself. Perhaps I was getting stale. Why didn't I have a shot at an adventure story. Leave out love. Something in the style of Wallace's *Bones of the River*. I was wise enough not to show him I was vexed and that I was thinking, well, if my yarn isn't good enough for the *Red*, perhaps it will be good enough for *Nash's* or the *Strand*, and maybe if they take it they'll want my nature stories too and pay a bigger price. Later I was glad I had been so wise. That story was to remain in my morgue for years and would not have been published at all had I not persuaded a very friendly editor of a not very well-known magazine to take it as a personal favour. He made it a condition that I should have Doyle and Olga married by a missionary.

I remained faithful to the *Red* (and the *Yellow* and *Green*) and the *Red* was faithful to me. I wrote an adventure story with a Colonial police officer and his dog the chief movers in it. The editor liked it so much that he asked me to do a whole series about the two, and his price went up to thirty guineas a story. I was doing well, if not so well as I'd imagined. My agent hadn't placed any of my work in America, but as he had said that was a very difficult market to land, and one day something happened to make our life in Kensington much more interesting and cured Claire of her immediate yearning for Paris and Italy. There was a restaurant called " The Good Intent " in the King's Road, Chelsea, only five minutes' walk from where we lived. It wasn't a bit Bohemian although it was frequented by artists occasionally. You could tell them by their black Stetson hats and often by their long hair, or if they were women, by their disregard for fashion. It was really respectable and rather dull but the food was good and cheap. We were having dinner when a very striking looking girl came in and sat at a table close to us. She wore a black hat, and a black Italian cloak, but when she took this off it revealed a brightly coloured dress cut with a tight bodice and long flared skirt in the Medici style. Her hair was raven black, her face pale, and she had dark eyes. Every one in the restaurant looked at her but she wasn't flustered. It was clear she was used to being looked at. But I was soon looking at her for a very different reason. I knew I had seen her before, and shortly she chanced to look towards our table and instantly she gave me a smile of recognition. Before I could rise she came towards us. It was Barbara Hepworth, but if she hadn't given her name I don't think I would have recognised her for it was the summer before the war when her father, the Borough Engineer to the West Riding, with wife and family of three daughters and one boy had stayed at a cottage close to the laboratory for several weeks, and Sam and I had become friendly with them. Barbara, then only a schoolgirl, had been making a collection of seaweeds and Sam had identified them for her in the laboratory. I'd had no idea then that Barbara had any artistic gifts. I felt a little incredulous when she told us that she had won a scholarship from the Leeds School of Art to the London Royal College of Art where, in the school for sculpture under William Rothenstein, she was now studying for the next year's Prix de Rome.

Clarie was thrilled. When we'd had dinner Barbara took us to her studio close to the Fulham Road. It was small, and, with blinds drawn over the top lighting, and with no other windows, looked like a prison cell. Barbara had a divan bed in it and there was just one small curtained recess for cooking and washing. The walls were covered with drawings, mostly nudes, and on a stand in the middle of the studio was an uncompleted head and shoulders of a woman modelled in clay, life size. I knew it was good, but how good I was not competent to judge. The drawings too were extraordinarily powerful, mostly done in chalk, and in line, but again it was not easy to express exactly what one felt for it was impossible at present to separate the work of art from the artist herself. I could still hardly believe that Barbara was the same long-legged, skinny, school kid Sam and I had known at Bramblewick before the war. Claire however had no difficulty in saying what she felt, and I could tell that Barbara had little doubt as to her sincerity although she laughed as she put back the wet cloth with which the modelling had been draped when we came in, and said modestly :

" Oh, it's not really so good as that, you know. You ought to see what the other students can do, especially the men. Especially Harry Moore. Thank heaven anyway he's not in for the Prix. I think I stand a chance, but you know the judges always give the sculpture prize to a man if other things are equal. They feel that woman's place is in the home, and that she only should take up art as a hobby."

I don't think that Barbara was being cynical, but I noticed a sudden hardness in her eyes and in the lines of her mouth, almost a pugnacity, and I saw how like she was to her father, a dour, hard-headed Yorkshireman who I believe had worked himself up to the high post he held by a quiet but very great force of character and ability. He was a man of great charm, but it was a devil of a job to make him talk and join in the arguments Sam and I would start in the laboratory at night, but when he did speak he usually floored us completely and with a devastating economy of words. He was a good tennis player who was never flurried, and never brilliant, but won his games without giving you the feeling he had beaten you at all. He was, I suppose, an ideal fishing companion, for he scarcely ever spoke even when we got into a big shoal of mackerel, and yet he managed to convey later that he had really enjoyed himself. Barbara was anything but dour but she had a good measure of his character, his determination and tenacity. And I thought there wouldn't be much she wanted out of life that she wouldn't get, including the Prix de Rome!

It was the start of a long intimacy, mostly pleasant, especially so for Claire. Our flat became a regular " looking-in " place for Barbara and many of her fellow-students. We met Harry (later Henry) Moore. He was another Yorkshireman and I believe his father had been a village blacksmith, and Harry had started carving in self-quarried sandstone in the back garden. He was short and

broad shouldered, and although there was nothing Jewish in his
face, I thought he bore an extraordinary likeness to Jacob Epstein,
especially in the width and shape of his forehead. Barbara considered him to be a finer sculptor than Epstein. But with Harry as
with most of the other students I felt out of my depth. They were
very modern, which is to say very primitive. Their discussions
were about " cave " drawings, and " bush " and Chinese and
Thibetan and Egyptian and Assyrian and Aztec and " negro " art.
They were supremely contemptuous about the British Royal
Academy and things like the Cavell memorial. There were a
few British painters such as Constable and Augustus John and
Frances Hodgkins whose work was not too bad. But the only
sculptor was Epstein and he was not really British but a Russo-
Polish Jew born in New York and only British naturalised. I
could admire the technical skill of Moore's sculpture, but it was
hard to follow either his or Barbara's critical explanation of it,
but that probably was because visual art cannot be explained in
words. Either you respond to it or you don't, and the fact that
you don't doesn't mean that it is not a work of art but just that you
are not ' in tune with ' the artist. And yet I sometimes wondered
if they were as good as they sincerely thought themselves to be.
Their contempt for the Academy tradition of art seemed to amount
to an obsession. Although all these young artists could if they
wanted make amazingly accurate and life-like sculptures and drawings of people and things they seemed to regard this simply as
practice in technique. Barbara, for example, showed us a drawing
of a dove with detailed drawings of the feet and bill and eyes
and individual feathers, as accurate as the tinted illustrations to
British Nudibranchiata. A camera could not have reproduced them
better. But the work that both she and Harry considered her best
to date was a pair of doves sitting head to tail, carved life-size from
a single block of marble; they were eyeless, feetless, and had neither
visible bills, nor individual feathers, only what Barbara called
" significant form," and so little of this I thought that unless I had
been told, I would not have recognised them as doves at all. But
then I was not supposed to. They represented (if that word was
allowed) the beauty the artist experienced when looking at her
models, and she did convey that beauty for her carving made you
feel quite a different emotion to what the drawings did. But was

her inspiration directly drawn from observation ? In their obsession for originality were these artists not, subconsciously at least, deriving from and even copying the primitive ? I did not know. Their talk and their art was above my head most of the time, yet I did think it was all sincere, that they felt everything they said and did and that there was no pose about them.

They did not often talk about writing, and never about my work, which I thought was rather unfair seeing that they had the run of our larder and drinks almost every night, and this out of my nature stories and the *Red Magazine*. Barbara once said she would like to read something I had written and I gave her *The Last Born*, but she forgot to take it with her and never referred to it again. At least once a week we had a bottle party, and sometimes the students turned up in fancy dress and we danced, and there was no talk about art, which was a relief to me. The truth was that the bug of Africa was starting to stir in my blood again. The stories I was writing had something to do with it, but what upset me more than this was that several big game and African travel films had been running in London and drawing big houses, and none of them was anything like so good as the one I had planned. I tackled my agent about it again. He told me frankly that I'd be a fool if I left London just when I was beginning to make a reputation for myself, as well as making such good money out of the *Red* and other markets. When he'd first advised me to travel he'd had no idea that there was going to be such a terrific boom in fiction and that so many new magazines would be coming out. While the films I was envious of were apparently doing good business, I must remember that they cost almost as much as ordinary films to produce and that their appeal was limited, especially in the provinces. I might think that it was the public who decided what films should be shown in the cinemas. That was wrong. The cinema owners were mostly in the hands of the film renters and distributors, and these were in the hands of the big producers (mostly Hollywood), and they had their highly-paid stars to keep before the public so that they were dead against any privately produced film being shown at all regardless of its merits. To make money out of the film business an author must write a successful novel, a world best seller like *If Winter Comes*. Then he would have all the film companies bidding against each other for the rights and it wouldn't matter if the novel was suitable for a film or not. It was its name that mattered. I'd do better to forget about films for the time being and keep going at my short stories. Until I'd got a really crashing idea for a novel these were easily my best line. I inferred that he didn't think I had any promise as a novelist, and indeed I had thought so myself after the publication of my thriller, which had received only three reviews and none of them favourable, and had so far sold less than a thousand copies. I felt the agent was right, and I tried to stop thinking of Africa, but I could not stop thinking about films. We went to cinemas regularly, and as I had become friendly with the editor of one film trade weekly, I went myself to many trade shows and very rarely saw a film without feeling critical, and thinking it could be bettered, both as regards story and direction. This of course was before the advent of the talkie. I did not feel that about Chaplin's early films of course, or Duggie Fairbanks or the Griffiths dramas or the majority of the Westerns, which usually went so fast you hadn't time to be critical. But it seemed to me that the majority of the films failed because their producers did not realise that the film was only another medium for *telling a story*, that its purpose must be to possess the mind of the viewer so that he forgot himself and became as it were temporarily bewitched. This needed all the tricks of ordinary story-telling. You had to create character and setting and both had to be believable. There never was a human being who looked or behaved exactly like Charley Chaplin's tramp. But then Charley's tramp was a caricature, and like all successful caricatures had its basis in truth.

Setting again need not be literally authentic. As in my device of a ring fence for getting shots of a wild lion, the fake might be more authentic than the real thing provided you did it carefully and that your concern was the truth and sincerity of the whole and not just the part. It did not bother me that the houses or streets in many of the plays I saw were obviously plywood and plaster and the land-scapes a painted backcloth, or ships just cardboard models moving in a tank. Inconsistences such as the classic Hollywood version of an English hunt ball with the gentlemen in their riding kits and wearing spurs were irritating but they did not matter so much if the story was all right. And it was the story that counted. It did not matter whether it was a comedy, farce, drama or melodrama, the story-telling must be there, characters must be brought to life, things must happen to them, situations, problems created and in the end resolved with a kiss or a hanging or a reconciliation and all the time the viewer must be intrigued, bemused and perpetually in suspense so that he never knew exactly what was going to happen next. I itched to write and direct a film story myself. I knew the agent was right about the big companies wanting best-seller novels, but I felt the producers themselves were wrong in not realising that they were working in an entirely different medium, and that they would make better films if they got writers to produce original scripts. I read all the books on film craft and scenario writing I could lay hold of, and I started taking the film trade papers, British and American. Then one day I read in one of the popular daily papers an article deploring the flood of American films, and the trashy quality of so many of them, and saying it was time that Britain challenged this monopoly. We had the actors, the writers, the technicians and the capital. We lacked Californian weather for open-air photography, yet the sun was known to shine and surely it was worth the patience and expense to show the world some of our unique scenery, that of our cities as well as our countryside and coasts. The article went on to raise the very point about novels being unsuitable for films and argued that original scripts would be better and that there was plenty of British talent available in this respect, and it led up to the news that a newly-formed British company was offering a prize of £500 for the best original script offered to them by a certain date. It had to be English in its setting but it could be either comedy or drama or thriller or all three combined. It must however contain a strong love interest.

The morning I read this article I had to go to Farringdon Street with my latest completed story, and having handed it in I walked up to Cheapside and boarded a bus for the Mansion House and from there sauntered along to the Monument and London Bridge. I liked this part of London much better than the West End. Here were the big banks and financial and commercial houses, the offices of the big shipping companies, and once you got in sight of the river you realised that London was first and foremost a seaport. There were steamers made fast to the wharves just below the bridge discharging cargo into warehouses or into lighters. There were tugs fussing about the lighters, some sheering off and moving up stream with the loaded ones, others navigating empty ones along-side the ships. There was a constant rattle of chains and the hissing of steam and men shouting orders. There was a smell of ships, the mingled odour of coal, smoke and oil and spices, and a faint smell too of fish from the nearby Billingsgate market. I stood on the bridge a long time. I watched two very pretty shopgirls leaning against the parapet eating their lunch out of paper bags and offering crusts to the herring gulls which swept down to them. The tide was at half ebb. Here and there under the warehouses strips of evil looking mud were bared. It was a dull misty day and the river itself was almost the same colour as the mud and as sinister. A hawker wheeling a hand-barrow of fruit stopped opposite the girl and shouted :

" Yer y'are, lydies. Tyke yer pick afore the copper sees us. Not allahed to stop on the bridge yer know. Apples er oranges. Tyke yer pick."

He was a typical coster, young and handsome. He wore a check stable coat and a cap set at a jaunty angle. He looked as though he had gypsy blood in him. The girls bought some oranges. They chivvied each other in true Cockney style and then the youth with his eye on the nearby traffic policeman moved on to the Southwark end of the bridge. I saw a small motor launch steaming up river against the tide, with two river policemen in her stern. The boat swung round and bore into a jetty immediately above which an iron derrick projected from a second floor warehouse hatch, with a rope hanging from it so that it looked like a gallows. The police-men made their boat fast at the foot of an old stone stairway slimy with river mud and one of them climbed up and moved, stealthily it seemed, along the wall of the warehouse as though searching for some one, wanted or suspect. And I experienced the sudden thrill of creation. I had conceived a story, a film, the setting the very scene I was watching, the Pool of London. Within sight of me were all the characters I wanted, at least for the germ of it. The pretty girls, the handsome coster, the river police. It was a crime story, a thriller. One of the steamers I had been watching discharg-ing cargo was Dutch. I could have a member of its crew engaged in drug smuggling from the Continent. There must be a West End gang, a " go-between," some sort of dockside tough engaged too in warehouse pilfering, just the chap those river police might be

looking for now, although it was possible the officer had gone
ashore merely to buy a packet of fags or a cup of coffee. The hero
must be my coster, but he must not be left in that humble state of
life at the end of the play. Local boy must make good. I had
noticed one of the girls moving her feet to the Charleston dance
rhythm while they had been ragging each other. We had gone with
Barbara and some of her friends to the Hammersmith Palais de
Danse one night and seen an amateur championship competition
run, I think, by the *Daily Sketch*. I had been amazed by the quality
of the dancing and I had imagined that the winners would have no
difficulty in starting business as professional teachers. That must
be the climax to the story. The plot began slowly to grow in my
mind, but it hadn't grown far before I began to feel doubtful about
having a coster hero and a shopgirl heroine. They were not
romantic enough.

I crossed over to the Surrey side of the bridge and walked
behind grim warehouse walls towards the Tower Bridge where the
river came in sight again. I walked on, still on the Surrey side,
towards Rotherhithe and the Surrey Commercial Docks, recognis-
able by the great stacks of imported timber and the funnels and
masts of large steamers rising above the dock sheds and warehouses.
It was not an elegant district. There were rows of warehouses and
occasionally streets of mean cottages and slums. There were pubs
with shady looking characters lounging outside them. I saw negroes
and lascars and Chinese and sailors' doss-houses and smelly fried fish
shops and pawnbrokers' shops, and all the time I was thinking of
my story and trying to work out the plot. I thought backwards to
my starting point, the police boat, the steps and the gallows-like
derrick. I realised that I had passed dozens of such derricks on my
walk and I suddenly thought, imagine having committed a murder
or being suspected of one, and being hunted by the police and seeing
these grim symbols of justice and retribution everywhere. As
suddenly I picked up, as it were, one sure thread of the tangle of
the plot. The hero suspected, wrongly accused of murder. The
real murderer the dock-side thug. The murdered man my river
policeman who catches the thug in a warehouse at night. The
character of my hero grew. He had to belong to the dock-side
himself. He could be a river boatman, roughly dressed in his job,
but a bit of a dandy at home. Somehow he had got involved with

this thug. He was trying to run straight, now helped by his sweet-heart, say, the daughter of the skipper of a tug. . . . I pulled myself up here with a start. I was getting perilously near O'Neil's *Anna Christie*, one of the plays I had recently seen and greatly admired. But I quickly reflected that no story could be completely original, and it needn't be a tug, but a barge, a Thames sailing barge, the girl living on board with her father (a fine character part), only again I must not make him too much like Anna Christie's father. She and the hero dance at some east-end dance hall every Saturday night where the elimination rounds for the London amateur championship are held. They win, but while waiting for the great final the murder takes place. Suspicion falls heavily on the hero. He knows he is being watched by Scotland Yard detectives now. He feels the net closing in on him. He is a haunted man and those derricks terrify him. His nerve breaks and he escapes in his little boat down river in the fog, the police chasing him, with his girl playing some sort of dramatic part in his escape and capture and exoneration. And of course the end is the dancing championship and success.

I wandered round the Surrey Docks. There were so many foreign ships and so many foreign sailors about that I could have imagined I was a thousand miles away from South Kensington. I caught a bus to Greenwich and crossed to the north side of the river to the Isle of Dogs and made my way north and then west through dockland into Limehouse and Shadwell, where the slums became grimmer and the waterside more sinister with the coming of dusk, for the lights accentuated the darkness of river mud and water. I passed a dockside police station where several notices were displayed, one headed BODY FOUND. It gave a detailed descrip-tion of a corpse that had been taken from the Thames on Limehouse Reach : height, weight, approximate age, colour of hair and eyes, shape of nose, other distinguishing marks, clothing, and where to be viewed. I was tempted to go and have a look at it for it gave the address of the mortuary, but I thought quickly that my story needed only one corpse, and that I would be complicating it if I introduced another, that it was indeed too complicated already. I ought to cut out the Dutchman and the drug smuggling and the West End gang. It should be a story of the river only, a drama, not a melodrama, one of real life, with every setting and character and incident feasible and authentic. And as I walked along, still in dockland, still within sight and sound of the Thames over which night was deepening, I began to see it as a *film* as a spectator would see it from a comfortable seat in a modern cinema. There would be music from the orchestra or organ, perhaps a few passages from the famous Water Music. The title of the film (I hadn't thought of one yet) would be shown on the censor's certificate, then the various credits (including one I hope to the author), the list of characters and then, still to the introductory music, the first title :

THE POOL OF LONDON
WHERE OLD FATHER THAMES MEETS
THE SEA AND THE SHIPS OF ALL THE
WORLD——

and the film would start with a travelling " day " shot taken from a launch moving down river through an arch of London Bridge showing the wharves and shipping on each side, the Tower Bridge in the foreground, this dissolving into a close view of a ship discharging sacks of grain into a sailing barge, fading out to a black screen and then the words,

NIGHT IN THE POOL

followed by a night " montage " (this would be studio made) showing the wharf, the last sack of grain being hoisted by the gallows-like derrick into a warehouse hatch, the hatch being closed and locked, the police patrol boat and a sub-title,

WHILE LONDON SLEEPS,

the patrol boat again, a close-up of a sack of grain, a rat gnawing at the sack until the grain spills out, dissolving into a close-up of a packing case being prized open with a jemmy, moving to human hands holding the jemmy, then of a vague figure moving stealthily under a warehouse wall, the police boat again, the figure pausing under a street lamp lighting some jetty steps, the light suddenly falling on the face of the thug showing satisfaction that his theft has not been detected, a fading shot of the derrick with its rope hanging like a noose, then the title

BUT IN THE LIGHT OF MORNING

and here the music would change to a dance tune and there would be a sequence showing the barge moored in the river, the heroine cooking breakfast on a stove on deck while her feet shuffled to a tune played on a portable gramophone, and the old man shaves. Then a shot from the barge showing the hero in his pulling boat, then him coming alongside, their love and their ambition established when they dance a few steps together. I saw the hero now as a composite of Duggie Fairbanks, Fred Astaire and Clifford Morrison (whom I had seen in a comedy of Harold Brighouse at the Hampstead Everyman, this long before he had earned fame in musical comedy). I could not think of any actress to play the girl, but she must be English, and not just a picture-postcard beauty. The part called for real acting. I had seen Sam Livesey in an American stage play and thought he would make a grand job of the barge skipper. For the thug I fancied someone like Franklyn Dyall. . . .

I wrote the full synopsis that night. I gave it the provisional title of *Smiling Morn*, that being the name of the barge. I gathered that the company only wanted a synopsis, but I thought it would be as well to have a scenario ready and in three days I completed it : and although the " competition " did not close for six weeks I sent it off, registered and express. I was not completely confident that I should win the prize, but I thought that no film director with any sense could fail to see that with a good cast, good direction, good photography, *Smiling Morn* would be worth a dozen Hollywood society dramas. It had I believed everything that a popular film needed, movement, suspense, pathos, comedy, characterisation, atmosphere. A film like this would show America (and the world) that stars, big names, authors or actors were not everything. That even as a " location " England had something as good if not better than California. And I also felt that this was by no means the only film story I could write. As I was well up to schedule with my *Red* and *John O' London* writing and had enough cash in the bank to keep us going, I wrote another, this time a pure farce, suitable

I thought for an English Harold Lloyd, and with the text-books to
help me I actually made this into a shooting script : but as there
did not seem to be an English Harold Lloyd, I hopefully sent it to
the man himself at Hollywood. I continued to go to all the trade
shows I could get tickets for. Some of these took place in real
cinemas in the morning with an orchestra in attendance. But mostly
they were in private rooms at the distributor's office, without
even a gramophone to drown the sound of the projector, and this
made one all the more critical. One film was so bad that I wrote a
scathing review of it for the trade paper and showed it to my
friendly editor. He was a Scot and he grinned when he had read it.
Then he pointed to a double-page coloured advertisement of the
very film in his paper and said :

" Guess the price of that advertisement ? "

I shook my head.

" Five hundred pounds, and they supplied the colour blocks."

" But it's a damned bad film."

" Aye. Maybe. But you're not going to ask me to say so. I'd
have the sack to-morrow if I did." Then he added, " Would you
like a bit of advice ? Keep out of films unless you've got a heart of
stone. It's the biggest and the cruellest racket in creation."

Perhaps I would have done better if I had taken that advice
there and then, but the fever was on me and it had to take its course.
Smiling Morn was not rejected in the same way as an unwanted
magazine story is rejected. It never came back at all, although the
manager admitted (by telephone) that he had received it and that
it was under consideration. The result of the competition was never
announced. A long time after (and after the company had gone
into liquidation) I saw the one film that it had produced. It was
set in England all right ; it had an all-English cast, and the story
was not based on a novel, in fact it didn't say anything about the
story, but it was obvious that the whole thing was nothing but a
very poor crib of a not too particularly good Hollywood film,
which, however, because of its star, had been a big box-office
success.

My fever cooled but was not completely cured. My bank
account was getting low and I had to get back to stories for the
Red. I had exhausted the literary possibilities of my police officer
and dog combination. I wrote one good nature story about a

swallow that got shut up in a barn when the local flock started its great migration flight, and had to make the journey alone. As I had discovered that there were authentic records of swallows marked in England wintering in East Africa, I made it do this astonishing trip (very topical because of the attempts then being made to fly by plane to Cape Town) and it gave me a chance to use my knowledge both of West and East Africa. I only got twenty-five guineas for it, but to complete the itinerary I had to read up Central Africa and I was carried away by a long description in one travel book of the pygmies of the Ituri Forest. It gave me the idea for another series of tales with the main character the son of a pygmy chief. The pygmies are exclusively forest people and hunters. They grow no crops but have a passion for plantains grown by the tall races outside the forest. With them they have a system of barter, plantains for meat. But gradually the agriculturalists are encroaching on the forest, cutting down the trees to grow their crops. The pygmies are threatened with extinction, and my hero must organise and lead his tribe to put an end to this. I conceived him not as a Mowgli or a Tarzan gifted with supernatural powers, capable of conversation with the jungle animals, but as an ordinary primitive hunter following the individual and tribal instincts of self-preservation. Against him I pitted an authentic figure from one of Stanley's books, a rascally Arab slave trader. I had no sooner started the first tale however than I began to think what a good film it would make, and only the knowledge that I had to make immediate money kept my emotions in check and stopped me writing a scenario of it.

Once when Barbara and a few more friends were with us and every one was talking art, the door bell rang, and there was Sam. I had been out of touch with him for a long time and I was very glad to see him. He seemed a bit put out when he saw all the people in the room, and when Barbara recognised him and got up and shook his hand he was more surprised than I had been and looked quite dazed for he did not recognise her. Then I reminded him about her seaweed collection and he suddenly got his nerve and his old self-confidence back and he shook Barbara's hand again and said:

" Why yes, of course. I remember. Delighted to meet you again. And how's your father keeping? Remember that long argument we had in the laboratory about parthenogenesis (this was to me), and how he floored us in the end ? Still keeping up your interest in British Marine Algæ (this to Barbara again). There was one specimen, a fucoid I think, that beat us. Wonder if I could identify it if I saw it now ! "

I thought that Barbara was getting almost as embarrassed as Sam had been and I could not help feeling slightly pleased that the others seemed also to be uncomfortable and that the discussion on art had been irrevocably interrupted. Fortunately Sam didn't wait for Barbara to answer his questions. After being introduced to the others he pulled a copy of the *Red Magazine* from his pocket and slapped me on the back, and said, as much to the company as to me :

" Congratulatiions, old boy. This yarn beats St. Mars into cocked hat. Absolutely grand. Written by a sound naturalist too. No mush about it. No sentiment. That's the way a nature story ought to be written. Scientific groundwork. Knowledge. Accurate observation. I've never been to Africa myself, too busy over here. But reading that yarn I just felt I'd been transported. I'm proud to think that I had a small hand in starting you on popular nature writing. I bet you didn't guess, Miss Hepworth, that one of the two young men who helped you with your collection of Yorkshire Marine Algæ would turn out to be a famous writer of nature stories. You'll have read this yarn about a lion of course ? "

Barbara looked really uncomfortable.

" No, I was going to read it," and to me, rather shamelessly I thought, " that is the one you promised to lend me ? Do let me have it to take home with me."

But Sam had turned on the others, who were all hurriedly finishing their drinks and giving other signs that they were about to depart.

" I always said he'd be a writer. He'd got the gift. Heredity partly. You know of course his father's an artist ? I hadn't. It was the purely academic side of science that appealed to me. Microscopy, parasitology. We were doing some interesting work then. Parasitic infection of a nudibranch by a degenerate type of crustacean, *Splanchnotrophus*. Degenerate ? Not so certain that it was. It's a moot point in zoology as to what constitutes degeneracy of a type. A free swimming crustacean evolves into an immobile type.

But is mobility proof of advancement ? Not necessarily. The proof of a species efficiency is in its survival as a species. I think myself that *Splanchnotrophus* had by its unique habits done rather well and the loss of its power of mobility in the process you might regard that as economy rather than degeneracy."

I don't suppose that any of the students would have been shocked if Sam had described in full detail the unique habit of *Splanchnotrophus* but I was relieved that he saw in time that they were not interested. He did not pursue the subject. He said that he mustn't stay as he was doing some work at the Royal College of Science and was on his way to the laboratory when he'd remembered the address I'd given him and thought of looking in and perhaps persuading me to go along with him. He had a most interesting experiment in progress. As Barbara had some drawings to show Claire we all went out together, parting in the street, and Sam and I walked towards Exhibition Road and the College. I was really glad to be with him again. He paid me many more compliments about my story, wanted to know how much brass I had got from it, and he whistled when I told him. He wanted to know more about Barbara. He admitted he'd been quite flabbergasted when he learnt who she was. Just couldn't believe that a kid like that could have grown into such a handsome woman. But why on earth had she taken up a thing like sculpture. Surely that was a man's job. And surely there couldn't be much brass in it. Still with her looks she ought to get a husband easy enough. He didn't think much of the others. They seemed a very queer lot, particularly the way they dressed. Still if they were artists, they could please themselves, and anyway some of the professors he'd met had been a bit eccentric in their dress. The one he was working with now had his head screwed on the right way. Groom. The timber man.

We turned left opposite the College of Science and entered some temporary wooden buildings which Sam explained was the timber section of the Department of Botany. But of course I did not know (it was my own fault for not answering letters) that he was back to science again. The boom in home-grown timber had petered out. The firm was reducing sail, and his father was quite capable now of carrying on alone. But timber itself was still a No. 1 world commodity. One of the most important problems connected with it had been accentuated by the post-war boom in building and the furniture trade. That of seasoning and preservation. He had told me before about the damage done to timber by pests, notably the powder-post beetle. Well, after a refresher course in general and applied botany at the College, he was now on the track of this pest. His investigations might lead nowhere. On the other hand, they might be epoch-making and affect the whole technique of timber seasoning.

We entered a laboratory. My nostrils were assailed by a mingled odour of ether and formalin and I felt a powerful nostalgia for the old days at Bramblewick, and Sam must have felt it too for he said wistfully:

" I wonder what happened to Rachel and Jenny?"

I was able to tell him that they were both married to Bramblewick sailors and that both of them had children.

" Oh," Sam said thoughtfully. Then, " Do you know I was really quite keen on Rachel. But it wouldn't have done to have got tangled up so early in one's career. It would have been a very big mistake, wouldn't it?"

He gave me no time to consider that rather unexpected problem for in suddenly very matter-of-fact tones he said:

" Well, here's where I'm working now."

He pointed to a bench on which was a microscope, a microtome, dissecting lenses and many glass jars with gauze covers containing small sections of wood. Other larger sections, planks and slabs were piled on the floor. Sam picked up a piece of wood that looked as though it had been sawn from an old four-poster bed. It was riddled with " worm " holes and when he shook it a fine powder like pepper fell from the holes.

" *Lyctus,*" he said. " Powder-post beetle. Millions of cubic feet of timber destroyed by it every year. And that's nothing compared with the damage to buildings and furniture. And it's getting worse. Even the War Office is getting bothered with it. Rifle butts are made of walnut. Walnut's particularly susceptible to it. Immunity, and not complete at that, can only be given by treating the wood with certain chemicals, creosote, for example, but you can't creosote furniture and the others are expensive. The life history of the pest is pretty well known. Female beetle lays her eggs in minute cavities in surface of wood, eggs hatch into grubs which tunnel the wood in all directions. No British hard wood, even the hardest like oak and ash, is naturally immune, but I'm checking up on that." He pointed to the jars. "I've got sections of almost every sort of British timber under observation. There's live *Lyctus* in each of those jars. But the most interesting thing I have to show is this."

Leaning in a corner of the laboratory was a fairly large and heavy plank. Sam laid it on the bench under a bright light. I could see that it had been sawn almost down the centre of a big and unusually straight oak. It was not planed. You could see the marks of the circular saw by which it had been ripped. Sam pointed to a small area on one edge of the plank. It was badly " worm-eaten " but the rest of the plank seemed quite whole.

"Funny thing, isn't it ?" Sam went on (and it was just as though he was giving me my first lecture on *Doto*) " that one patch should be infected, and the rest clear. Looks as though this plank may hold the solution to the mystery, solve a problem that has been vexing the world's timber experts for years. It was lying in a sort of store in the department of botany when I came here a week or so back. And, by the way, I ought to tell you this is a private research I'm doing. No money in it yet, and I've still got to go back to the estate occasionally. Anyway I came across the plank just by accident. I was looking for something else. But I noticed the *Lyctus* tunnels and that started me thinking and I mentioned it to Groom. He told me that he had an idea the plank and the rest of the junk in that cupboard was from the Great Exhibition of 1851. That was in the Crystal Palace by the way, built originally in Hyde Park and opened by Queen Victoria, and afterwards moved to its present site at Sydenham. The site of the various colleges and museums in South Kensington was bought out of the profits of the Great Exhibition. The minimum age of the plank (as a plank) was therefore established. It proved that there had been plenty of time for it to be attacked. If it was immune then the thing to discover was why ? What was its history prior to the exhibition ? What process of treatment, accidental or otherwise, had it undergone ? "

I asked Sam how he proposed to find out. He became rather ponderous.

"One of the pitfalls of scientific investigation," he said, " is drawing conclusions from insufficiently examined and tested evidence. It's so easy to interpret evidence so as to fit and prove your theory. One mustn't put the cart before the horse. It's only assumption that the plank is immune. I've got to cut pieces from all parts of it, including where it has been attacked, and expose them to fresh attack. As a matter of fact we're not strictly right in saying that it's only in that one small area where *Lyctus* has been at work."

He turned the plank on to its other face, and made me examine it with a lens. I saw that there were many small holes here, but that they were not real tunnels disappearing from sight, but that they were like blind burrows made by rabbits and abandoned when they encountered a stone or root.

" What happened here ? " Sam continued. " Looks as though the female laid her eggs all right, but that the grubs didn't survive long. Obvious assumption food supply was there, but very limited. Now notice another thing about this face compared with the first. It's darker than the other. The saw marks are coarser. I've measured them. It's a safe bet they were made with a 48-inch saw and that this was the first cut made. The other face is lighter, the saw marks actually made by a 22-inch saw, and at a later date as evidenced by the lighter and cleaner colour. That's all-important. But it's far from giving us the complete picture of what happened at the mill. That I hope to find out in time."

I told Sam that I thought he was marvellous, that the whole thing was as exciting as a detective story. What a triumph for him if he solved it. Certainly this was more exciting and a thousand times more important than his research on *Splanchotrophus*. There really ought to be a fortune in it.

Sam laughed dryly (although I could tell he was pleased with my enthusiasm).

" A fortune ? You might think so, if I saved all that annual loss by putting paid to *Lyctus*. But I doubt it. This is pure science, remember, not commercial. When a doctor isolates the germ that causes a disease, his job is only half done. And when he finds the cure he can't take out a patent on it. He can't put a sign outside his door—Doctor Sawbones, inventor and sole owner of the Sawbones patent cure for influenza. I don't know if I have done the wise thing in getting back to pure science again. Don't think I'm rude, but I don't suppose you'd be able to draw even a tolerable student's diagram, say, of the nervous system of a lion. Yet you write a story about a lion and get twenty-five guineas for it. I'll be lucky if I make that at the end of this job even if it's a success."

I am sure that Sam did not say that enviously. I was just as sure in that moment that he had nothing to be envious of, for if I could write stories and sell them they were only magazine stories without any lasting literary worth like the stories of Stevenson, Chekhov, Kipling, or D. H. Lawrence or Katherine Mansfield. Whatever else I felt about Barbara and her friends I knew that their work was art and that they were real artists and that I was not, but only a writer of pot-boilers. I thought that Sam was fine in regarding work as a doctor might, putting the general benefit to humanity before personal gain, and I told him so, but he laughed and said, but quite unconvincingly :

"No, I'm not a Louis Pasteur. I'm a Yorkshireman. Only I'm taking the long view. Success in this particular job won't bring much in the direct way of reward, except perhaps a bit of kudos. But it may lead to something big, something very big . . . Anyway the job's only starting. It may lead to nothing. And that plank doesn't mean anything until I've found out exactly what the brutes find in wood that's good to eat. Remember how we started our first microtome picture of *Doto* ? I've got some *Lyctus* grubs fixed and embedded in wax ready for slicing. . . . Let's make a start. Only I wish we were back in the old laboratory, and we could hear the sea roaring on the scaurs. And," he added wistfully, " we were meeting Rachel and Jenny. . . ."

3

ALTHOUGH Barbara knew she was easily the best sculptor of her
year at the R.C.A. she had other doubts apart from the prejudice
against her sex, about winning the famous prize. The selectors were
nearly all elderly, and definitely Royal Academy in their outlook.
She knew for certain that if she submitted the work that she and
Harry Moore knew to be her best, she would not stand a chance.
The prize, she complained, was not given for the best sculpture,
but for what the selectors *thought* was the best sculpture ; in other
words, what they thought would be most suitable for exhibition
in Burlington House, or for permanent show in a London park as
a reproof to Epstein's *Rima*. Good taste was their motto. Thus
she knew that if she was to win the prize she must forget all she
knew and felt about the primitives and the ultra moderns and
significant form and deliberately come down to Academy level.
If she carved a pair of doves she would have to give them heads
and tails and eyes and feathers so that the selectors would not have
to look at the title to know what the carving represented, and if she
carved a human torso it must not look like a gorilla or a sea lion.
I gathered that Barbara and her friends had no higher opinion about
the sort of sculpture that was taught in the English School of Art
in Rome, and I wondered why she was so anxious to win the prize.
The answer was that no modern student took the actual teaching
seriously, that what made it worth while was the money, the
travelling allowances, free board and lodgings, a free studio and
models and material, and the opportunity that living in Italy
afforded for seeing and studying in its museums, galleries and
churches, some of the finest art in the world. The Italian masters
like Leonardo, Michael Angelo, Duccio, Giotto, Donatello,
Raphael ; the Greek and Byzantine sculptors were accepted by
Barabara as the real thing.

Of course to a sculptor who thought of his art only as a
means of livelihood, the Prix de Rome was as good as an M.A. to
a teacher or a D.Sc. to a chemist. It would be likely to impress
(perhaps more so than his actual work) provincial committees

charged with the task of erecting a war memorial in the town square, or a statue of a deceased alderman or public benefactor. Barbara had no illusions about ever making money this way or by executing commissioned portraits for private clients. She wanted to make money but the only way for a conscientious and independent artist to do it was to exhibit in the private galleries like the Leicester and the Redfern and sell either to private collectors and connoisseurs or to the few discriminating public collections which in defiance of good taste were buying Epsteins, and the paintings of Picasso and even hotter revolutionaries.

I forget the exact conditions and regulations of the Prix de Rome contest, which was open to the students of all art schools, but I think the judges had to form their opinion from a varied collection of each student's work, modelling, carving, direct studies from life, design and drawings. But at least one exhibit was a " set " piece, and in Barbara's year it was to be a decorative *bas relief* plaque to be placed above the main entrance of a hospital. It was to be modelled in clay, cast in plaster of Paris, and must be suitable for ultimate casting in bronze. We saw Barbara soon after she had been informed about the plaque. It was, she said, just the sort of obvious thing the Prix de Rome committee *would* think of ! How Burne-Jones would have revelled in it. Obviously they would expect something Biblical complete with quotation such as " Christ healing the sick." Well, she'd have to do it, and make it as conventional as possible. She'd been warned that the selectors were very hot on technique. She'd put in all she knew. Have all her figures draped of course. She believed they actually gave marks for drapery, far more important in their opinion than anatomy, which *should* be the most important thing of all no matter how abstract your conception might be. She had just heard, by the way, that the hot favourite of the Slade School was a man called Jack Skeaping. Harry had seen his work, and was much impressed with it, but he was original and independent, and it wasn't likely that he would make any concessions to the smug ideas of the selectors. Unfortunately however he was a man !

Claire was anxious for Barbara to win the prize. If she did it would make our long-deferred visit to Italy much more exciting. We might be able to take a small villa in Rome. It would be fun to entertain Barbara and the new crowd of students she would meet at the school. But of course we must spend some of our time in Florence and Sienna and other places famous for their art collections. Also we must see Naples and Capri and Vénice. I certainly did want to see all these places, but I had a growing feeling that you could have too much of a good thing, even of good art and particularly if it was not the art you were directly interested in. What I wanted, next to Africa, was to go to the South Seas, or Central or North America. I wanted to see fresh animals and natives and meet real men, sailors and pioneers, prospectors, ranchers, remittance men, beachcombers, district commissioners, for I felt that these were the things and the people I wanted to write about, and more than that, make films about, although my prospects of ever selling a film story or having anything to do with the making of one seemed more remote than ever.

It was unfortunate that the very day after I met Sam he got a wire to say that his father had been taken ill and that he was needed to take charge of the estate and mill. Temporarily his research on *Lyctus* was stopped, and he did not know when he would be able to continue. I was terribly disappointed to hear this for being with him that night had recalled and half reawakened an old love and before I'd left him we'd talked of going up to Bramblewick for a few days, and if the laboratory and cottage were vacant, staying there and doing some collecting and fishing. I'd almost forgotten what it was like to fish. I was not happy. And yet I was doing well with my writing. The editor of the *Red* was immensely pleased with the first story I wrote about my young pygmy chief. It was longer than usual and he agreed to pay thirty guineas for it and the same price for as many as I cared to write of the same length. He also thought that he would like to have special illustrations for it, something out of the ordinary, and wondered if I knew an artist. I mentioned this to Barbara who was always complaining how hard up she was. I thought if she was prepared to sink to the level of the Royal Academy in order to win the Prix de Rome she might not be above the *Red* seeing that it would only be negroes and animals she would have to draw and that she could if she wished use another name. But she did not rise to the suggestion nor did she even ask to read the story. She had just done a rough sketch for the plaque, and I think I must have annoyed her by my instinctive enthusiastic admiration. It really was fine, and Claire agreed, but more discreetly. I remember it only vaguely now, but it was a long rectangle with many figures standing on each side of a beautifully conceived Christ. There were lame and blind among the figures and a mother carrying a child, and although she had only roughed out the faces the whole composition conveyed in a most powerful way the drama of sickness and healing.

In successive weeks we were to see that rough sketch improved and completed and then modelled in clay, every figure and every face and every feature done almost as intricately as a Chinese ivory carving, and yet without (to my eyes) detracting from the unity of the whole design. But the better it got the more Barbara seemed to dislike it, and when it came to having the plaster cast done she said she felt like smashing it up and withdrawing from the competition altogether. She had not let Harry see it in any of its stages and dreaded his comments now. But Barbara had too much of her father in her to give up. She was out to win the Prix, and win it she would. The cast was made. It was Spring before the judges started their tour of inspection and a considerable time had to elapse before their decisions were made known. I had met Sam several times, but he had only been able to make short visits to town and his research therefore had not proceeded very far. He had made one important discovery however. In the digestive organs of the *Lyctus* bugs he had discovered starch in various stages of assimilation. Starch is found in the cells of wood. It was a fair bet then that the food of *Lyctus* was this substance. But again he had not conclusive proof. So long as his father was ill and the responsibility of the estate was on his shoulders *Lyctus* must wait, and I began to feel that after all that detective hunt which had started so excitingly was going to peter out. I had forgotten hat Sam, like Barbara, came from Yorkshire.

We had decided to go to Italy at Easter. I had finished three of my pygmy stories, and felt justified in having a break. If Barbara won the Prix she wouldn't go to Rome until the autumn, and I guessed that this trip of ours was to be a sort of initial reconnaissance, that we were going to look for some place during our tour that would be suitable to return to semi-permanently later on. Barbara was now waiting for the result, and on the whole she was calm. Harry Moore, who was a great friend of William Rothenstein, had told her that there was not the slightest doubt that the judges had put her work top in the R.C.A., Harry himself having at last seen the plaque had congratulated her on its brilliance, not as a work of art, but as a satire on the Royal Academy. At the same time there was disquieting "inside" information from the Slade. Skeaping's work had stood out from that of the other students in the same way as Barbara's had done. It was reported that the selectors had appeared to disagree about his "set" piece, which made no concessions to Royal Academy traditions and was almost Epsteinish in its broad treatment : but that they had been deeply impressed by his drawings, chiefly of animals, and by a "straight" torso carved in wood. Harry thought it looked like a dead heat with the prejudice of sex perhaps swaying the balance. But the day before the result was to be declared came a new and very dramatic piece of information. Skeaping, who had been over-working to get his Prix de Rome exhibits ready, was dangerously ill with appendicitis. He had been rushed to hospital and it was not yet known whether the operation would be in time to save his life.

Barbara had not met Skeaping. She would not have been human not to have felt in some measure jealous and resentful of so dangerous a rival after the way she had worked and sacrificed her artistic pride. She had more reason still to be resentful if he won without playing down to the judges. But now that he was ill her emotions must have been very mixed. Whether he won or she won, she could not wish a fellow-artist, even if he was an enemy, personal harm, let alone death. Yet she could not be blind to the fact that if anything did happen to him the Prix de Rome would be hers for certain. Again, she would never feel happy if it did come to her that way. She would feel she was living in a dead man's shoes.

I never knew in what manner the decision of the judges was conveyed to the competitors, whether personally or through the principals of the colleges. We were by ourselves at tea-time when Barbara came in. She stood for a moment dramatically by the door. She looked unusually pale. Then she smiled and said :

"God—give me a drink, will you? Something strong. And a fag."

I did so. Claire asked her to sit down on the divan beside her in front of the fire. None of us spoke for a full (and very painful) minute, while B. drank neat whisky and smoked her cigarette. Then she said :

" What a damned good drink. Can I have another ? "

I gave her one. She sipped at it. Then, without a tear in her eye, without a sign of emotion in her voice, yet with a peculiar hardness in her whole face that made her look more like her father than ever before, she said :

" Well, that's that. Jack Skeaping's won the Prix de Rome."

We sympathised. Barbara lit another fag. She remained quite calm. She had just come back from the college. Every one there had been very nice about it, particularly Rothenstein. Harry of course had been a bit ironic. Said she hadn't sunk quite low enough for their lordships. But anyway she was runner-up to a very good man. Rothenstein thought there was a good chance of her getting a travelling scholarship to Italy later on. But she didn't like being beaten.

" But what about Skeaping ? " I dared to ask. " Is there any news about him ? "

Often I have wondered what Barbara was thinking then, whether in that moment that queer instinct that we call a woman's intuition was at work. She blew another cloud of smoke from her mouth and looked at the fire and said quite calmly :

" Oh, he's all right, Harry told me. Operation a perfect success. I suppose the news will knock at least a week from his convalescence. Harry's met him, by the way. Says he's quite fascinating. Expect we'll all meet some day. How funny ! It would be like a boxing match, wouldn't it, loser congratulating winner, winner sympathising with loser."

Barbara finished her drink and said smilingly :

" What damned good stuff whisky is. Do you think I could have another ? "

4

WE WAITED until after the Easter holidays to go to Italy so that trains would be less crowded and hotels cheaper. For once we did not stay in Paris, but went straight on and did not break our journey until Lausanne. It was my first sight of the Alps, and I would have liked to have spent a week there climbing at least one of the lesser peaks, fishing in the lake or in some of the mountain streams. But Claire was eager to get to Florence and we only stayed one night in Switzerland. I had never seen anything quite so lovely as the scenery we passed in the train after leaving the Simplon Tunnel. We passed quite close to Lake Maggiore. The weather was fine but not too hot, and there was a breeze which filled the coloured sails of many beautifully shaped boats. There were wooded islands with romantic looking castles and villas on them, and to the north of the lake huge snow-capped mountains. And yet there was to me something unsatisfying about this scenery. It was theatrical, too beautiful to be real. It was like looking at an endless succession of Academy pictures by the best English landscape painters and it made me almost long for something ugly.

We found this at Milan where we spent one day. Here was industrial Italy, big engineering works, furnaces, mills, war factories changed over to the making of commercial cars and agricultural machinery. Mussolini was now in power. On my long war-time journey from Taranto up the east coast of Italy and to the French Riviera I'd seen a cross section of a country which had been rotten ripe for a dictatorship, and it was not all war weariness that accounted for the filth and incompetence so apparent everywhere. I remembered the station lavatories. The swarms of beggers who had crowded round our train whenever we stopped near a town, the lazy insolence of railway officials. Milan was ugly after the mountain scenery, but there was something invigorating about its busy streets with plenty of buses and smart looking private cars, and smartly dressed men and women. It had an air of prosperity, so different from the Italian towns I had seen before, and in particular I noticed that there were no beggars, which reminded me that in the London we had left, despite the boom, there was scarcely a main street in the West End without its ex-servicemen pavement artists, and bands of hurdy-gurdy players, and match sellers. There were plenty of black-shirts about, but apart from the dinginess of their dress, there was nothing offensive about them. At the frontier all the officials had been polite, and apart from that we had never been asked for our passports. I felt that there must be something fine about this man who in such a short time had achieved such a miraculous change. I had read of his ruthless methods, the assassination or deportation of those who had stood in his way, the castor oil. But I had already been convinced that most of the war-time atrocities attributed to the Germans were either false or exaggerated for propaganda purposes and I thought it was likely that it was the same about the alleged acts of the Fascists. How gullible I was ! I was ready to believe that Mussolini had invented a technique of government which at a stroke did away with all the muddle of politics, and clumsy old-fashioned legislation, and just got on with the job of reconstruction, and the creation of national and individual prosperity. I felt quite proud to think that in the stories I was writing about my pygmy chief planning and fighting to save his people from extinction I had in a way anticipated Benito Mussolini, although it might have been that reading about Benito in the papers had subconsciously helped to inspire the stories.

We had plenty of money—or at least I thought so. The lira rate was even better than the franc, and at Florence we put up at a first-class hotel within sight of the River Arno and the famous Ponte Vecchio which, with its houses and shops built on its arches, was like a small edition of the original London Bridge. I liked Florence. Its streets and houses retained much of their mediæval character. I had recently read the classic autobiography of that gay, swashbuckling, hot-tempered artist adventurer of the sixteenth century, Benvenuto Cellini, and wandering through those narrow streets intersected with dark alleys, it was easy to conjure up the atmosphere of the Renaissance when artists were made or broken, enriched or imprisoned by noblemen and cardinals and popes. Here Cellini was born, learnt to play the flute and practise the arts of gold and silver smithing and sculpture, which were to make him the temporary favourite of popes and princes. Here he loved, fought duels, carried on the political intrigues for which he was expelled. He lived at Bologna and Rome, later in France, but returned to Florence to execute under the patronage of Cosmo de Medici his famous bronze " Perseus with the Head of Medusa," which, ironically enough, was one of the few works of art on show in Florence that I did not see at all.

Art in the showman's sense was still the dominant activity of Florence, and the mainspring of the tourist trade, which certainly seemed a more legitimate one than the Grotto of Lourdes. Although the holidays were over the galleries (most of these like the Pitti in the original palaces of the Florentine nobles) were thronged with tourists, English, American and German, some in parties complete with a lecturer. I have often thought that there is no greater test for a man's honesty than to go round an art gallery and give a candid opinion on every picture that he sees, or even to answer like a witness under cross-examination a straight " yes " or " no " to the question does he like it ? What man of ordinary intelligence or education brought face to face with a picture bearing on its frame the name of Leonardo da Vinci dare answer " no " even though it did not arouse his emotions half so much as a photograph of his favourite film star ? Personally I could not appreciate any serious work of art if other people were gazing at it at the time. I wanted solitude and above everything I wanted *time* to disabuse my mind of everything I had heard about the artist, to forget whether one *ought* to like the picture because the best critics acclaimed it, to attain complete emotional detachment. I knew the critics could not be wrong, that these really were great works of art, and while I believed that the majority of the tourists were incapable of seeing what the critics or even their lecturers saw, that their expressions of deep admiration were largely feigned and hypocritical, it was obvious that there were many others whose admiration was completely sincere. I had no doubt whatever of Claire's sincerity. What defeated me was her *capacity* for admiration : how she could derive an ecstasy from one picture, and go on to another and another, like a bee among the flowers of a June garden.

I felt that the criterion of any picture should be its capacity to give out, and to go on giving out a form of energy transmitted by the act of painting from the artist's mind, as magnetism is transmitted from a magnet to a bar of inert steel by contact. It is an energy born of the artist's knowledge and experience and his controlled and disciplined vision. True that all visual art is dead without light, that a painting is only a device for reflecting and modifying the light vibrations of the sun in such a way that they produce through our optic nerves the sensation we call beauty. Every pigment or combination of pigments juggles with the stream of sun " waves " to reflect its own characteristic sensation, red, blue, yellow, green, grey. But the artist juggles with them all, weaves them into a pattern, and the measure of his skill in doing this is in their continuing to radiate in the same pattern so long as the pigments withstand physical disintegration. To me neither the physical identity of the artist, nor his period mattered, nor the subject. But I knew also that as with music your appreciation became deeper as you studied and understood the subtleties of composition. That appreciation was itself nearly an art, requiring a conscious discipline and constant practice. I felt that if I was to get at what undeniably was great in any of these masterpieces we saw, then I must have it to myself, live with it, and not take a mental snapshot of it over the shoulders of a hot, fat German before moving on to the next and the next.

Claire resented what she called my marine biological theory of aesthetic appreciation. I was not certain that I was right about it and am not now. She accused me of being bored. I was not bored exactly, but even after we discovered that we could see the galleries in relative solitude if we went immediately at opening time, I felt that there were far too many galleries for one town and far too many masterpieces in them, and that I was being stuffed. Our night life did not offer a complete relief to this. There were many genuine artists and art students living or staying in the town and we soon got to know quite a crowd of them, and it was just like Paris although there was a predominance of English and American, so that I could at least understand the words of a discussion if I could not always follow its drift. We drank together, dined together in Florence's best known " artist " restaurant (I think it was the Bucca), we had studio parties. Claire thought that Florence would be an ideal place for us to live in for at least a year, particularly if Barbara got her special scholarship. But I argued that we should see a little more of Italy before deciding anything. I wanted to see Rome and Naples (where there was a marine biological station almost as famous as the one at Monaco) and Capri and perhaps Venice, although I did not mention this as it would be more or less on our way back to England (for which I was getting more than a vague longing). At last we went to Rome.

I'd wanted to see Rome ever since, as a boy, I'd discovered there had been a Roman fort on the highest part of the moors at Bramble-wick. A stone with Roman lettering on it had been discovered there and was one of the most interesting exhibits in the Whitby Museum. Also I'd had to learn by heart that poem of Lord Macaulay's in *The Lays of Ancient Rome* about Horatius keeping the bridge and plunging into the Tiber and swimming across it after slaying the commander of the invading enemy in personal combat. I wanted to see the Tiber and the Colosseum and the Forum and the Vatican, and other antiquities because they were tangible monuments in the story of the world, because they were marvellous and romantic. And I did get a thrill from seeing them, although it was tinged with disillusionment in the case of the Tiber, which, being very low, did not suggest that Horatius's feat in swimming across it with his " harness on his back " was as notable as Macaulay's description of it. The Colosseum excited me profoundly, so did the Trajan column and some of the city gates and bridges, the Pons Fabricius and the Ponte Sant Angelo with its central arches still as Hadrian had built them. But of the Forum little remained but the stumps of pillars, and I could not help feeling that as in the case of the Egyptian pyramids most of these antiquities would have looked more exciting if they had been restored to their original condition, with the original portions clearly marked for those who insisted on the genuine antique. Clarie agreed with me in this. She thought that ruins were depressing and more so if they were the ruins of something that had been very beautiful. But again it was the " galleried " art in Rome that interested her most.

On the whole I liked Rome better than Florence. I should not have minded spending a month there, but the weather, which had so successfully spoilt our other continental trips, now tormented us in another way. It became almost unbearably hot. We both longed for the sea. But I was also getting worried about money.

It would be necessary for me soon to do some work. Naples promised to be hotter than Rome, in spite of the sea air. Capri now sounded much too expensive. We decided to go north to the Ligurean Riviera, which we were told had all the natural and artificial attractions of the French and real Italian Rivieras but with cheaper accommodation. We tried Rapallo first. It was a moderately sized township built on the shores of a bay from which mountains climbed steeply. There was a real native Italian part, but mostly it consisted of hotels and boarding-houses, all of which it seemed were full of visitors from Germany. We pushed a little farther along the bay to a smaller resort called Santa Margarita, which was more native but also full of Germans. Then at the head of the Bay we found Porto Fino, which had a real harbour with fishing boats in it, and practically no Germans. After two nights in a quiet moderately priced inn we found a furnished villa and took it for the rest of the summer at a rent of two pounds a week.

Porto Fino was what the guide books call an artist's gem. It reminded me in one respect of Bramblewick. Its original native houses were packed so close together along the water front that there had been no available sites for hotels and boarding-houses and the old part therefore was unspoilt. The houses were tall and many storeyed. Their walls were lime-washed with tints of red, yellow and blue. The harbour was deep with the water clear and usually dead calm so that it mirrored the houses and the olive orchards on the hills that rose above the port in the same way that pool in Dad's best selling subject had mirrored the red roofs of Bramblewick. There were fishing boats in the harbour and their sails were of almost every conceivable tint. Wherever you stood near the harbour or on the rocks at each side or on the hills above, Porto Fino made a perfect picture. There was no jarring architectural note for even our own villa was discreetly hidden by trees. But we were both rather disillusioned with Porto Fino before long. In spite of it being an artist's gem there were very few artists (in Claire's meaning of the word). Those we saw sketching or painting were either amateurs or professionals engaged on "selling" subjects. One was a well-known exhibitor at the R.A., and the R.W.S., and I remember seeing his work in *The Studio* before that last journalistic bulwark of the Academy tradition went "modern."

There was no Bucca at Porto Fino. No studio parties. Everything was most respectable. I was not so unhappy about this. My disappointment was the sea. It was very beautiful to look at. My North Sea, even in the calmest and sunniest days, was never such a blue. It was warm too, so that if you'd wished you could have bathed in it all day. But you daren't dive or swim for any distance without first of all seeing that the water was clear of jellyfish. These were not the ordinary stinging medusæ of British summer seas. They were shaped like a string of sausages, anything up to a yard in length. They were practically translucent and therefore invisible. except at short range. If you encountered one it wrapped itself round your limbs like a tentacle of an octopus, and everywhere it touched you were stung as by a nettle. There was also a small sea-urchin which had the habit of hiding under weed. It had spines about two inches long and if you trod on one the spines were sharp enough to penetrate the sole of your foot. In spite of this Porto Fino was not very interesting from a marine biological point of view. As this was the Mediterranean there were no tides. If there had been it wouldn't have been any better, for apart from a narrow strip of shallow sand here and there along the coast, there was no beach. The mountains fell almost sheer into the sea, which was so deep a few hundred yards from the shore that no ordinary hand fishing line would reach the bottom. There were no fish anyway it seemed. The boats were sardiners, and they fished a long way out. I had to write however and Claire, who was hopeful that we should go back to Florence as soon as the weather got cooler, taught herself Italian. I had started another story about my pygmy chief, partly because our financial position was looking really alarming, partly because my agent had written to say the editor of the *Red* was wondering what had happened to me. I had by the way given up my *John O' London* series of nature articles as the editor had turned down two in succession and I'd felt that really they were a waste of time.

I had written to Sam asking if he had any news to give me about *Lyctus*. His answer was disappointing. His father was better but not quite well enough to take full charge of the estate. He'd only been able to devote a little time to research and he'd discovered nothing new of importance. But continued tests had confirmed beyond doubt that starch *was* the food of the grub. That was all.

but he still had a hunch that the plank held the secret and that some day it would be revealed.

There had been no news from Barbara since we had left London although Claire had written to her several times, and sent her reproductions of some of the pictures we had seen in Florence and Rome. We wondered if she was ill or had taken her failure to win the Prix too much to heart. In her last letter Claire had told her that we had taken a villa at Porto Fino, that she doubted if the place would appeal to her as an artist as it was on the " pretty-pretty " side, but that it certainly was a pleasant place to spend a holiday in and that it really wasn't so far from Florence, to which she expected we would return when the weather was cooler. Would she care to come and stay ? Claire got an answer at last and it contained a staggering piece of news. Barbara was very apologetic that she hadn't answered Claire's letters or thanked her for the photographs. It wasn't because she was ill or moping about that silly competition. As a matter of fact she had never been so happy in her life. She had some very great news. Did we remember that the man who had won the Prix was Jack Skeaping ? Did we remember how jealous she had felt about him although of course she had never met him or seen any of his work. Well, thanks to Harry, she had met him. She had seen his work and it was marvellous, but so was he. He was tall, dark, very handsome. He had quite recovered from his illness. He had liked her own work too. He had told her that in some way it seemed to be the complement of his own. They had got on awfully well together. He was passionately fond of dancing. So of course was she. In fact it seemed that they had the same tastes in everything. They liked the same music, the same plays, the same food. They had the same philosophy of life and art. Could we guess from this what her stupendous news was ? No. They weren't married yet. But they were passionately in love with each other and they were going to be married soon. Perhaps they would come and spend at least part of their honeymoon with us, and start learning Italian. The other news she had to tell us was perhaps just as exciting. She had got her scholarship. That would mean they would be able to live together in Italy, so of course, whether they came now or not, we'd all meet soon.

Claire wept when she finished the letter, I suppose from the same emotion that makes most women except the bride weep at a wedding. But I could think of nothing but Barbara's father and his stubborn jaw and mouth, and how these characteristics were in Barbara's face too. She'd won the Prix de Rome after all ! Little did I guess however what the sequel to Barbara's victory would be. That a few years after we'd all be sharing a house in St. John's Wood, a house that was destined to be the Waterloo of our own marriage.

Book Five

I LIKED Jack Skeaping. I envied him too. He was, as Barbara had first described him, tall, dark and handsome. His father too was an artist and I believe that Jack and his brother and sister had been brought up in a very Bohemian household near Epsom Racecourse, which accounted for his interest in and love of horses. His earliest boyhood ambition he told me had been to be a racing jockey. All his spare time had been spent in the stables. His first drawings had been of horses. I forget whether he had had any proper schooling, most likely not. All three of them had inherited a powerful " artistic " strain. With his brother Kenneth it had been music. He was now violinist in the famous English Quartet. With his sister it had been dancing, and she was now in ballet. Jack, having outgrown his ambition for jockeying, had gone in for ballet too but he'd still remained interested in horses and other animals. He'd gone from drawing them to modelling, then to carving, and in sculpture at last he'd found his real career.

He was the most versatile man I had ever met, and he had a terrific energy and zest. He was a superb dancer, ballroom as well as ballet. Together (Barbara always exotic in her dress and outrageously defiant of fashion) they were the centre of interest at every dance or ball we went to. Jack could play any muscial instrument from the 'cello to a piano accordion. He could ride of course and skate and ski and swim. He could talk brilliantly on almost every subject except literature (in which, ironically for me, he had a blind spot). He had a brilliant gift of mimicry (especially of Cockney character) and with his face and figure could have made a big name for himself on the stage or in films. I was not so certain about his sculpture. The fact that I liked all of it instantly made me distrust it. It did not fulfil my conditions of great art. It did not go on giving like some of Epstein's sculpture I had seen. It had a brilliance, and I felt it was a superficial brilliance. Actually none of it excited me as much as Barbara's. But his craftsmanship was superb, especially in his drawings and his quick modelling of

247

animals. He was a Fellow of the Royal Zoological Society, and a
constant visitor to the Zoo. Carrying a tray like that used by a
cinema attendant for selling chocolates and cigarettes, he'd stand
outside a pen of deer or gazelle, all of which might be gambolling
like March hares, and in a matter of minutes he'd build up on his
tray a clay model of one of the animals, perhaps in the very act of
leaping, and as alive as the creature itself. If he was drawing he'd
produce with just a few lines for each animal a whole group almost
as quickly as it would take a business man to write a few paragraphs
of a letter, or me to write one sentence of a nature story. In many
ways Jack made me think of Benvenuto Cellini. One of the most
exciting passages in *Cellini's Memoirs* (I had read the *Everyman*
translation by Anne Macdonell) and to me one of the most dramatic
pieces of writing of all time, was the account of how he had made
the bronze casting of the Perseus of his Perseus and Medusa masterpiece (the very one I believe we had missed seeing in Florence).
This had been commissioned by the Duke of Florence, Cosmo de
Medici, under whose patronage Cellini was working after leaving
the employ of Francis the First, In Paris. The relations between
the Duke and Cellini were not too happy. Another of the Duke's
sculptors, Bandinello, was intensely jealous and tried to persuade his
Lord that Cellini despite the excellence of the clay and wax model
was not capable of carrying out the tricky job of casting. This
infuriated Cellini and made him determined to do the thing by his
own methods, which in many ways varied from those practised by
the professional founders. First he had to cover the whole figure
(which was of burnt clay with a facing of wax) with the clay that
was to form the mould. This was reinforced and bound with iron
on the outside. The next thing was to heat the whole contraption
so that the wax facing of the positive would melt away, leaving a
half-inch space between the burnt clay of the figure and negative
impression of what had been the wax facing on the mould. Then
the mould with the original figure inside it, but separated by that
space of half an inch all over into which the molten metal had to
run, was lowered into a hole in the ground and earth was piled
round it. The furnace, for which Cellini had got several wagon
loads of pine logs, was lit. It burnt so well that the roof of the shed
under which the operation was taking place caught fire. The
weather was cold and rainy. Without the roof the furnace started

to cool. Cellini and his assistants worked madly to keep it going. Then Cellini himself collapsed and had to be put to bed. He recovered later to find that his assistants had nearly let the furnace out. He fiercely ordered them to bring more wood. The metal started to melt, and then boiled over, blowing off the furnace lid. Cellini's next anxiety was that the metal had fused. He ordered his assistants to fetch every pewter dish and porringer and plate that was in his kitchen and throw them into the brew. The metal at last started to run freely into the mould. The job was done and two days later when the mould was chipped away it was proved to be a complete success.

I don't think that Jack ever attempted bronze casting, but he came home one day with a Chinese Ming period earthenware model of a duck that a collector and connoisseur who was interested in his own work had loaned him. It was an exciting thing to look at, exquisitely modelled, and about life-size. Jack had no interest in copying such a thing. What interested him, quite apart from its beauty, was how it had been made. It was hollow, just like a bronze casting. The shell was little more than half an inch thick. He found that this shell was laminated, made up of many very thin layers, and assumed from this that when the mould had been made from an original clay model, it had been filled with clay so thinned out with water as to make it virtually liquid. The mould would be emptied leaving a thin coating of clay inside. This would be allowed to dry, then successive coatings would be made until at last the clay shell was of the required thickness for firing. He decided to test this. He made some drawings of ducks in the Zoo. From these he modelled one life size, and it did not take him more than an hour. For the mould he first of all made a thin ribbon of clay about an inch in width, and when his model was fairly dry he fixed this on edge like a fin completely round the duck from the breast under the belly, over the back and the head to the breast again along a central line, so that the thing was divided. He covered one-half of it with plaster of Paris, pressing this up against the vertical ribbon. When it was set in a minute or so, he removed the ribbon, leaving the half-mould with an even wall, an inch deep. He thinly painted the surface of this all the way round with almost liquid clay. Then he covered the other half of the model flush up with the wall of the first so that the whole thing was enclosed. But you could tell where the dividing line had been by the almost hair-like mark of the clay. He next plunged the whole thing in water. This made the film of clay expand sufficiently to part the two halves of the mould. He eased them clear away from the model, left them to dry for a while and then put them together. The mould was complete, except that he had to make a hole under the belly to pour in his liquid clay.

He may have used ordinary clay for this. If he did he must have mixed other ingredients with it. The process of building up the shell inside the mould took a long time for each film had to dry, and there was a long wait before he dare remove the two halves of the mould which had been tied together. The result was perfect. There was only a very fine line where the joint had been and this he removed with a moist brush. The now hollow duck was identical with the original.

I don't suppose Jack realised how excited I was about his duck and particularly about the firing of it, or he might have asked me to see it done. He went down to Epsom to his father's house for this operation, not taking even Barbara with him. He returned three days later, very tired but triumphant, with the duck fired and not a crack or a distortion and almost unrecognisable in its colour and surface texture from the one of the Ming Dynasty. It was just as beautiful. He had designed and made his own kiln in the back garden of the family home. He had bought a load of logs for fuel. Like Cellini he had had a bad fright for the kiln had to be kept going day and night at an even temperature. Some of his logs had been green and refused to burn. In the middle of the first night it had rained, and he had been obliged to sacrifice a dog kennel and most of a chicken house to keep the thing going. Yet to him the whole business had been only an experiment, an exercise in versatility. He had no ambition to be ceramic artist. If he had, he could have had not only fame but money. But I do not think it was an artist's singleness of purpose that steered him away from the paying sidelines of art. He was not indifferent to money. He was not above pot-boiling when occasion demanded. It was just that he had an extraordinary zest for activity, for doing things, and for doing them quickly and getting on to something else. Compared with him Barbara was slow, almost stolid. But I believe she was the better artist.

Our house was of the Queen Anne period, in a terrace, not far from Acacia Road. It had four storeys, with two rooms on each and a basement with three rooms, one of which gave on to what originally had been a garden. Some tenant however had built this over to make a billiard-room with a top light. The Skeapings had the basement rooms to live in, and the billiard-room was their studio. It was ideal for sculptors except in one respect. There was only one entrance, and that through the basement passage which was too narrow to take anything like a big block of stone for carving. Jack was already talking about doing a life-size carving of a racehorse ! Barbara shared his love of animals but she was particularly fond of birds. They had an aviary made to occupy the entire length of the studio walls, and they had it stocked with budgerigars, canaries, Java sparrows, love birds and, of course, doves. The seed they fed them with got spilt about the floor and attracted swarms of mice, which got quite tame.

Claire had been left some money by a distant relative, and she let herself go on the decoration and furnishing of our part of the house. It had been allowed to get into a bad state of repair by the previous tenant. It had been lit with gas. We had electricity installed for cooking and heating, as well as lighting : all the old wallpapers were striped and the walls distempered, and the furniture was either modern from Heals, or Queen Anne from the antique shops in Baker Street. Jack gave us some of his animal drawings to hang on the walls, and we had some full-scale facsimiles of Cezanne and Van Gogh and Gaugin, as well as one or two small carvings of Barbara's. I had a sort of attic back room to write in. Its windows looked down on the studio and beyond that to some very old mews, which curiously enough were roofed with exactly the same red pantiles as the cottages of Bramblewick. Beyond these again were tall buildings so that I could only see a small patch of sky. I was still writing for the *Red Magazine*, and the *Yellow* and the *Green*, but I had dropped nature stories altogether and doing nothing but " straight " fiction. I got more money for these but they took me more time and I was still a long way from earning even a thousand pounds a year.

One terribly ironic thing had happened. My agent had been unable to place any of my stories in America. One day I picked up an American magazine called *Adventure*, and there was a nature story in it, that I thought was not so good as some I had written.

I sent the editor copies of several that had already appeared in the *Red* and its companions, and one that the *Red* had bought but had not published. About a month later I got a letter from the editor returning all but the one that had not been published and saying that he was keeping it and that a draft would be forwarded for it in due course. It was, he said, one of the best nature stories that had ever come into his office and he could not tell me how vexed he was having to reject the others. But it was the unalterable policy of his magazine not to publish anything that had appeared in England longer than a month before. When the draft came it was for fifty pounds, the highest price I had yet got for a story. That meant that if I'd landed him from the first my income would have been more than doubled. I immediately wrote a new one, but he rejected it saying that it was not up to the standard of the one he had taken. The editor of the *Red* did not turn this story down but he made it fairly clear that he was only taking it because of our " gentleman's agreement." I was angry and felt like breaking with him, but I cooled down when he asked me if I thought I could do a full length adventure serial, for which he would pay me at the rate of four guineas a thousand for first British rights. That, he pointed out, would leave me free to have it published in volume form. He would like to have an African setting, and although my pygmy stories had been popular with his readers, he suggested that for a serial I must have white people for the main characters. He did not suggest that I might also sell the film rights, but that aspect came quickly to my mind. It hadn't taken me long to hit on a plot with a sadistic German called Von Schomm and a Bolshevik revolutionary, Dr. Recco, for its villains, a Sanders of the River Englishman for hero. Von Schomm, a sculptor studying primitive art in German South-West Africa when the war starts, becomes an officer in the German colonial army. The campaign in G.S.W. was a short affair, for there was no commander comparable with Von Lettow Voerbeck. But before the colony surrenders, the gold in all its banks is collected and my villain is ordered to transport it across Central Africa to German East. He is captured by a tribe who practise the " leopard " fetish. He wins a psychological victory over the chief " leopard " man and goes one better on the fetish by making the gold into a great effigy of a leopard with a mechanical foot to do the sacrificial killings, all this in a temple that he decorates with sculptures compared with which Mr. Epstein's would have looked as innocent as the Cavell memorial. Schomm, gone sadistically mad, forgets his mission for the Fatherland, but a white German N.C.O. who was with him escapes and the secret of the golden leopard becomes known to Dr. Rocco, who is organising a great revolution of the African blacks. It also becomes known to the hero, who holds a roving commission from the British Secret Service.

I did a synopsis of the story and the editor liked it but insisted that it should have a love interest. As most of the action was to take place in the worst possible country I didn't like this. I saw that it would mean unending complications. I argued with the editor that most of his readers would hold the view that a woman's place was in the home, and would have little sympathy for one of the modern he-man type, and that she'd have to be that unless I had to have my hero spending half his time protecting her from tarantulas and scorpions and tsetse flies, not to mention big game and leopard men, native as well as German. The feminine type of girl would find it most difficult to keep herself looking attractive in the bush. From the point of view of construction there was the difficulty that wherever the girl went (in Africa) the man would have to go. She could have no independent action. Neither could he. In fact she'd be a damned nuisance. But the editor was firm. He said I needn't trouble about making it too authentic. It was fiction after all. I capitulated, for I thought that if the thing was ever published as a book it would very much increase its chances of being filmed if I had a lovely girl in it.

I don't think I had ever hated anything so much as the writing of that serial. Scores of times I gave it up, and only the fact that I'd agreed to write it made me go on. I modelled my heroine's general appearance on Barbara's. I made her dark, foreign looking, and before I moved her out to Africa, I made her wear very much the same sort of clothes. I had to make her look rather vampish however so that she should create a false impression on the hero and stop them falling for each other too soon and too easily. My plot did not allow her to be an individual hunter for the gold, so I had to bracket her with the Bolshevik and I made her his niece, and I gave her a French name. I quite liked her in London where she first met the hero and they dined and danced together. In one of Barbara's frocks, with some red in it to make a contrast with her raven hair, large grey mysterious eyes, a dazzling smile, she was a credible person, enough at any rate to set the heart of a one-time big game hunter and now Secret Service agent beating a little faster. But once I got her embarked on the soil of Africa and setting out on a journey that might have made David Livingstone quail she became the pest I feared she would be. Even in a topee and jodhpurs she just would not fit in to the setting of jungle and swamp and dark perilous forest I required for my action. It wouldn't have been so bad if I could have left her somewhere while the others went on. But I knew that no reader having read my first description of her would stand for that. She had taken the stage and she insisted on keeping it even to the final chapters where she was taken prisoner by Schomm's leopard men, and brought for sacrifice to the golden leopard, from which fate of course the hero saved her, he having already squashed her uncle's plan for an African revolution.

I wrote this terrible tale between my pot-boiling short fiction stories. I was never tempted to try and discuss it with the Skeapings, who indeed seemed to regard my activities in the top room of the house as something completely remote from their lives and interests. Their job was more interesting anyway because you could see it happening. There was always something going on in the studio. They were having a struggle to make a living out of their art. They'd had one or two shows in the West End. They'd had a very good press and they'd sold quite a lot of their work, but they had to put a lot of money down for the use of the gallery, and they had to pay a big commission on all sales. Jack was so hard up one week that he and his brother Kenneth, who happened to be in a similar fix, put on old clothes and wearing black masks made the round of the theatre queues, Kenneth with his violin, Jack with his piano accordion. They made more than ten pounds in three nights. It was during one of their leanest periods that Jack was approached by the "art" manager of a famous Midland pottery firm who asked him if he would do a series of models of animals suitable for repro-duction in glazed china. The idea was to start a rivalry to the products of the famous Copenhagen ware which was on sale at Heal's and many of the new "arty" furnishing stores in the West End. They were to be quite small, and I believe that the fee offered for each one was twenty guineas. I don't know what Barbara thought about this proposition, but I had a strong feeling that if she had been offered six times the fee to do a work to order, to be reproduced mechanically and sold *ad lib* in shops, she would have refused, this in spite of her Yorkshire blood. It was beyond all doubt, pot-boiling. Jack did not seem worried by any such scruples. There was no need even for him to go to the Zoo, for by this time he must have sketched or modelled almost every sort of animal that was there, and I believe he could have done them blindfold. They were lovely things that he did, especially the gazelle and a kangaroo and a Mongolian pony. He modelled them in clay and then cast them in solid plaster, and it wasn't long before they were on sale at Heal's, reproduced in highly glazed buff china and exhibited in one of their special showrooms which was a " suggestion " for the drawing-room of a modern flat, completely furnished and decorated. Only a pair of the dozen or so models Jack had made were on show, tastefully spaced on the mantel-shelf above a chromium-plated electric fire. There was nothing to suggest that there was a crate (or perhaps several crates) of them, gazelles, ponies, giraffes, polar bears, in the basement store. They looked as exclusive as the beautifully designed and apparently hand-made unstained oak furniture, and it was not easy to realise that any number of persons with sufficient money could buy duplicates of the entire contents of the flat, and have them installed in their own homes : which might of course create a situation as embarrassing as that of the lady going to a reception in an exclusive Paris frock and finding her hostess dressed in a copy of it.

But the Skeapings hadn't to do much pot-boiling. They were getting known. The tip was going round among the dealers and private collectors that their work was likely to have a rising value and would prove a good investment. Many of these people called. One evening the most famous of all private collectors arrived in a Rolls-Royce. It was the Greek millionaire, Eumorfopoulos, whose collection of modern art alone was supposed to be worth hundreds of thousands of pounds. Naturally we kept out of the way while he was in the studio with Jack and Barbara (Barbara wearing her most exotic frock). He stayed a long time. But when he had gone and Barbara came bounding up the basement stairs there was no need for her to tell us that his visit had been a success.

Jack had already dashed out for a bottle of wine. The millionaire had bought sculptures from each of them, and I believe some of Jack's Zoo drawings. I forget what the price was for everything but it ran into hundreds of pounds, and in addition to the bottle of Chianti which we shared and a dinner at the Cafe Royal, Barbara got a new frock, the population of the aviary was increased by several prize budgerigars and canaries, Jack bought a huge aquarium and some Japanese goldfish, and the Skeaping firm invested in several blocks of sculptor's marble, and some very special woods with which Jack was going to do the initial and experimental studies for " building " a life-size racehorse.

Yes, I envied Jack. I was not envious of the financial success he looked like achieving in time. Nor of his more certain coming fame. I was jealous of his creative gift, which was apparently effortless. His hands were like those of a magician. He had only to touch a piece of formless clay or chip at a block of wood or stone to start transforming it into something beautiful. Alone in my attic room wrestling with the plot of a short story for the *Red Magazine*, or with a description of scenery or the appearance of a character, I'd hear the thump, thump of Jack's or Barbara's mallet from the studio below my window and I'd feel almost sick with disgust at my own craft, and I'd wish to God I'd never learnt to write at all. If only I'd learnt an art that needed my hands and muscles instead of just my mind. If only I'd learnt to make pottery or furniture, something I could see and feel and use when I'd done it. Modelling and carving looked so easy. But if I took a piece of clay in my hands and tried to model a gazelle I felt as helpless as a baby, although when I shut my eyes I could see whole troops of gazelle, not in the Zoo as Jack saw them but on the African veldt where they belonged, and as clearly as though I had been there. . . .

I had lost touch with Sam for a long time. I assumed that he was back on the estate and that he had abandoned his *Lyctus* research and felt diffident about admitting failure. I had an idea too that he did not like the highbrow atmosphere I was living in. I was overjoyed when I got a letter from him asking me to meet him at the Strand Palace Hotel. He had one or two interesting items of news for me. He anticipated the telling of his first item of news by introducing me to a pretty and charming girl. It was his wife and they were on their honeymoon. I had never known Sam look so happy. We had lunch at the hotel. Gladys was a graduate of Sheffield University. Not his year of course, by a long shot. She'd been teaching English literature in a north country private school. They'd met at a students' social gathering in Sheffield and the next thing they'd known was they just wanted to get wed, and here they were, happy as sandboys, having a real holiday in London before settling down to the grim realities of married life. Gladys, Sam told me, had been looking forward a long time to making my acquaintance. He'd given her many of my stories to read. But why on earth had I stopped writing nature stories? Some of the others I had written were all right, but (and Gladys would agree with him) my best line was nature. Popular science, with a human appeal, but with a background of real science.

Gladys did agree. She said she particularly liked the one I had written about a swallow. That only someone who had lived in the country and observed wild life very closely could have written a story with such sincerity. She felt about my other stories that although they were good I hadn't *felt* them so much. They didn't *live* in quite the same way.

"Yes," Sam joined in genially. "But perhaps it doesn't much matter if the other sort make more brass. That's the test when all's said and done. We've been having pretty much the same argument, haven't we, Gladys? Science or commerce. Timber or the laboratory? We've come to a compromise, if you can call it that. I'm hanged if I know though whether it's for the best."

Sam announced his second item of news. He had got an appointment at the Royal Veterinary College as Professor in Zoology. It wasn't perhaps so important as a chair at even a provincial university, but he'd got his Ph.D. now, there'd be opportunities for research, and it might lead to something bigger in time. I was thrilled and congratulated him enthusiastically, but seeing he had mentioned research I was waiting for him to tell me what had happened about *Lyctus* and as he said nothing I asked him. He laughed.

"Yes, I'll tell you about *Lyctus*. But not now. Gladys must be getting sick of the sound of that word. And I am myself as a matter of fact."

I

Gladys had some feminine shopping to do after lunch and Sam and I strode down Villiers Street to Charing Cross Gardens, that pleasant green refuge which forms a sort of undercliff between what was then Adelphi Terrace and the Thames Embankment. We sat down. I thought it might interest Sam to know that both Shaw and Barrie lived in the terrace above us and that at this moment we were probably not more than a hundred feet away from them, but Sam only said " Oh yes," and he offered me a fag. I felt he had something dramatic to tell as a climax to the news he had already given me and I was very expectant. I was completely surprised all the same when he suddenly announced quite calmly :

" Oh, about that *Lyctus* job. Of course I solved it. Easy as falling off a log. Or falling on to a log might describe it better."

It was my turn to slap him on the back.

" You've solved it. Splendid ! But why the devil didn't you tell me before ? You mean to say just as calmly as that you've found the antidote to the powder post beetle, the thing that does thousands of pounds' worth of damage——"

" Steady," he cut me short, and I had a horrible feeling that his calmness was not a mask for jubiliation. " Don't jump to conclusions. You asked me if I'd solved the problem of *Lyctus*. So I have. I did that shortly after I wrote to you in Italy, or at least I'd reached the point when I needed only practical confirmation of a theoretical certainty. You remember that Exhibition plank ? "

He took a letter from his pocket and made a sketch on the back of the envelope. It was a section of the plank showing where the area of " worm " holes had been.

" Remember that ? " he went on. " That was the only part of the plank that had been seriously attacked. But there were a number of blind tunnels on the dark face, the one with the big saw marks. Now the main infestation was near to what had been the bark. The bark was then off, but looking close to where it had been I noticed a significant thing. The wood near the tunnels was dark and mouldy looking, different from the rest, where the bark had apparently stayed on for a number of years. I suppose no one who hadn't actually been in the timber business would have spotted what that meant. To me it was clear that just where *Lyctus* had been at work the tree had received a wound in felling. The bark had been scraped off, leaving that part of the wood exposed to the air and perhaps frost. That would mean death to the living cells of the wood in that area. Follow?"

I did, completely fascinated. I knew of course that a tree like all other living things is made up of cells, which have an individual life. I knew from my own observation that a cut in the bark, such as a boy would make cutting his initials, would if deep enough darken the exposed wood and seemingly kill it. But I hadn't thought how. Sam continued:

"Remember that I'd discovered that *Lyctus* grubs were feeding on the starch granules in the wood. The obvious assumption then was that there was starch in the wood adjacent to the wound, but none or next to none where the bark had stayed on after felling. Now what does happen to a tree after felling? These days it's lopped and topped as we say, cross-cut into conveniently sized logs and hauled to the mill, sawn into timber and then kiln dried. But supposing it isn't; that it's left in log form as it was in the old days. The tree as a tree is dead, but actually it's not, for you'll have seen how a fresh-cut sapling driven into the ground as a fencing post will bud and produce leaves in spring. In the case of some trees, the sallow for example, new roots may form and the thing lives and grows. But in most cases it's only a temporary extension of life, if you like, a slow dying. The wood cells continue to live on their food reserves, notably starch, until these are exhausted. But the condition for this is that the wood cells should not be killed by other means, first say by exposure to the air, summer heat or frost, or for that matter, kiln seasoning. The bark on a felled tree affords this protection. Conclusion. Fell a tree. Leave the bark on, seal all other wounds, leave it to die of starvation. By the time it's dead its starch is used up. There's nothing for Lyctus to feed on. The timber is immune."

I repressed an impulse to slap Sam on the back again for I had half guessed he was moving to an ironic anti-climax. He re-lighted his fag which had gone out.

"That at any rate was the logical conclusion," he went on. "But to get back to the plank. Remember the blind tunnels on the dark surface which had been sawn by a 42-inch saw. That the smoother and lighter coloured surface was free? The coarser cut

had been made sometime before the other. The picture I got was
that it had been made after the log with its bark on had only partly
starved. Some starch was left, enough to attract the female beetle
and to cause her to deposit eggs but not enough to keep her larvæ
going. What happened was that a single slab had been cut from
the log leaving one bare semi-vulnerable surface. Then, as would
be the custom in those days, the log would be put on one side for
seasoning (or if you like slow dying). The second cut (with the
smaller saw) was made when this process was complete. By a piece
of pure luck the cut was made so that it included that part of the
perimeter of the log that had the wound on it."

Sam stopped. I was a bit bewildered but I said—

" Then it *is* possible to make timber immune from *Lyctus*."

He laughed a little grimly.

" Yes. I've done it up at the estate. For my own satisfaction I
wanted to prove it. I've had trees carefully felled so as not to
damage the bark. I've had every cross-cut or lopped surface sealed
with wax, to keep the logs reasonably moist. It's taken more
than a year, but the timber's virtually starch free, and consequently
immune. The problem that has been vexing the world's timber
scientists for years has been solved by yours truly. In brief, if you
don't want *Lyctus*, season your timber exactly as our grandfathers
did before the Great Exhibition. *Which is exactly what the modern
timber man cannot afford to do !* "

I felt furious and very sympathetic.

" And so it's all come to nothing ! "

Sam laughed aloud. " Not exactly. I read a paper on it not so
long ago to a very distinguished scientific society. Remind me
and I'll send you an excerpt from the *Proceedings*. I think that had
a lot to do with the new job. Come on. We've got to get back
to the Palace by three. Gladys will hate it if I'm late."

I was very glad that Sam was making such a success of his life :
that he had found the right girl and the right job, and that he had
really made a victory out of his defeat with *Lyctus*. I did not feel
certain that I was making a success of my life for all that I was
still earning plenty of money out of short-story writing. I felt
there was a lot of truth in what he and Gladys had said about those
stories, that they were saying only what the Skeapings had implied

by their complete indifference. But I had run the entire gamut of nature stories both in subject and in treatment. I was sick to death of the struggle for existence, and the mating and home-building and young-bearing habits of the animals of Africa. I was just as sick of the district commissioners, and police officers, and big-game hunters and natives too of the Dark Continent, and if the old nausea asserted itself occasionally, it was an urge for Africa itself, not what it offered as a subject for literature or films, and it was never so violent as it had been in the early days of peace. When I was working in my room late at night, after the buses had stopped running and the wind was from the direction of Regent's Park I could hear the lions roaring from the Zoo, and the yapping of jackals and the wailing of hyenas, but it was an adventure and not a literary emotion they aroused. And just as strong sometimes was the emotion aroused by a rare beam of sunshine falling on the sooty but still red pantiles of the mews beyond the Skeapings' studio, for that would take me back to Bramblewick, and remind me of my boyhood there and of the exciting and very pleasant times with Sam. It would set me thinking of the Bay on a calm summer's day and old Captain Bunny and the *Lydia*, of Tom Bell Nick and the billet, of winter gales and things washing up on the beach and of my scaur-line. And I'd think of the Mill Dam and the woods and the moors and finding flint implements, and Juggerhowe Beck and Adeline. But then I'd think of the times when Claire and I had gone there always in summer time, with the place crowded with visitors coming in char-a-bancs, and how nearly all the fishermen I'd known were either dead or retired, how there was very little fishing going on and how most of the boats were just used for " taking visitors off," and I felt I had no wish to go back there again for it was dead.

One day however, when I was struggling with still another *Red* story about a district commissioner, I found myself staring at those tiles with an unusual intensity. It was just as though I was back in Bramblewick on a lovely summer's day in June, with the red roofs shimmering in the heat and the sea dead calm under a pale blue sky. I could see the boats in the Landing, and just a few well-dressed visitors on the beach and even on the scaurs : and then suddenly I was seeing and feeling and even smelling all this, not through my own senses but through those of another person, of a Bramblewick sailor far from home and longing to be back : and from this emerged, again like the image of a photographic plate in a developing dish, the figure of Joe Stubbs, not a sailor in fact but a ship's cook. I had noticed him on one of our summer visits to Bramblewick soon after the war, a scraggy-looking chap, round-shouldered with a pale, weak, insignificant face. He wore a fisherman's guernsey and he had a small pleasure boat rather like the *Lydia*. I had not recognised him at first as a fellow-schoolmate. What attracted my attention was an enormous scar on the back of his neck reaching practically from ear to ear. It was only when a lady visitor I happened to meet had told me that she had been out on the Bay with him for a " trip " and that he had fascinated her with the story of how he had come by that scar, that my curiosity had been aroused. It was a knife wound. The story was that his ship had been sunk by a German raider in the Indian Ocean, and that after many days on a raft he and several shipmates had been cast on an island inhabited by cannibals. They had been captured, bound to trees, and one by one his mates had been slaughtered. Then his turn came. One of the savages prepared to slit his throat with a knife, but he had managed to wriggle free and the knife, instead of cutting his throat, cut the back of his neck, and at that very moment a party of bluejackets from a naval launch had come to his rescue. . . . The lady told me that she suspected it was a yarn, but he had told it in such a convincing and dramatic way that she at least half believed it. It was then I remembered Joe as a schoolboy, and his reputation as " the biggest liar in Bramblewick." He'd had a pale face then, and he was very unhealthy. In fact Mother said I must never sit near him at school if I could help it as she believed that like his father, a baker, he had consumption. He was one of the village lads I never had fights with and even the bullies left him alone although they mocked him when he tried to put over his astounding yarns. Joe had actually seen fairies in a pasture along the cliff where there were toad-stools ring. He knew there was a Father Christmas because he had seen him in a sledge drawn by reindeers. The most exciting adventures befell him (when he was by himself). He'd been caught by the tide, and saved himself by climbing the steepest part of Low Batts cliff. He'd been chased by a bull, and a mad dog with foaming mouth, and a tramp had once run after him with a knife and tried to murder him, and he was such a liar generally that if any boy doubted another's word he'd say, " Thoo's as big a liar as daft Joe Stubbs ! "

I had discovered the truth about Joe's scar. He was a ship's cook and although he had been at sea throughout the war no ship that he had sailed on had suffered from enemy action. It was true that his wound had been made by a knife, but he had received it during a dockside brawl at Marseilles. It seemed that he had bought a little pleasure boat the first summer after the war, but that he was going back to sea for the winter months. He had the reputation of being a very good cook and could more or less take his choice of berths in north country owned tramps. He always chose a ship bound on a voyage that would land him back in England not later than June and the visitor season. I did not give the game away to the lady visitor, and as I had found Joe himself rather diffident to approach I had thought no more about him.

The picture of Joe, or rather the series of pictures of him my mind invoked were extraordinarily vivid. I saw him as a boy, as a grown man. I had a picture of him as the lady visitor described him, resting on his oars while, with the same earnestness as he'd told us lads about his fairies and mad bulls, he regaled her with the dramatic details of his imaginary adventure. And I saw him too leaning over the rails of a ship at night, watching the phosphorescence and dreaming of Bramblewick Bay and his little boat and the visitors listening to his yarns ; and soon I had him conceived as the central figure in a story with a twist to it as ironic as any of Maupassant's or Chekhov's or Hardy's. There was nothing fantastic in regarding Joe's lying even from boyhood as the expression of an artistically creative gift. He was, at least for the purpose of my story, a born storyteller, lacking only the power to express this gift in writing. In a distant age Joe might have been a wandering minstrel in his own if he had been born " Up-Bank " instead of " Down," to a well-to-do sea captain like the father of Rachel and Jenny, instead of to a consumptive baker whose wife too was always ailing, he might have had health and a decent education and turned his gift to profitable and perhaps distinguished writing. But he'd only gone to the village school, and because of his delicate health had seen little enough of that. He was too delicate to join a ship as apprentice, as most of the village boys did on leaving school, so sailed as a cook's boy.

There was the start of my story, and the point to establish was that Joe's lying was artistic and not mere bragging. It was true that he was always the hero of the startling adventures he recounted. It was true that like most weaklings he longed to have attributed to him just those virtues of strength and bravery he so pitifully lacked. He was in fact a coward, as most persons of imagination are. But his lying had nothing, or little, to do with this. Joe lied, invented, dramatised for the sheer creative joy of it, and again for the purpose of my story, those dangers and strange happenings which are the lot of most seafaring men on their journeys upon the waters, storms, fires at sea, collisions, shipwrecks, adventures ashore in strange lands eluded him throughout his career as cook's boy, cook's mate and cook, for up to the end of the war all his service was on one ship which made a regular run from Cardiff to Monte Video. That fact (in my story) would not completely cramp his style as a teller of yarns, for he would hear plenty and his vivid imagination could twist and invent to make them authentically personal. But a sailor's greatest joy in yarn-telling is when he is ashore, at home or in the local pub, or wherever men gather together. Among the seafarers of Bramblewick his reputation as a liar persisted, there was always the risk of finding among his listeners some sailor who might challenge his facts, and it would not be until after the war when he had saved enough money to buy a pleasure boat that he found among the summer visitors (especially the ladies) an appreciative and uncritical audience. That boat and all that it implied would become his obsession. In autumn when the last of the visitors had gone, it would be hauled up into the Dock along with the other pleasure boats, turned keel up and covered with sail cloth like a piece of furniture in an unoccupied house. Bramblewick could have no interest for him now, and he'd cunningly accept a berth as cook in a ship that would have him home in time to clean and repaint his boat before the fine weather came. But even on these voyages nothing ever happened to him. All the yarns he told were either second-hand or pure invention, and while he remained a coward, he must have wished that it was otherwise : that provided he lived to tell the tale, at least one great adventure would come his way.

For once Joe is too clever in his choice of ships ! He signs on for a voyage to Cape Town, Durban and Mombasa and back. But at Cape Town the ship is unexpectedly chartered for Sydney, and Joe recovering from a mild shore spree wakes up in his bunk to discover that for one summer at least, his little boat will not be launched. The ship is old and slow. It is a long and little used track from South Africa across the Indian Ocean, but he has the bitter experience of seeing at least one passenger liner bound for home pass within hailing distance. Then comes the storm, a storm exceeding in violence anything he may have described to his summer audiences from imagination. He is terrified and fails even in his traditional duty as cook to keep the galley fire going and the hard-pressed hands supplied with hot drinks. The ship breaks her back, founders. Joe is picked up by the one surviving lifeboat, in command of a truly heroic second mate who, although badly hurt, navigates the boat with such skill that she weathers the climax of the storm itself. Not until then, with wind and sea abated, does Joe awake from what has been a coma of fear. He realises he has survived the storm and the foundering of the ship. And then he realises that provided they are picked up by a homeward-bound vessel, he may still get back to Bramblewick, and that this time at least he will have a real story to tell. When he learns from the second mate that their situation is still desperate, that they are hundreds of miles from the nearest land and well off the beaten steamer tracks, that their rations of food and water are very meagre, Joe seizes an oar and pulls like a madman. When the gallant mate dies Joe, the cook, takes command, and throughout twenty days of terrible privation inspires the rest to keep to their oars.

The tale of that voyage, the heroism of the cook become front-page news when the liner that picks the boat up eventually docks in London. The public has already forgotten that such voyages were commonplace during the war. The survivors (all except Joe) are interviewed and photographed. All agree that but for Joe, who kept them pulling (and pulled himself) they would have given in long before they were rescued. Joe is too ill to be interviewed, but there is a photo of him being carried on a stretcher to a waiting ambulance. He goes to hospital, and before the Bramblewick summer season starts he is home and his boat is painted and launched. But the story of the storm, the catastrophe, that epic voyage, is never told by the artist hero of it to his visitor ladies. For Joe has been stricken incurably dumb !

Once again I wrote at white heat, and I believed it was the best story I had ever written. Claire thought so too, and that it would be a pity to give it to the *Red*, for *Nash's* ought to jump at it. But the *Red* had been good to me, and while I half hoped he would turn it down I felt I must give the editor first chance. I got a shock when I called at Fleetway House, and was told by the reception clerk that the editor of the *Red* had resigned and had already left the office. I asked to see one of the sub-editors but was told that he was engaged and could not tell me when he could give me an appointment. Bad news travels quickly and in no place quicker than Fleet Street. I had scarcely turned from Ludgate Circus when I met a newspaperman I knew who told me that the Amalgamated Press (which had originally belonged to the now dead Lord Northcliffe) had been sold to a big trust, that many of its publications (including the *Green* and the *Yellow* " editions " of the *Red*) had been killed, and that the same thing was happening with certain other publishing houses. Men were being dismissed right and left, some who had been on the staffs of their papers or magazines for years. Newcomers were being pushed into their jobs. In some cases it looked as though the new owners were starting a ruthless economy, in others it was more like raving madness. But behind it all it seemed that a big financial gamble was going on. One famous publishing house had already changed ownership twice in a week. I did not at first realise the personal implications of what had happened, that my source of income for many years had suddenly dried up. I went on to call at the offices of the International Magazine Company (publishers of *Nash's*). I asked to see the editor, thinking by this time that my name would at least assure me of a short interview. I got a message to say that the editor was engaged, but that any contribution could be left at the office provided a stamped envelope accompanied it for possible return. I did leave it, but it came back to me within a week, and I did not in fact sell that story for many years when (in very dramatic circumstances) it was accepted by *Blackwood's* at half the rate my dead layer of golden eggs, the *Red*, would have paid for it.

It never rains but it pours ! I heard through my agent from the new editor of the *Red* that his office was over-stocked with stories and that as the *Green* and *Yellow* had been discontinued, it would be at least a year before he would be in the market again. My agent was hopeful as he always had been. He said that while I had lost a good market in the *Red*, there were plenty of other magazines, and if I kept on writing I should have no difficulty in landing one or several of them, but of course I must not expect them to offer me commissions. I did write several stories, but he could not sell one of them. I tried *John O' London's* to see if I could get my old job back. But they had got a famous scientist doing their nature articles now and there was no space for any of mine.

Then one day (it was late in January) the Skeapings announced that they had decided to go to Florence for the spring and perhaps for the summer, and that when they returned they would have to find a larger studio, as both of them intended to tackle big carvings. They suggested we might like to go with them, and Claire was very willing because it had been a gloomy rainy winter and she was longing for sunshine ; and there would be no point in staying on in St. John's Wood if Jack and Barbara were not coming back to it. We could either sub-let the house or surrender the lease and store or sell the furniture. I certainly did not want to live in St. John's Wood any longer ; neither did I wish to go to Florence. So Claire decided she would go with Jack and Barbara, and I decided to go to Bramblewick. There was no quarrel. We all parted good friends. But it was the end of our marriage.

Book Six

I

IN A BOOK called *Phantom Lobster* (the title was unfortunate as it made many people think it was either a ghost story or a thriller) I have told the tale of what happened when I went back to Bramblewick ; of how, disillusioned and at first rather sorry for myself, I lived in a once time fisherman's cottage in the same alley where my old friend Captain Bunny had lived ; of how, realising the futility of writing short stories which were neither works of art nor saleable to the popular magazines, I tried to sort out from the mass of my pre-war memories of Bramblewick and its people the theme and substance of a great novel, a great work of art. Of how in this task that needed all my powers of concentration and self-discipline, I was constantly frustrated by a desire to be out of doors, to be living in the present instead of thinking in the past, to be absorbing fresh impressions instead of regurgitating those I'd got, to indulge without restraint in the vice of sea-angling, and above all in the distracting company of my re-found friends, the Lunns—which led in the end to my chucking the book, and becoming an inshore fisherman.

It was a different Bramblewick to the one I had known as a boy. That was indeed dead. But it was also in February a different Bramblewick to the one I'd seen on my brief summer visits since the war. At least sixty per cent of the four hundred odd cottages which mostly had housed fishers or other seafarers had been bought by people in York and Leeds and other West Riding towns, either for their own use in the holidays or for letting. These like the hotels and " Up-Bank " boarding houses had been full in summer. Now they were closed. The streets and cobbled alleys I knew so well were deserted. The purely pleasure boats were hauled well out of the way of rough seas into the Dock. Yet two families of fishers and two cobles were still trying to win a livelihood from the sea. Old Luke Fosdyck, who'd been coxswain of the lifeboat when I was a boy, and Tindal his brother, who had been bowman, intended to keep at it so long as any one else did. Henry Lunn, who had emigrated to Bramblewick from a fishing village farther up the coast just within my memory, and had been regarded as a "foreigner" ever since, was still offering them a sturdy challenge. Luke and Tindal had their young ex-seaman nephew Tom to help them. Henry, whose pre-war partner had given up the fight and gone back to his native village, had been joined by his sons Marney and John, who'd also been seamen during the war.

Phantom Lobster was not fiction but a record of actual happenings. If it had an undertone of irony, of satire, that was because in retrospect I had looked at the things that had happened that way. All that I changed were the names of people and the places that were in it. But again the things that happened were not just the physical things, but the things that were going on in my mind. Whether I was a creative artist or not, I had inherited an uncomfortable measure of the emotions of one from Dad, and in the book I showed how these were directed, not into a work of art, but into the creation of something that should have been at least more useful. To that extent the chief "character" in *Phantom Lobster* was its narrator, and its theme the invention of a new kind of lobster pot, and how this intrinsically successful invention failed. But the real "character" of my tale, the real protagonist, was the North Sea, and the theme a deeper one than my puny bid to beat it.

It would have been impossible to tell this story without describing in some detail the village background, and the undying resentment of the Fosdycks against the Lunns, the Bramblewick native against all "foreigners." I had to describe my personal circumstances and what led me to make my first exciting experiments with the pot. Both families were still at their winter cod-fishing when I returned to Bramblewick. This, even in the old days, was a hazardous business. There was no real harbour. The Landing was merely a creek between two prominent scaurs reaching seawards, and with their ends marked with posts. At high water the scaurs were covered and the creek ceased to be. In rough weather the Landing was closed at all states of the tide. Winter fishing had always been a case of hit and run. Lines were shot but eyes were always on the weather. Let the wind veer a few points from north to the east and increase and the whole of the shallow Bay would be a welter of broken water, with rollers sweeping along the foot of Low Batts cliff and crashing on the scaur ends by the Landing. The fishers would hurry ashore, often abandoning their gear. The wheeled carriages would be rushed down from the Dock or the Slipway Foot, the cobles would be lightened of all movable gear, heaved on to the carriages and then hauled in turn up to the Dock and safety. But in the old days there had been no shortage of brawny men to help in this strenuous job. Now there were only the veteran Fosdycks, Henry Lunn and the three young men to do it, and perhaps the local policeman or postman if they chanced to be about. I hadn't waited to be asked to help in this daily job. And I hadn't expected thanks. But it wasn't long before the diffidence Henry Lunn had showed to me when I'd been at the laboratory, and fancying myself in my sports coat and flannel bags, completely melted and there started a big friendship, a comradeship between me and my once-time scholars of the village school, John and Marney Lunn. John, the elder brother, a bachelor, was rather dour and slow and gloomy, but a fine fellow. Marney had all of Jack Skeaping's vivacity and zest for life and doing things, and he was in a sense an artist. He was married and had a young baby, and he lived in a cottage perched on the north cliff not far from my boyhood home. That snug little cottage of Marney's became like a home to me.

From helping haul the cobles up I got to helping the Lunns gut their fish, and finally going to sea with them. But it was near the end of the cod season, and ashore they were feverishly completing the fleets of new lobster pots they intended to shoot at the first spell of settled weather. All their last year's pots had been smashed up in a gale. The earlier lobster fishing began the better the prices, but also the bigger the risk of loss. I helped to carry those brand new pots down to the launch coble one fine day early in March. There were ninety in all, the produce of a winter's work ashore and worth with their new manilla " tows " at least thirty pounds. The weather looked settled and we shot them close in along Low Batts cliff about a mile north of the Landing. No sooner had we come ashore than a fierce north-easter sprang up. We put back at once. By the time we reached the buoys of the first fleet a heavy sea was running. It had started to snow. It took our combined strength to haul the pots and stow them in the motor coble. Then we had to steam out across a tide rip and shoot them in deep water on soft ground where with luck they would survive the storm. But because of the bulk and weight of them we could only stow one fleet, and by the time this was shot the buoys of the others were hidden in broken water and we had to abandon them. The gale lasted a week. When it was over we found the deep water fleet but every pot was smashed. Of the other sixty pots and their gear we found no sign except the buoys which were washed ashore. John Lunn cursed gloomily at what had happened and predicted further catastrophe. Henry took it with philosophic calm, but Marney promptly set to making more pots and soon had his brother and father hot with lobster fever again. If for no other reason, they had to show the Fosdycks they were not beaten !

Lobstering had become the last hope of the Yorkshire inshore fisherman whose economic decline had started even before the war. The steam trawler, independent of weather, unlimited in its range and with well-organised facilities for the discharging, marketing and distribution of its catch, had beaten him hands down in round fish. But the lobsters were found mostly on rocky ground where trawling was impossible. There was no better way of catching them than in pots. The supply never exceeded the demand, and prices, especially at the start of the season, were high. Our first catch of eighty lobsters, for example, fetched ten pounds in the Whitby market. But against that was the loss of those ninety pots, and several spells of bad weather which, if they were not so disastrous, caused losses and damage, and more important, meant no catch. It was a chance remark of Henry Lunn's that started me thinking about this one day and wondering whether anything could be done about it. The pots which had been used by genera-tions of Yorkshire fishermen were quite different to those used in Devon and Cornwall, which were bee-hive shaped, woven with withies with a central vertical funnel, and very big. Ours consisted of an oblong slatted tray of wood, with three arches or bows of hazel fixed so that they formed the frame of a little house. This was braided over with twine and there were two horizontal funnels on opposite sides. Because it was buoyant it had to be ballasted with iron. Henry pointed out that the chief snag was the space it took up when they were shifting grounds in sudden changes of weather and that the same thing stopped them ever fishing certain rocky grounds many miles out from the coast. It wouldn't pay to make the trip carrying only thirty pots at a time. It was then I had my inspiration. Why not make a lobster pot of light steel instead of wood planks and hazel, shaped the same way, netted the same way, but designed so that when not in use the arches or bows would lie flat like a folding pram. It would not take a fraction of the space required by a rigid pot when stowed. Steel would be a hundred times as strong as wood. There would be no buoyancy to overcome so that ballast could be dispensed with. It would not be half the weight to haul. . . .

I described in *Phantom Lobster* how I made my first experimental model of a folding lobster pot out of an old parrot cage, a discarded baby carriage and an iron bedstead I salved from the midden across the green from my cottage. And I described what was going on in my mind while I was frenziedly sawing away at the old bedstead with a blunt and shrieking hack-saw in the middle of the night.

"I found an ever-growing satisfaction in my labour. The toughness of the metal increased my confidence in its ability to withstand the destructiveness of the sea. I could hear the faint roar of the smoothing surf whenever I was obliged to pause and rest my arm. There was a new and personal challenge in it, and as I laboured a revelation came to me. I was creating something which would put new life into the moribund inshore fishing industry, that might remove the blight of post-war unemployment from the young men of the coast and save their breed from extinction.

"Was there not something more noble in this than writing? Edison, Marconi, Ford had done a greater service to humanity than all the writers and artists of their age. It might be said that wireless telegraphy was a finer legacy to the civilised world than for example *The Last Supper*; or *The Fifth Symphony*, or *Hamlet*. And was there not after all a close analogy between an invention and a work of art? Both in their inception welled up or burst from the sub-conscious mind by that process called inspiration. Both were the products of observations taken and stored in. . . .

"I was not a writer. I was an inventor, an engineer, perhaps a captain of industry. The thought brought joy and a new energy to my aching muscles. . . ."

Seeing that I had never handled a hack-saw or a breast drill in my life before, that I knew next to nothing of mechanics, my invention was really clever, and in spite of the fact that folding lobster pots had been in use on the Kentish coast for sixty years I did not know this, and my design was original : although it was also true that any blacksmith or garage apprentice, given a Yorkshire lobster pot and told to design one in mild steel that would fold up, should not have had much difficulty in doing so. A bigger difficulty was to fit the net and the funnels so that these would collapse when the frame did, and it took Marney Lunn many nights of patient experiment to solve a problem that would have entirely beaten me. In the end it was mechanically perfect. Even old Henry was satisfied when we proved that it fished as well if not better than the hazel pot. You could shut and open it in three seconds. It was virtually indestructible. To prove this we moored it to the lowest marking post on the Landing scaurs and left it there throughout an equinoctial gale. The net was scrubbed but the frame was scarcely scratched. An old-fashioned pot would not have stood up to a single tide of such treatment.

I saw in it (and all the Lunns were in enthusiastic agreement with me) not only the solution of a local problem but a fortune for myself and my friends, although the only thing they wanted was one of the big motor vessels that were now fishing out of Whitby. Along the coasts of England alone hundreds of thousands of lobster pots were lost every year, and in addition to this there was the loss in fishing time : the hold-ups in fishing while new gear was being made. The production cost of mine if mass produced (and that of course was the idea) would not have been more than a wooden pot. It was simple, like the kink in the hairpin, but revolutionary. In time even the most conservative of fishermen would have to abandon his old pots in favour of the new, just as he had been obliged to give up sail and oars for an engine. But I did not wish to make a fortune out of *him*. God forbid ! I saw the whole thing as a big co-operative business, a British Inshore Fisheries Corporation, manufacturing the pots, selling or even leasing them to the fishermen on easy terms, buying his catch at a fair price, distributing it, retailing it in the company's own multiple shops, and if the increased catches it made possible resulted in over-production, starting a cannery. Everything would be profit-sharing and run on model lines, and it all sounded grand. The Ministry of Agriculture and Fisheries sent experts to see the pot in use. Their report was favourable and I was given a grant to have a fleet of " shut-up " pots made to carry out experiments on deep water grounds, where it proved completely successful.

But the Ministry's interest in the pot was technical and neither social nor commercial. I was to discover that to get the thing going even in a small way, I should need a capital of at least £2000 to secure full patent rights, and buy the necessary machine tools. I sought this in London. . . .

" London abounded with millionaires and philanthropists and wealthy business concerns to whom that sum would be insignificant. One had only to stand at Hyde Park Corner and count the number of Rolls-Royces that passed in five minutes, to realise it was no fairy tale that the streets of London were paved with gold. One had only to look at the palatial blocks of offices and flats and shops they were building and the new tube stations and picture palaces and popular cafes, and the six-wheel buses with their soft seats : one had only to watch the shopping crowds in Oxford Street and Regent Street and Kensington : or in the City to see the silk-hatted bank messengers hurrying along with black bags full of money to realise that London was a city of stupendous wealth. It was as though one could hear through all the roar of the traffic, the stir and tinkle of a perpetual stream of money, welling out of the banks, spilling over the counters of the shops, and into the tills of restaurants and pubs and theatres and picture palaces : into the bags of bus conductors, and the pockets of taxi-men, into the automatic tube machines, and cigarette machines, telephones and public lavatories ; and flowing back to the banks where you'd see men in dark clothes with pale bored faces shovelling heaps of coin with copper shovels and moving thick wads of pound notes about with no more concern than if they had been packets of cheap stationery. Yet the great electric cables buried under London's roadways were not more adequately insulated from leakage than the arteries and veins of this stream of cash. . . .

" Every morning I set out with my folded lobster pot in its canvas case, in my search for capital. . I had high-placed friends who, although not wealthy themselves, gave me social introductions to people who were. I was granted interviews with millionaires, titled philanthropists of international renown. All seemed deeply impressed by the pot and by the fact that it had been praised by the Government, all expressed sympathy with the inshore fisherman and saw how the pot would help him, but none offered to invest money in it. I showed it to the founder and managing director of one of London's biggest departmental stores, to the director of a famous shipping line, to a director of the Bank of England itself, without result. . . .

" It was the height of the great speculative boom which preceded the start of the great world depression. Every day the advertising columns of the press were full of the prospectuses of new companies. The public was invited to invest (and presumably was investing) in concerns for the exploitation of gramophones and gramophone records, of radio apparatus, colour photography, cinemas, patent mattresses and medicines, of greyhound racing tracks and dirt tracks, of automatic photography machines. Yet I could not persuade any one to take the responsibility of inviting the public to invest in an invention that was to save men's lives and a fine industry from languishing to extinction. It seemed to me that the whole country had gone pleasure mad : that people could think of nothing but listening to the gramophone or the radio, or going to the pictures or watching tame dogs chase an electric hare, or men falling off motor cycles, or having themselves photographed in six different positions for a shilling the lot."

But this was the approaching climax or rather anti-climax of my experience and also my tale. For the greater part of three years I had lived at Bramblewick fishing with the Lunns, not lobstering only but summer salmoning and autumn and winter lineing. In all that time I had not given a thought to writing. But now and again the old film fever had seized me, for there was a great pictorial beauty in the old village, and in the scaurs and the cliffs, when there were no visitors or char-a-bancs about. Despite that so many of the cottages had been bought by "foreigners" for holiday or letting, their outside character had not changed, and wandering through the twisting alleys at night with the gas lamps lit and throwing queer shadows on the cobbled pavements I'd think of all the films I'd seen showing rural or even English fishing villages as their background and there was not one to compare with Bramblewick from a photographic point of view. The scaurs and the panorama of coast either to High Batts or Low Batts were just as exciting, especially in winter storms. You'd see huge snow clouds, with the sun lighting the tops of them and grey walls of hail or snow reaching from their almost black bellies down to the sea beyond Low Batts point, advancing south and finally obliterating the point and then the Bay itself and finally High Batts : then with the squall passed there'd be a gleam of blue to the north and the sun would light up the snow on Low Batts top and travel down the cliff and spread an intense light on the huge waves rolling into its foot, and I could imagine how wonderful this would look to a townsman if it could be successfully conveyed to the screen even in monochrome. But this alone would never be enough. It was simply documentary, and while I was photographically thrilled by the sight of the cobles being launched or hauled up or crashing through the surf at the Landing mouth, or some incident while fishing, or just the sight of Henry Lunn holding the tiller and, shielding his eyes to search for a buoy in the dazzle of sunlit sea, I'd remember what I'd thought from the first about documentaries and my fever would subside.

Phantom Lobster was not my first book about Bramblewick however. In *Love in the Sun* I told how, having met Dain, we left Bramblewick, and made our first home out of a derelict army hut on the shore of a cove in Cornwall. How we made furniture out of driftwood that washed up in our cove and grew our own vegetables, and built a boat and were very happy, for in time we had a baby too : and how before we'd even made our roof water-tight I started to write the story of the Fosdycks and the Lunns : the Fosdycks sticking to their pulling and sailing coble and their old ways, dour and hard and never forgiving the Lunns for coming to take the bread out of Bramblewick folk's mouth by fishing in *their* Bay ; the Lunns, equally tough physically yet softer of heart, modern and go-ahead, joining the quarrel against their natural instincts and will, yet unable at times to disguise their satisfaction in the triumphs their motor coble scored for them over their rivals. And both families bound by common necessity to help each other in the hauling and launching of the cobles, and all their hates and resentments completely but only temporarily sunk when it came to a lifeboat rescue or one of their own families being imperilled by their common enemy the sea. Dain too had known the warmth and fascination of the Lunn family circle. I'd had no great faith in this book being a financial success. It was not the great novel I had wanted to write in the early days of my return to Bramblewick. As we had next to no money and I had many debts, it might have seemed wiser if I'd tried writing short stories again. I wrote it just because I had to write it and because Dain felt the same thing too, that it didn't matter whether it made money or not, and her faith and enthusiasm meant everything to me in doing the job.

Looking objectively at the books I have written I can see how they are like that nursery toy which consists of a series of boxes fitting inside each other, and with this book, as it were, now holding the lot. I did not fashion them like that deliberately. It just happened. I did not mention my patent lobster pot in my first book, which I called *Three Fevers*. It was written in the first person, but that was because I had to do it in the simplest way and instinctively I knew this was right. I had to convey *reality* to make the reader feel that he was actually on the spot, seeing and feeling what I had seen and felt. Yet the " I " of *Three Fevers* had no part in the tale beyond that, whereas in the final scene of *Phantom Lobster* where I had to disclose to the assembled Lunn family the failure of my invention, I described how from their calm and kindly acceptance of a bitter disappointment I had my first inspiration " to write a book about them and the Fosdycks, and their conflict with the sea, without frills, without any attempt at ' art ' or cleverness, making it real, making it live so that it would be a record that in my time such men existed."

Phantom Lobster was the box that held *Three Fevers*, but *Three Fevers* was also to hold *Foreigners*, which was a close-up of my boyhood at Bramblewick within the time space of one year. *Love in the Sun* fitted over the lot, but later I was to squeeze in a " sequel " to *Three Fevers*; *Sally Lunn*, wherein I resolved the age-long quarrel between the Fosdycks and the Lunns in Romeo and Juliet manner without the tragic ending. Were these books true or were they fiction ? That question was asked by many reviewers as each one was published. One reviewer called *Three Fevers* journalism, good journalism he admitted, but journalism all the same, and he said it as though this was an accusation. But although I had been careful to point out in a foreword that *Phantom Lobster* was a true tale (I even gave the latitude and longitude of my admittedly disguised village of Bramblewick) most reviewers reviewed it as a novel. The answer is that they were all written about real people living in real places and with things happening to these people as they happened in real life. But these people and places and happenings were as *I* had seen them, and in a way, chewed them over in my mind, and as I was not a " reporter " responsible to an editor and a public for a strictly accurate record of facts it did not worry me if I changed or invented so long as I was faithful to the main truth of the book itself, the main idea, the thing that made me write it.

The main idea of *Love in the Sun* was to give a picture of a man and girl escaping from the turmoil and complexities of the post-war world to a life which despite the somewhat sophisticated profession of its " hero " was essentially primitive and Edenesque. I did not in this case write a foreword to say whether it was true or partly true or completely fictitious. Actually it was autobiographical. But in writing it I had to do what Barbara Hepworth did with her eyeless, featherless, marble doves. I had to select from the experiences of three years the significant form and ruthlessly eliminate everything (no matter how intrinsically important) that did not belong to the master design. I had to preserve balance and this occasionally at the expense of literal truth. And the biggest problem of all was in the ending of it where a shadow fell upon our happiness in the shape of a wealthy major planning to buy our home over our heads and turn us out. This happened to be partly true. He had offered our landlord three hundred pounds for the hut and the land and cove that went with it, and we had only a short period in which to exercise our option to buy. *Phantom Lobster* had been published then and although it had received a good press it had been a financial flop. But I wrote *Love in the Sun* long after we had returned to Yorkshire and the film of *Three Fevers* had been made. I was regarding our Cornish adventure in perspective. The news about the major had not been so tragic. We had by then got our second baby. We had heard that the Lunns had left Bramblewick and were fishing in a bigger boat from Whitby. We had very reluctantly come to the decision that although our hut had been ideal for the two of us and even for one baby, it was not suitable for two babies and certainly impossible for the really large family we hoped to have. We had decided to quit, and even if we'd had no money we would not have bought the place. But I thought of how all the desert island stories I had ever read from *Robinson Crusoe* and the *Swiss Family Robinson* to the *Blue Lagoon* had been spoilt for me by the coming of the rescue ship or party, and I didn't want to spoil my book with such an anti-climax. Actually it was then I sold my story of Joe, the artist sea-cook, to *Blackwood's*. And so in the book I exercised what I think was a legitimate poet's licence and translated this into the sale of the film rights of *Three Fevers*, which in reality happened a year later, and the reader should have put down the book with the feeling that the flowers would still go on blooming in our garden by the sea. But the price I got for the film rights was exactly three hundred pounds. That too was the exact price of the piece of land near the moors above Bramblewick (and on the very stream which runs into the Mill Dam) we were to buy for the building of our second home, and with the self-same money. Fiction should never seem stranger than truth, so I increased the sum to a thousand pounds. And I thought ironically that perhaps the two multi-millionaires who spent nearly forty thousand pounds on making the film might read the book, and note the error and send me the balance as conscience money. But of course they never did !

2

WE WERE living at Whitby when out of the blue I got my first exciting letter about the film. Accommodation was scarce, and we had been obliged to take an ugly modern villa about a mile and a half from the town and close to the cemetery. The Fosdycks had at last been obliged to give up fishing. Tindal, in helping heave the coble on to its wheels, had strained his heart. Luke could not carry on with only Tom. Besides young Tom had put an end to the feud so far as his generation was concerned by falling in love with and marrying one of the Lunn girls. The whole Lunn family, Tom now included, had " flitted " to Whitby, and were living close to the harbour and were partners in a mule, a boat considerably bigger than the coble and completely decked. It was of a type that had been used at Whitby long before the war, and was equipped with a very primitive internal combustion engine. It had been superseded among the progressive Whitby men by the keeler, a broad-beamed, deep-keeled and much larger vessel, powered with a Diesel engine, and a wheel-house and cabin accommodation for the crew. The Lunns' mule indeed had been laid up for several years and was scarcely seaworthy. But their last season at Bramble-wick had been their worst on record, they had not enough capital to think of a keeler, so the old *Faith* had been patched up, and her bottom tarred, the engine had been overhauled, and as there was no longer a landing Bar to limit fishing activities, they were doing well. I had made several trips with them but my practical fishing days were over of course.

We did not like the place we were living in. Bramblewick itself offered no attractions now that the Lunns had gone. But we had found what we felt was a perfect site for our new and permanent home, once we got enough money to build it. It was a " parcel " of rough farm land and copse high up on the very stream which runs into the Mill Dam where I'd poached the Squire's trout when a boy, and measured forty-two acres in all. One of its boundaries was the open moor, and there was a short track across this to the main road to Whitby with a frequent bus service. And close to the stream and with a spring above it was a solitary farm building, divided into stables and cowshed, with its roof broken in but its stone walls still erect and substantial. It had originally been part of the Squire's estate which had been broken up and sold on his death. The man who had bought it was old and as his own farm was three miles away, it was too far for him to manage and he had offered us the whole lot, building and land, for three hundred and fifty pounds freehold, and he had come down to three hundred pounds on our paying him a deposit of thirty pounds. Our idea was to use the main walls of the building as they were and increase their height to make a second storey. The site was just ideal for it was below the level of the wind-swept moor, yet it had a clear view of the moors to the south. To the east there was a lovely aspect down the thickly-wooded valley of the beck into Fylingdale with its level mosaic of fields reaching to the cliff edge, and beyond this, framed by the slopes of the valley in the near foreground, a wide enough segment of the bay to give us the sunrise and the moonrise out of the sea, even in winter.

We were perhaps too far from the sea, and we were going to miss our boats, and many other of the attractions and distractions of our abandoned Eden, but there was a path running alongside the beck through a narrow rocky gorge which shortly opened out on to an almost level rabbit-cropped sward fringed with oaks and alders. Here the beck had been divided by a mass of rocks, and we saw how we could create a barrier here and a pool four yards wide and reaching about twenty yards up stream. There were small trout in the beck and remembering how the trout in the Mill Dam fattened in a season, I thought that this place, which Dain had already christened The Island, would go a long way to make up for our cove. I could make a little boat too for the children and a sandpit, and there was a stunted oak with a long level branch that would be perfect for a swing.

We had discussed the plans for our new home with Will Cornforth[1] who, son of the late Squire's estate carpenter, had just started on his meteoric career as a builder and contractor with his headquarters and sawmill an old Whitby shipyard which the Government had reopened during the war for building concrete barges and then abandoned. He was still in his twenties, had had

[1] Now Major-commanding an R.E. Construction Co. in the Middle East.

no education except the local school and an apprenticeship to a local builder, but he had an amazing ability in all practical branches of building, was full of enthusiasm and go, and had already landed the contract for Whitby's big new housing estate in the face of county as well as local competition. He knew our place well for his father had often done repairs to the building. He was as enthusiastic as we were and offered to do the job at the lowest possible price. He agreed about our keeping the original walls so that it wouldn't clash with the farm houses in the neighbourhood, but of course we wanted modern metal-frame windows with long horizontal panes so as to make the best of the sunshine and the views. Dain insisted on a straight staircase with low steps because of the children, and it was almost as exciting building our dream house on paper, contriving where the nursery and the bathroom and the kitchen and larder and living-room and bedrooms should fit in to and upon the shell of the old barn as it had been making our Cornish hut into a home. But it was still on paper, and still a dream when the letter came. Our hopes for buying the site and building the house were founded exclusively on *Foreigners*, still unpublished, and remembering what had happened to *Phantom Lobster*, they were not very strong.

The letter was not an offer. It was from the managing director of British National Films, and as there is no need now for novelist's licence, I give it in full :

" Dear Sir,
                    re : Three Fevers.
We have read this book and believe that it contains distinct filmic possibilities—provided that it is treated something on the lines of *Man of Aran*—but we should like to know from you whether conditions to-day in any part of Northumberland or Durham are approximately as they are described in your book.

We should also like to know if you are ever in Town, or if you are likely to be in Town in the near future, in order that we might have a chat on the subject generally.
                    Yours faithfully,
          FOR BRITISH NATIONAL FILMS LTD.
                              JOHN CORFIELD,
                              Managing Director."

The name John Corfield was last in the list of three directors appearing on the heading of the letter. First was Lady Yule, next Arthur Rank, D.L., J.P. I had never heard of British National Films before, nor had I heard of Lady Yule or Arthur Rank or John Corfield. Had I known at my first and decisive interview with John Corfield that Lady Yule was the widow of Sir David Yule the banker and financier and had been left a fortune of several million pounds, that Arthur Rank was a son of Joseph Rank the millionaire Wesleyan flour king and was himself worth millions, it is possible that I would not have so readily accepted John Corfield's offer of three hundred pounds for the world film rights of *Three Fevers*. But I don't know. The sum (the exact price of our land) was significant enough to be an act of Providence. And anyway it was only an advance on a royalty of five per cent on the nett profits of the film, which I felt would be prodigious.

The whole thing generally seemed so like a dream come true, that I believe that if Corfield had offered me ten guineas I would have accepted. For everything seemed so wonderfully right. Corfield was nothing like any film man I had ever met. (Indeed it was his first adventure into films.) When I informed him that *Three Fevers* was set not in Northumberland or Durham, but in Yorkshire, that the village of Bramblewick was not only as quaint and unspoilt as I had shown it in the book but that from a filming point of view it was probably unique in the whole world, not only as regards its cottages and streets but in its superb coast scenery, I thought I had rarely seen a man look so pleased. He was short, middle-aged, with a pale and pleasant face and he wore large horn-rimmed glasses. He beamed and rubbed his hands together when I told him that Henry Lunn and Marney and the Fosdycks were all real persons, and that although they had now given up fishing at Bramblewick, the Lunns were only six miles away. They still owned their small motor coble, and there were plenty of sailing cobles available. It would be quite easy for the purpose of the film to re-create the " fishing " situation there exactly as I described it. The lifeboat also had been taken away but there were several on the coast and the Institution would be only too glad to help because of the publicity and their collecting boxes. He seemed so pleased that I went on to tell him how it had been my ambition for years

to make a film such as this and to give him my ideas about the
British documentary and he didn't seem taken aback when I said
that *Man of Aran* was just *not* the one to model this upon. The
scenery and the photography were grand, but in his attempt to
give a picture of a primitive community struggling for existence
on a barren island Flaherty had made his characters behave like
those in a Wagnerian opera. There was no story. No suspense.
You didn't convey the character of people by their looks but by
their actions. There was action in *Man of Aran*, but apart from the
shark sequence it was to me meaningless.

I heard later that Mr. Corfield had taken a personal dislike
to me from the first few moments of our interview, but he
certainly did not show it then. He pointed out quite mildly that
Man of Aran had made a great deal of money and had been
acclaimed the best film of the year in America, where they were
supposed to know something about films. But I said, what I still
feel to be true, that it had scored by its photography and setting
and by being so completely different from anything Hollywood
had ever produced, and that as a work of art it was not a patch
on Flaherty's first and really magnificent *Nanook of the North*. We
could get scenery effects every bit as good as *Aran*. but the main
thing should be the people and the story. . . . It was just then
that we were joined by another gentleman. It was the company's
film director, Norman Walker. He too was completely unlike
any film director I had ever met or heard of. He was about my
own age with a smooth pink face, wore glasses and had the most
charming manners. He asked me to call him by his Christian name
and he called me by mine. My liking grew as he showed that he
shared my views about *Man of Aran* and the British documentary
in general, and that his conception of *Three Fevers* as a film was
practically the same as my own. Certainly we should get into it as
much natural beauty as possible, village streets, quaint houses, the
sea and boats and especially storm effects. But the story, the
human characterisation was the main thing. As he saw it the
theme of the book was the feud between two families of fishers,
one standing for the old ways the other for the new, and
how the quarrel was forgotten when, as I had got it in the
book, the Lunn brothers were caught in a storm and all joined
in the rescue. But of course we must make some concessions

to popular taste in films. In the book I had my hero already married and with a baby. It wouldn't be out of keeping with the character of the book if, as well as the families uniting in a sea rescue, there was a Romeo and Juliet romance between a Lunn and a Fosdyck.

It should have been clear to me by the way they both talked that the company had already decided to buy the book. I had reason to believe later that if I had stuck out for £2000 I should have got it. But when they told me that the company had been formed with an idealistic as well as a commercial objective : that it was out to raise the quality of British films, to fight the baneful effect of Hollywood : that they intended to spare no expense in making their first film in every way exceptional, I just felt I was among understanding friends, and that one of the greatest ambitions of my life was near achievement. When I had agreed about the price we continued our discussion. We were agreed that it would be hopeless trying to get the real people to act in the story. They (and I felt pretty certain the Lunns would be agreeable) would do the dangerous and professional parts like the coble getting into the Landing in rough weather, the lifeboat launch, but we needed professional actors and actresses wherever they had to talk and face the camera. I was thrilled when Norman Walker suggested that the actor most suited to play the part of Henry Lunn was Sam Livesey, for I had seen him with Tallulah Bankhead, in an American play called *They Knew What They Wanted*, and I'd thought him very fine indeed. For Marney he suggested Duggie Fairbanks, Jun., who was then working in English studios, and again I was thrilled only I didn't know whether his accent might not be against him. But these were only tentative suggestions, he explained. They must select the cast very carefully. The first thing to do was to have the shooting script prepared. This would have to be done by a professional script writer. But Norman himself must come up to the coast for a few days to take a look round. He was banking on my co-operation in the actual making of the film. Perhaps I would act as technical adviser, for above everything he wanted this film to be free of the silly mistakes that occurred in Hollywood film versions of English life. He would look to me too as a sort of liaison officer with the fishermen. I had the courage to suggest to this proposal (which again delighted me) that I should receive something for it, and I had a suspicion that Mr. Corfield looked rather displeased, but he said the company would pay me six pounds a week while my engagement lasted. If I'd known that this was considerably less than what was paid to the production's carpenter I might have protested, but again I don't know. I was riding on a rainbow, and a few minutes' later after we had fixed the time for our next appointment, I was in the nearest post office writing a telegram to Dain :

Three Fevers ! Three Hundred Pounds ! Three Cheers !

3

IT WOULD take an entire book in itself to describe in physical and psychological detail the making of that film which in due course was to be shown to the public under the title of *Turn of the Tide*, with a brief acknowledgment that it was " based on the novel of *Three Fevers*," with my own name added. All the wisest people agree a novelist should have nothing to do with the filming of his own novel. It has been said that if an author does sell the film rights of a book, he should have the transaction carried out entirely through his agent and bank manager, never under any circumstances meet any person connected with the filming company, and make up his mind from the start that the script writer, the producers, the directors will do precisely the opposite to what he himself would do if he wished to express his story, its plot, characters and atmosphere through the medium of talking moving pictures. Also that if he has any feelings about his story (and it is certain that between some authors and their books the relationship approaches that of mother and child) he will strongly resist any temptation he may have to see the film when it is made. The nervous shock might finish him.

But my case was different. My desire to make films had always been at least as strong as my desire to make books. I knew that the film was an entirely different medium from writing. I did not imagine that *Three Fevers* as I had written it *was* a film story or that it possessed anything but—to use Mr. Corfield's peculiar phrase—filmic possibilities. I wasn't highbrow either, in my conception of it as a film. I thought of it first as entertainment, something the public would pay money to see and enjoy. But I also felt that film people were inclined to under-estimate the intelligence of their audiences and that they could and would like what was artistically good if it was done the right way. Would an average suburban London audience be able to spot the difference between a live cod and a " props " one. Perhaps they wouldn't, but if in our film we did get an actual shot of lines being hauled at sea and a real live fish coming into the coble, even if it was gaffed by the real Henry Lunn " standing-in " for Mr. Sam Livesey (who would speak the accompanying line of dialogue to the action) I believed that subconsciously at any rate the audience would respond to the authentic.

Curiously, it was on this very point that Norman and I had our first breeze. There was a sequence in which we had to show Henry Lunn pacing along the shore of the Bay after a night's storm in which his two sons have been caught in their small boat while salmon fishing. Henry finds a dead salmon among the weed at the sea's edge. In it is a gaff with his own initials marked on it. It is dramatic evidence that the boat had capsized. It so happened that soon after the production started we got a north-easterly gale exactly like the one I had described in the book. There were intervals of bright sun, and the tide was exactly right. But this sequence did not come until the end of the book and I had not realised that in outdoor filming you take what you can get according to the weather and never mind the script. It was a silent shot, no dialogue. We found a perfect location, with scaurs in the foreground of a patch of sand and lines of scaurs reaching beyond this with monster rollers crashing on them and raising a salt-water mist through which High Batts cliff was just visible. By taking the shot against the sun the effect would be that of moonlight (a well-known trick of the amateur photographer) with the figure of Henry in black silhouette against the glitter of broken water. Dressed in yellow oilskins with sou'-wester, wearing sea-boots and with very little make-up, Sam Livesey was the living image of Henry Lunn. He was " shot " first moving along the scaurs with the rough sea beyond him and the wind ballooning his oilskins, then stopping and looking seawards and then to the mass of weed the storm had cast on to the patch of sand. And it was not until then that Norman remembered the fish which was to be the climax of action. He asked me if I had got one. I had not. Could I get one, quickly while the tide and light were favourable for the shot ? I had to tell him that the fish had to be a salmon, that salmon fishing did not start until May and it would be quite impossible to get one locally. He said then it would have to be some other sort of fish. I had to tell him that as the gale had been raging two days, even at Whitby fishing had been suspended, and that I was certain we could not get even a cod. Norman did not swear but I could tell he was angry and that he blamed me, but I did not feel I was to blame seeing that he had not told me he was going to make this particular sequence. I suggested the only thing to do was to defer the shot of the actual discovery of the fish. He went very pink, and said that would be quite impossible as we'd already got the other part of the sequence and the whole must match in lighting or the effect would be absurd. He would have to use a " props " fish.

Where that " props " fish came from I never knew, but it was produced in less than twenty minutes by the company's " Props " man. It was indiarubber, a sort of balloon which at that time were on sale at most toy shops. It was certainly shaped like a fish, and it had a fin and a tail, but I thought that nothing I had ever seen in a Hollywood film could match it in absurdity, and I couldn't help telling Norman what I thought. But he ignored me and the gaff was hooked in one of its fins (so as not to puncture the air-filled body) and it was placed among the seaweed, and Norman gave the word " action " to Sam, who walked along the beach again, fixed his gaze on the weed, lifted the fish up, and registered the appropriate facial emotions as he looked at it, although the fish itself (supposed to represent a 16 lb. salmon) was floating almost horizontally in the gale and would have ascended like the balloon it was if Sam had left go.

We saw what are technically called the " flashes " of that sequence in a Whitby cinema a few days later, the negative having been sent express to London and a print made. The photography was superb and so was Sam's acting. Seeing it I felt that Norman and Sam and the cameraman had all got the very spirit of that dramatic episode (which in *Three Fevers* I had partly based on a real occurrence). But even Norman had to admit when the fish itself was shown that the stupidest person could not mistake it for anything but a rubber balloon. He had to decide to re-take the whole sequence. But he never did. It was decided later to cut the whole of this episode from the film and give it quite another ending.

I did not care a hang whether the film was " faithful " to the book or not. It was at my own suggestion that we took one completely benign character, old Isaac Fosdyck, uncle to the brothers, and built him up into a sort of villain and gave him a grand-

K

daughter Ruth, and invented a love affair between her and the
bashful John Lunn, an affair which was to be resisted by the other
members of both families, but especially by Isaac. It was my
suggestion that we should not model the film parts of Luke and
Tindal Fosdyck on the physical appearance of the real fishermen,
for quite apart from Tindal being ill and Luke retired I knew that
no money on earth would persuade them to do " owt so daft " as
take part in the production. I think I would have had some difficulty
in persuading the Lunns to take part but for an extraordinary thing
that happened the day I did my deal with John Corfield. On that
very morning the motor mule *Faith* with all the Lunns and Tom
Fosdyck on board was just passing out of Whitby harbour when
she encountered a moderately heavy but not breaking sea which
caused her to pitch and to drop. It would have been nothing to a
keeler or even to a mule if she had been really seaworthy. But the
Faith was not seaworthy. Her back was broken, her planks smashed
in and in less than two minutes she had foundered. The crew were
rescued by a keeler that happened to be near and none of my
friends was physically the worse for their dipping. But although
they had been doing well they had not been able to save enough
money between them all for a keeler. They had only their old
motor coble, and although I had to promise them that they would
not be called upon to do anything that would make folks, especially
Bramblewick folks, laugh at them, they were quite agreeable to
accepting Norman's offer of five pounds a week each with an extra
five pounds a week for the use of the coble. Two old Whitby
salmoners, Tom Dryden and Henry Welham (ex-coxswain of
Whitby lifeboat) were even more willing to become the Lunns'
protagonists at five pounds a week and another five for the use
of their coble which otherwise would have been laid up until May,
when salmoning started. But as all of them wanted to get home
to Whitby every night and the winter bus service was awkward,
Norman had to agree that both parties should be transported the
double journey by taxi. Not the least fantastic of the many fantastic
sights of Bramblewick during the next few weeks was the daily
one of five fishermen dressed for fishing, coming down and going
up Bramblewick Bank in a Rolls-Royce the Company had hired
from a Whitby garage, some of them occasionally smoking cigars
on the homeward journey.

Wilfred Lawson (I must have seen him scores of times in the plays of Bernard Shaw, and later he was to play Dolittle in the film version of *Pygmalion*) was cast for the part of Luke Fosdyck, and George Moore Marriott (famous as a character actor before his comedy association with Will Hay and Graham Moffatt) had Tindal Fosdyck's part. It did not bother me that George modelled his part on the psuedo Tindal, Tom Dryden. But it did bother me that Wilfred Lawson, having borrowed from Henry Welham a genuine guernsey, and patched pants and sea-boots and equipped himself with a cunning imitation of old Welham's moustache, should model his part on the pseudo Luke, for Luke himself was bearded and grim and a powerful hater while the ex-coxswain of Whitby lifeboat was one of the gentlest of men. Norman had been unable to get Duggie Fairbanks, Jun., for the part of Marney. It had been given to John Garrick, who was better known for his singing than for his acting. Marney was the male " star " of the book, but now that we had got our love interest the balance inevitably swayed towards John, and for this part Norman had booked a comparative new-comer to the screen, Nial McGinnis, later to make a hit in the stage play *Mice and Men*. Beautiful Joan Maude, daughter of Nancy Price, was cast for Marney's wife. That famous old character actor J. Fisher-White had the built-up part of old Isaac Fosdyck. The company's publicity agent had run a press campaign that a boy film actor was wanted for the part of Steve, and as he had given my name with the story I had been inundated by letters from parents enclosing photos of their young sons, in the hope and belief that a new Freddie Bartholomew was in the making. But Norman had already engaged an experienced boy actor called Derek Blomfield ; and for the part of Ruth Fosdyck he believed he had got a real potential star, Geraldine Fitzgerald, from the Abbey Theatre, Dublin.

I had many arguments with Norman Walker, many disagreements, and one final row in which I told him that I wished to God I had never written a book called *Three Fevers*, or even heard of British National Films Limited. But this happened at a later stage of the production, and as I liked Norman, and Norman liked me, we became greater friends still later on. I had indeed many just grounds for exasperation and anger. So indeed had Norman for there were times when it must have seemed to him that everything in earth and heaven was conspiring against him to make the film a flop. To start with, the contracts of the artistes were muddled so that most of them arrived at Bramblewick and came on to the pay-roll before the technical apparatus, camera and sound was ready for action. This apparatus by the way was hired, and at a staggering price. Next, when artistes and machine were ready we were still waiting for the shooting script. The gale had come then, with a terrific sea, better than anything we could have prayed for, for there was plenty of sunlight too. To start shooting without a script was an extremely risky and almost unheard of thing to do, but Norman could not stand the sight of the unemployed apparatus and artistes, and he picked on certain scenes in the book, which he was confident could not possibly be excluded from the script, and he asked me to adapt the dialogue for them. One scene was between John and Marney Lunn at the Slipway top, the morning of a fishing trip. The weather is calm but threatening, and before father comes it is uncertain whether the cobles will be launched or not. John, always pessimistic, looks at the weather and growls :

" Sea's growing ! "

The gay-hearted and ever venturesome Marney laughs derisively and says :

" Gan on. It's smooth as a mill-pond. It'll be hours before it's breaking across the bar."

The light was just right for the taking of this scene, but it happened that the tide was high (whereas in the book it was low). It was also exceedingly rough, and to my alarm Norman decided that the brothers should meet by the hauled-up coble in the Dock and that the view should include the Slipway top up which the biggest of the seas were running. I pointed out that this would make Marney's remark that the sea was like a mill-pond quite absurd, but Norman took no notice, and when Garrick and McGinnis had rehearsed the scene several times and the camera and sound men were satisfied, the clapper man stood before the camera and mike and did his act, and then Norman gave the order for action. At the precise moment that Garrick said " it's as smooth as a mill-pond " a big wave rushed up the Slipway and broke against the old coastguard wall sending up a cascade of spray almost as high as the cottage roof ; and like the shot we took of Sam and the indiarubber fish, the photography and acting were to prove excellent. The breaking sea of course made a retake necessary. I was really sorry for Norman. There was another scene, a part of the same sequence where old Isaac Fosdyck had to encounter a coastguard in the street. The coastguard says :

" Now, Isaac. What do you make of the weather ? "

And old Isaacs croaks back with a sinister leer :

" Why, we're in for a blow. A hard 'un too."

The local coastguard was persuaded to play this simple-seeming action in person. He was a hard-bitten ex-naval petty officer with a double row of ribbons and a great reputation for personal bravery, but when he came to make his speech he stammered like a child reciting a poem at a concert, and the scene had to be rehearsed a dozen times before Norman was satisfied. By that time the sun was obscured and we had to wait. The wait however destroyed the coastguard's confidence again, and he dried up immediately the camera started rolling over. The sun was hidden again. Half-way through the next take, when the coastguard delivered himself of the complete speech and Isaac began to answer, a shout came from the sound-recording van to say that there was a breakdown. When the fault was mended the sun had gone, but so had the coastguard who, like the weaving girl at Bamako, had had enough.

All this must have been very trying to Norman's nerves. But it was equally trying to mine. Norman was chiefly worried about his expensive and idle cast. I was worried that while we were taking shots like these and spending so much time over them the most fickle actor of all, the weather, was putting on its very best act—a full north-easterly gale, with superb cloud effects, alternating squalls and brilliant sunny intervals, and that we were missing a chance that might not come again for weeks. I knew of a dozen places along the coast where with the sea as it was we could get wave effects at least equal to those in *Man of Aran*. But in answer to my suggestions that we should take the camera along the cliffs or shore Norman, with some justification, threw back at me my criticism of Flaherty. He reminded me of my own contention that the scenery should be the background for the human action, and the story. He gathered that at present the sea was too rough for the cobles to go out. It was, and, to use a Yorkshire saying, I'd have only been showing my ignorance, if I'd asked the fishermen for confirmation. But it was Henry Lunn himself who broached the subject indirectly.

Henry was not happy. None of the fishermen had had anything to do since they'd started their daily Rolls-Royce riding between Whitby and Bramblewick. The Lunns in particular disliked inactivity. But above everything they disliked being what they called "made game of," folks laughing at them being in the limelight. They were in the limelight all right. The company's publicity man had done his work well. Normally at this time of the year Bramblewick would have been a deserted village. Now, apart from the people connected with the film, crowds were coming over daily from Whitby and Scarborough to watch the production. The "story" had also gone out that we were to put a real steamer on the rocks and stage a dramatic lifeboat rescue. In addition to sightseers there were press photographers and reporters by the dozen. The Lunns were "interviewed" and Sam and McGinnis and Garrick photographed, standing with their "doubles," and I knew that Henry in particular was hating it, and especially so because it was all happening within sight of his old enemy Luke Fosdyck. Tindal was still confined to his cottage. But Luke, dressed in his best Sunday breeches and guernsey, and wearing his lifeboat coxswain cheesecutter (although he was retired and the lifeboat station closed), was never absent from the scene of activities. He stood aloof from the crowd, leaning against a coble or a cottage wall, grim as ever, but with a look of supercilious contempt in his eyes, which Henry felt were just mocking him personally.

It was while we were waiting to get a re-take of the scene between Marney and John, that Henry expressed his emotions to me. He pointed to Luke who was standing by the now empty lifeboat house.

"Look at him, standing there as though he owned the spot, and laughing at us inside him. I tell you I'm getting fed up with this job. Why the devil don't they get on with it. They no sooner get one thing right than summat else gans wrong. It strikes me that none of them knows their job. It's nowt but a lot of daftness. What do they want us chaps for, that's what I'd like to know. I don't like taking brass for doing nowt."

I told Henry that we were waiting for the written play of the film before starting in real earnest, but that what the company really wanted him and John and Marney for were the fishing bits, and particularly for the coble coming into the Landing in a rough sea, and that of course it was no good while the sea was as rough as it was at present. To my surprise he answered angrily :

" Who said it was too rough ? What the devil do they know about it ? Have they been talking to old Luke ? Of course it would be too rough for *him* ! We've come into the Landing many a time when it's been just as rough as this, or at least almost, aye, and gone out too when there's been lobster pots to save. If they want us to gan out in our coble we'll do it. It'll be a damned sight better than sitting here on our backsides doing nowt."

The motor coble had steamed over from Whitby (with the sailing coble of the psuedo Fosdycks in tow) before the gale had come and both were in the Dock. I had an awful feeling that Henry was making his suggestion from pique and bravado and I felt extremely diffident about telling Norman. Not for all the films in the world would I have Henry and his sons risk their lives. But Henry took that responsibility from me by approaching Norman direct, and as the tide was at half ebb it was decided to make the shot. I was frightened. I knew that it *was* too rough. At the same time I was excited, for I felt that if the coble could make the passage out and in between the Landing posts we should have something better than anything in *Man of Aran*. Norman was excited too. Again there was no dialogue, and he said that if the sequence did not come into the script then we should re-write the script so that it did. We'd begin with the actual launching of the coble—take a " pan," follow it from the Dock down the Slipway to the beach and then to the sea. The camera was moved to the right position. And by a miracle we started getting clear interludes of sun, in one of which the action started : and for a time I forgot my fear, for this was a business I had taken part in so many times myself, and I'd thought so often how exciting it would look on the screen.

We got the " pan " of the launch to the dry Slipway bottom. I admired Norman's coolness in that he had the operation repeated three times and three " takes " made, before proceeding to the actual business of the Landing passage. The scaurs on each side of it were now bare. The camera was taken down the easterly one, which was more prominent and reached farther seawards. We hadn't noticed the gale itself in the Dock. Here we were fully exposed to it, and my heart quailed as I watched the huge rollers that were breaking from post to post of the Landing entrance not more than a hundred yards away from where in the lee of the scaurs the water was relatively smooth. In spite of what Henry said I knew that no threatened lobster pots would have persuaded him to tackle that passage. Not that any extra bribe from the company would have persuaded him to do it. It was pride that was obsessing him, a determination to show his enemy Luke that the Lunns were not going to be beaten and laughed at even when it came to making a film !

The coble was wheeled into the water, then launched from its carriage. The three Lunns got in, but Sam and McGinnis and Garrick, all clad in oilskins identical with those of the Lunn family, stood by on the east scaur. The camera had been taken out to the tip of this scaur but the wind was so strong that big stones had to be placed against the tripod legs. John started the engine. Marney began to pole the coble seawards with the boat-hook and as soon as the water was deep enough Henry shipped the long rudder which in a coble acts partly as a keel. He shipped the tiller, and then after a steady look seawards he waved his hand to indicate to us on shore that he was ready. I could not have felt more frightened if I had been in the coble myself. Even in a lifeboat with ten men to pull, it would have been a risky job. The coble's freeboard at the bows was not more than three feet. Amidships it was less than a foot The waves breaking across the Landing were rising fifteen feet and more at times. And all that the coble had to drive through them was a six horse-power paraffin engine at least twenty years old. Norman of course did not appreciate the risk. The camera-man was ready. Norman shouted through his megaphone to Henry to carry on, and I believe that if it had been any one else but Henry in command I'd have shouted at Norman " For God's sake tell them no. It isn't worth it." But I knew Henry.

The coble gathered way. It was still in the lee of the west scaur and in smooth water, but the rollers were breaking scarcely twenty yards ahead. It rose to the wash of the first. The second was higher but it had broken and flattened, and the coble rode it comfortably. But by the time the next one came the last lee of the scaur was astern and its lip was just turning as the coble struck it. A broader beamed boat could not have withstood its impact. It would have stopped it dead, and swung it round broadside to the following wave. But the bows of that grand little coble were like a knife. It sliced through the very crest of the wave and bounded on to meet the next which, slower at breaking, it swung over like a hurdle, disappearing entirely from our sight in the trough for seconds. . . . But the coble appeared, this time rising almost on end and seeming to poise on the very crest of the following wave before disappearing from sight again. And by the time it appeared again it was seawards of the marking post of the scaur. The rollers were no longer breaking. The passage had been made, and Henry carefully choosing his time, swung the coble round and began the equally hazardous passage back. I did not watch that passage. I turned my back and waited, either for a shout of terror from the rest of the men who were on the scaur or for what I fervently prayed for, a shout from Henry himself that all was well. What I did hear, and it seemed hours afterwards, was a shout from Marney, the real Marney :

"Eh, did you get it all right ? Or do you want us to do it again ? "

We saw the rushes of that scene and the one of the launching in the Whitby cinema a few nights after. The launching scene (we saw the pick of the three " takes ") was superb. It gave one first a complete sense of security, the coble safe ashore in the sheltered Dock : then Sam and McGinnis and Garrick moving to it, removing the chocks from the wheels, adjusting the launching gear. At this point the real Lunns took charge (by Norman's orders they had taken care never to show their faces) and the coble was moved to the Slipway top, and you saw it moving slowly down past the coastguard wall, until suddenly it cleared and you got a view of the Bay as far as High Batts cliff with the sun shining between the storm clouds and throwing coble and men into silhouette against the glitter of the sea. It was superbly photographed. But more important, it gave one a mounting sense of conflict and impending danger. And this was only a prelude to the double landing passage. Even in the security of the cinema, and with the knowledge that the venture terminated safely, it made my heart thump with fear. The outward passage looked even more hazardous than it had seemed in reality, and the inward passage, on which I had turned my back, simply made one gasp. It looked miraculous, for the coble

disappeared entirely from sight between two monstrous waves :
then it appeared poised on the breaking crest of one of them, running with it like a Hawaiian surf-rider, then sinking again and rising
more slowly to the next pursuing wave, which did not break but
appeared to push the coble gently past the marking post into the
security of the Landing. Never had I felt such an intense admiration
and pride for my old friends. When the coble was seen moving
into shallow water, and the " Lunns " got out and faced the camera
and you saw that it was Sam and McGinnis and Garrick (who had
adroitly changed places with the real Lunns at an appropriate
moment) I momentarily forgot that this was a film story and felt
furious that any one should be led to give three landlubbers credit
for such a performance. But I had a quick reaction, and I slapped
Norman on his back and gave him my wildest congratulations, and
he slapped me back and congratulated me, and we both congratulated Henry and Marney and John, who of course had been invited
to see the " rushes," and I felt indeed that nothing could stop our
film being one of the greatest films of all time. I felt triumphant,
and I shook old Henry's rough hand again and gave him a special
word of thanks. But all he said was :

" Why it was nowt. Only I wished you'd invited awd Luke
Fosdyck to see it. It would have made him grin t'other side of
his face."

But unfortunately the crossing of the bar was only one small
section of the film. The rest was the story and the story had to be
played not by the Lunns but by professional artistes. I had accepted
that. I was dead against it becoming a documentary, and when at
last the shooting script arrived I was prepared for some shocks, but
not for a mortal blow to every ideal I held about films, fishermen,
humanity, art and above all truth. In the names of the characters
(apart from the new one of Ruth) it certainly was faithful to the
book. But in what these characters said and did it bore resemblance
neither to the book nor the fishermen themselves, nor in fact to any
other community of decent human beings. The writer had converted the whole thing into a melodrama with a sugary love affair
settling the almost bloodthirsty feud between Fosdycks and Lunns,
a feud in which the fishermen snarled and fought with each other,
cut each other's buoys adrift, cheated and double-crossed like

gangsters. In the book I had, and I think with success, tried to show the nobility of both my families. That the Fosdycks' only fault was their hardness and fierce jealousy of the newcomers : that these very traits were in a way a reflection of the hardness and cruelty of the sea. But they had a high code of honour and of essential decency. Feuds, hate, jealousies were all sunk when it came, for example, to a lifeboat rescue, or any fellow-fisherman being in peril. This was the very spirit of the book. There was none of it in the script and, apart from anything else, I knew that if the film was faithful to the script then it would be a deadly insult to every fisherman I knew. That I'd never dare look one of them in the face again.

But fortunately Norman shared my consternation at the script. Corfield had arrived, together with the art director and several other gentlemen. We had a conference at the Victoria Hotel which lasted until the early hours of the morning, in the course of which the script was read aloud word by word, and that reading itself lasted more than two hours. Whether the other gentlemen were friends of the script writer I did not know but they were all against me in my heated criticism of it, and so I felt was Mr. Corfield, who accused me of being highbrow. But Norman backed me up. He said he simply would not have the confidence to direct the film to this script. That in any case it would have to be cut by at least an hour's running time. And to Mr. Corfield's protest that it might take another fortnight to prepare a new script, that meanwhile all the artistes and technicians and apparatus would be idle, that the unit must move to the studio in less than three weeks as floor space had already been booked, Norman made the daring rejoinder that he would take the responsibility of seeing that all the unit was at work and not wasting the company's money, that he and I would make a shooting script of the outdoor stuff together.

The gale dropped. The wind backed to west and we had three days of rain in which Norman and I worked at the script with very little break for sleep. I was not happy in that collaboration (for which incidentally I received no extra pay). If Norman had backed me up against the others I did not feel that he had grasped the spirit of the book. I was soon so confused I could hardly grasp it myself, for when I started to write lines for Luke Fosdyck I started to think of benign Henry Welham and Wilfred Lawson's " interpretation "

of him. The character of Marney was completely changed now
that John had become the star, and again I was seeing him as John
Garrick, whereas McGinnis was more like the real Marney and
utterly different from the John of the book or reality. Old Isaac
was easier because he had an entirely different role to play, and
somehow or other although he'd only played in that one futile
scene with the coastguard, Fisher-White had brought the character
to life. Sam too was so good that I could make him say anything
the real Henry would say. But I was lost when it came to Ruth.
Geraldine Fitzgerald was lovely to look at, and it was obvious later
that she was a fine actress. But she was Irish, with a bewitching
Irish brogue, and I could not see her as a Fosdyck, although she and
McGinnis looked capable of acting some effective love scenes
together, and we invented one where she discovers John in a copse,
cutting hazels for lobster pots. She steals on him unawares, and,
girlishly, throws some pebbles at him and then greets him :

" Now, John. What are you doing ? "

And he answers with fatuous sarcasm :

" I'm cutting rhubarb for your grandad's dinner ! "

But I could almost hear Geraldine saying "phwat" for "what,"
and whenever I gave her a longer speech the temptation to use the
phrases of J. M. Synge in the *Playboy of the Western World* and the
Tinker's Wedding were almost irresistible.

I had the horrible conviction before we started shooting again
from this ill-constructed and uncompleted script that the whole film
was destined to be as big a failure as my first African travel and
natural history film had been. What made me feel worse about it
was that here we had the money, the best technical apparatus and
technicians, a very fine cast of artistes and a priceless opportunity
for producing a masterpiece which was being thrown away. That
conviction deepened with the making of the next scene, part of the
sequence taken from the opening chapters of the book, where the
cobles are cod-fishing in winter. A storm comes on. The Fosdycks
rush for shore, but the Lunns hold on to the last moment, and have
to make their hair-raising entry into the Landing. We had built
this up by showing the anxiety of Marney's wife and Ruth. There
would be an interior scene for this later, but the outdoor action was
Ruth and Amy (admirably portrayed by Joan Maud) rushing up
the cliff and anxiously watching the coble come in. It happened

however that the wind was now due west and blowing almost at
gale force from the land. This meant that the sea or at least the Bay
was, to use Marney's phrase when the wave broke as high as the
cottage, "smooth as a mill-pond," but in spite of my protests,
Norman posed Geraldine and Joan on the edge of the cliff, and
filmed them as they stood with the west wind blowing out their
hair, and great white clouds sweeping the sky above them and
throwing shadows on the sea, while they registered first terror and
then relief as the coble was supposed to make that breath-taking
passage we had already filmed. I saw the rushes of this shot. Again
the photography was superb, the pictorial composition perfect, and
both girls were faultless in their acting. Yet there in the foreground
was the sea that was supposed to be crashing on the scaur ends and
across the Landing, smooth indeed as a mill-pond.

But it was not until we moved to Elstree that I plumbed the
depths of despair and had my final bust with Norman and British
National Films. My first impressions however were favourable.
The art director, whose name unfortunately I forget, had spent
several days at Bramblewick, making sketches of the streets and
alleys, and actually taking plaster casts of the paving and cobble
stones and cottage walls and pantiles. There was one famous scene
in the village, beloved by Dad and many other artists, where two
alleys converged into another, with a quaint street lamp fixed with
a bracket on the dividing cottage. It was called the Openings and
the director had built an exact full-scale replica of this scene complete with lamp and even the stepping-stones to the cottages. It was
uncanny. Looking at it from the camera's point of view I could
have scarcely told it from the original. Yet moving slightly to one
side I could see how the whole thing consisted of plywood and
plaster, shored up with wood battens. He had also built the forepart
of the Bramblewick lifeboat house, and the forepart of the lifeboat
itself, the side of the Lunns' coble (but only that), the interior of
Marney's cottage, and also old Isaac's (this entirely imaginery), the
Lunns' warehouse, inside and out, the latter with a blackcloth
panorama of Bramblewick Bay stretched behind it.

I felt almost hopeful again. I felt that if any one could take all
this care, and spend so much money on our film, they must be
certain they were going to make a success of it. Norman at any

rate seemed quite confident still. He told me that I could not
imagine what a relief it was to him to get working in the studio
and to be independent of the weather and light. As soon as the final
script was ready he'd soon make up for lost time. The script was
not ready of course, and soon I was introduced to John Monk, who
had been with Flaherty on the production of *Man of Aran*, and I
was told that he was to work on the script with my collaboration,
only that before we started work we should all meet in conference,
with Norman, the cutter, the art director, Mr. Corfield, and several
other gentlemen he had asked for expert opinion. There were so
many of those conferences, so much was said about so many points
that I could not remember what happened at any particular one,
but I formed the impression that in the opinion of the experts who
had been called in *Three Fevers* was a most unsuitable novel for
making into a film at all, that the company would have done better
if it had left it alone, but that as it was committed, the only thing
to do was to make the best of a bad job. The sea bits already taken
(they'd been shown to the experts) were good in their way and
they would certainly get praise from the highbrow critics, but
they'd leave the renters cold. The only hope was to concentrate
on the love interest. There was no doubt that in Geraldine and
McGinnis we had got a pair of potential stars with a big box-office
appeal. The next thing was to pitch up the drama. The only
exciting thing in the book from a box-office angle was the steamer
going aground and being salvaged by the lifeboat. If the company
was willing to go to the expense of putting a real steamer ashore
that might make a high spot. And a good end too. Have the girl
on the steamer perhaps. Anyway get the families together and end
in wedding bells. But the whole thing needed pepping up.

I found a friend and sympathiser in John Monk. He had read
Three Fevers, liked it and genuinely regretted the drastic surgery
he had to perform. We cut the end as I had it in the book which
disposed of course of the indiarubber salmon. Corfield had declared
that the directors were prepared to have a real steamer put ashore
for the salvage sequence, but as that was not to be " studio " we
left it and concentrated on the beginning   John suggested that as
the thing that caused the Fosdycks' greatest resentment against the
Lunns was the engine the " newcomers " had installed in their
coble, we ought to build that up, " dramatise " the engine itself,

show it arriving at the village station and being brought in a crate down to the Dock, the villagers trying to guess what new " daftness " the Lunns were up to. John had read *Foreigners* too, and *Phantom Lobster*, and he admitted he'd got the idea for this scene from *Phantom Lobster* from my description of how we shipped our first fleet of patent lobster pots into the coble without the Fosdycks seeing them. I didn't mind. I didn't object to our lifting some of the atmosphere and action in *Foreigners*, and starting the script with a fight between Steve Lunn and the village boys who rag him and call him " foreigner," thus establishing not only the " feud " but Steve himself.

Norman approved of all this, and was so pleased with one or two scenes that he decided to get on with the shooting without waiting for the completed script. But he'd no sooner started than he found he wanted certain alterations in the dialogue. He'd come into our office and suggest extra shots, with appropriate lines. As we ourselves did not know yet how the whole story was going to work out, this was almost as bad as working without a script at all, but we appreciated Norman's worries and helped him all we could. I was not happy however. I walked into the studio on one occasion. The scene was an exterior of the Fosdycks' warehouse, Luke and Tindal baiting lines and arguing with old Isaac, and Lawson and Moore Marriott and Fisher-White were rehearsing it. The dialogue was all right as I had written it, but for once the lines I'd given Lawson were genuine " Fosdyck " and Lawson was completely Henry Welham, mild and good-natured. In addition he and poor George were making an unholy mess of the baiting job. I told Norman what I thought was wrong and he more or less told me to mind my own business. I reminded him that my job was that of technical adviser, that he himself had asked me to point out any silly mistakes and that I thought Wilfred Lawson was turning the part of Luke Fosdyck into that of a Sunday school superintendent. Later we apologised to each other and shook hands on it, but my belief in the final success of the film had suffered another reverse and we had another disagreement very soon after. This concerned the " engine " sequence. A brand new 20 h.p. marine petrol engine had been hired from Thorneycrofts, who had works on the Thames. It was powerful enough to drive a large cabin cruiser, and its weight was at least a quarter of a ton. A fisherman or yachtsman would know that the cost of it would be in the neighbourhood of £250 and that it would be a most unlikely thing for a poor fisherman to invest in. I did not mind this. What made my heart sink was that the props man had produced a light grocer's hand-cart with spidery wheels, and that Norman proposed to use this to carry the engine down Bramblewick's cobbled alleys to the Dock. The sheer weight of that engine (and it would have taken six strong men to lift it on to the cart) would have caused those wheels to fold up as though they had been made of match stalks. It was more absurd than the indiarubber salmon, and I told Norman so. He retorted that he had no intention of putting the actual engine on the cart, only the crate, and that the crate, with the engine in it, would be opened at the coble (or rather the section of coble the arts director had had built). I said empty or not, the audience would know that the crate was supposed to contain an engine. They could not help but see the absurdity of it. The thing should be brought down with a horse and cart or failing that a motor lorry. If we were going to pass this sort of thing then I had no doubt that when we came to towing the steamer off the rocks we'd do it with a fishing line. Norman went very pink and he said he was directing the film and that he would do it exactly as he wished to do it : to which I answered " Of course. Carry on. But why not engage Harry Tate instead of Sam Livesey for the part of Henry Lunn. With that engine and that cart and the indiarubber salmon he'd bring any house down ! "

Of course I apologised, and Norman apologised to me and said he quite sympathised with my feelings as an author and that he would get a heavier hand-cart, and that he would in future get me to vet every set and rehearsal before it was shot, although I must be very careful not to make any criticisms about the artistes, at least not in their hearing as they were all very touchy. But I felt it was wisest not to go into the studio again, and John Monk and I worked hard at the script and got it finished all except the end and I think then I could have calmly resigned myself to the death of my hopes and gone quietly back to Yorkshire, if Norman had not suddenly decided to have my opinion on all the studio stuff he had taken to date, to help him pick out the best of the " takes." We went into a stuffy little studio cinema for this ordeal. I wouldn't have minded if he'd shown some of the shots we'd taken at Bramblewick too. I could have watched the launching of the coble and the passage through the Landing a score of times and not been bored But these were all " studio." They were not connected in any way and for each one there were at least three " takes " and of some as many as six. I could get no sense of illusion from them. Each one began with the " clapper " man holding a board with the number of the scene and calling this for the sound track. However real the set looked, I could not disabuse my mind of the plywood and timber battens behind it I certainly could not tell Norman which " take " I liked best, for even if I could have seen and heard them in a normal way I did not know whether to " measure " them by the script, or the book, or the real people. I was dazed when it was over : and then as it was after shooting hours Norman insisted in going into the director's office, and reading through the whole script aloud, stage directions too, with his watch on the table to get the exact timing. He did not make any attempt to read the dialogue properly. He used exactly the same voice as he did for the stage directions, and he might just have been reading through a list of words

Poor Norman ! He didn't know that every word he read of that script was like another breath blowing up an already over extended balloon. He seemed surprised but not at all angry at the explosion, at what I said and the vehemence with which I said it : and was not angry when I told him I wished to give up my job with British National Films then and there and get back to Yorkshire.

Later I wrote to him a letter of apology and I got a nice one back from him saying that he quite understood my attitude, which was that of any novelist seeing his own book cut to pieces, and he'd been surprised I had stuck it so long. He thanked me for my expert technical help, and especially for my work on the script that would go a long way to making the film the success they all thought it was going to be, and he hoped we should all meet for the first night and have a celebration.

I thought again when I read this letter, poor Norman ! for by that time I had resigned myself to the film being a complete flop. Indeed I found a consolation in the certainty that it would be. It would never be shown in our local cinema. I would be spared the humiliation and vexation of defeat, and the Lunns would not be able to blame me for " having folks laugh at them." The company came back to Bramblewick to complete the outdoor shots and especially the salvage sequence. I met Norman several times. We were friendly, but I didn't want to be involved in the business again and Norman showed no desire to have me back in the production. I was glad to observe however that during a short repetition of our winter gale, he had the cameraman out along the cliffs getting *Man of Aran* shots at the very places I had indicated to him. A large steamer was duly brought into the Bay one day (when the sea was dead calm) and carefully allow to ground on a patch of safe sand, and dry out on the spring ebb. This, strange to say, was closely faithful to the incident as I had recorded it in *Three Fevers*. A steamer had gone aground one day in thick weather. The lifeboat had gone out (it was before the Bramblewick station had been closed) and the skipper had accepted the lifeboat's offer of service in taking out an anchor to deep water so that when the tide flowed the steamer would be able to haul herself off. It had been difficult to explain this operation in the book. I had felt it was impossible to explain it on the film so that an ordinary audience would grasp it. Besides the real drama of the incident was psychological. For a salvage tug comes on the scene. The master of the tug plays on the young steamer master's nerves, warns him not to rely on the lifeboat but to engage the tug. I had suggested to Norman that it would be far better not to worry about the technicalities. To show the steamer in distress, then resolve the action into a race between the lifeboat and the tug, the one that gets to the steamer first being the one to win the salvage prize. But Norman had rejected this suggestion. He thought he must do it just as I had got it in the book. And he was prepared even to make an artificial fog to make it look completely authentic. Actually this was not necessary, for by a miracle no sooner had the steamer grounded than a real fog descended on the coast exactly as I had described it, and Norman told me that the " rushes " had exceeded his fondest expectations. But I saw neither the real thing nor the rushes. I wanted to forget. I had found an anodyne to my disillusionment in the building of our new home.

4

OUR HOME was built. We moved into it. We made gardens, paths, a road across the moor. We cleared the Island. We made a dam across that very stream which, a mile and a half nearer to the sea, runs into the Mill Dam where I had poached the Squire's trout. But I daren't make it deep as the Mill Dam because of the children, and although there were trout in it our first-born refused to let me catch them as they looked so pretty. We made a swing, and a miniature lido by the dam, and I started building a small boat. *Foreigners* had had a good press but it hadn't made much money. We'd had to borrow from a Building Society for the building of the house but I'd started writing *Love in the Sun*, and Dain was going to have another baby. I didn't hear anything more from Norman but I read in the papers that British National had begun their next production under the direction of Norman Walker, and I thought, well, the directors have still got faith in him despite the failure of *Three Fevers*, which they must have decided to scrap.

Then towards the end of October, we received a printed invitation from British National Films Ltd. to attend the first trade presentation of their first production, *Turn of the Tide*, adapted from the famous novel of a Yorkshire fishing village, *Three Fevers*. It was signed John Corfield, and whether this was accidental or not, it arrived the very day the trade show was to be held, so that there was no chance of our seeing it. There was no reference to it in the papers next day, or the next or the next, which was Saturday. This I took as a clear sign the press critics hadn't thought much of it, and that when they did give it a notice it would be down at the foot of their column under the latest Hollywood successes, and they'd not say anything very nice, which would at least convince Corfield and Co. that I'd been right about it. To get our Sunday papers I had to cycle down to the village of Hawsker three miles away. I went that Sunday for our usual *Sunday Times* and *Observer*, and I opened the *Observer* before I left the shop. Miss Lejeune was doing the film reviews of that journal then as now, and I had always regarded her views as perhaps the soundest among British film critics, which is to say that they agreed with my own. If any one would give *Turn of the Tide* a slating she would.

I gasped when I read it. Her column was headed ENGLAND AT LAST, and *Turn of the Tide* was at its head. It began,

> This picture is a surprise packet. With no justification at all most of us had expected unimportant little items trying without much imagination or many resources to put England on the screen. What has emerged is a sane salty story beautifully presented, of the Yorkshire fishermen and the little things done against wind and weather that makes their lives dramatic.
>
> The film was adapted from the novel *Three Fevers*, but the title has suffered a sea change. The author, who has lived among the fishermen, knows their idiom, and has himself adapted the story for the cinema and is largely responsible for the spare pawky dialogue. An author as every one knows is not always an asset to a film company, but in this case he has behaved himself with genius.

There was a full column of description and praise, for the direction, the photography, the acting, and it ended,

> *Turn of the Tide* would be easy to overpraise and spoil. But as one of the most persistent advocates of films of England and English life I should be ungracious if when at last we got one I didn't say thank you. I am grateful for the story, and the setting and the north country words that sound so rich and earthy.

I turned to the *Sunday Times*. Sydney Carroll, who had once been a theatre critic and notorious for his forthright denunciations of any play or actor he did not like, would certainly not be deluded the same way Miss Lejeune has so obviously been. But again I gasped. His column was headed BRITISH SEASCAPE. *Turn of the Tide* was his top film and he said, in the course of a column,

> To do it justice one cannot avoid superlatives. . . . Exquisite results are achieved with the camera. There are seascapes of sweeping beauty ; the grandeur of the coastline, the moods of

the ocean calm or angry, the forerunning signs of storm, sullen banking clouds, eerie gusts lifting up from the craggy shore, shivering through the reeds on the cliff top, swirling in the narrow cobbled streets of the village. . . .

This picture is a perfect example of the combination of technical skill, artistic direction, and ideal casting.

I bought a copy of every Sunday paper and cycled home across the moor, wondering all the time if I was suddenly going to wake up and find the whole thing was a dream. Dain, who'd shared my hopes and then my disillusion and finally my resigned pessimism about the film, was equally dazed now when I read Miss Lejeune's notice to her. We looked at the other papers. Every one had starred it and given it big space. We read bits out.

The Empire News said,

Here is something from a British studio that rings true and will have a large slice of interest for all fans who do not crave the glitter stuff in their films all the time. . . . Miles in front of other films of similar type. You'll love it. . . . Director Norman Walker has my applause. . . .

The Sunday Graphic said,

. . . a thoroughly entertaining picture with a laugh here, a tear there, and your attention riveted on the screen so that you don't mind the chap in the seat behind breathing down your neck. . . . A gem of a film. Love scenes handled with beautiful restraint and naturalness by Geraldine Fitzgerald and Niall McGinnis. Magnificent acting. A fine picture.

The Sunday Chronicle said,

Man of Aran was showered with praise for its "real drama." *Turn of the Tide* is not so artistically pretentious but I found it infinitely more dramatic. More human too. The characterisation is delightful, the photography in line with the general excellence.

If I had a big drum I'd bang on it until the whole twenty million of you went along to see it.

The Sunday Pictorial said,

Nothing more delightful has been seen in pictures. *Turn of the Tide* will make friends of film-goers wherever it is shown.

The News of the World said,

Congratulations to British National Films for their courage, to the actors and actresses for their acting, and a well-earned bouquet to spare for Norman Walker. . . . Definitely a film to see.

In the whole batch of Sunday newspapers there was not one that did not give the film the highest possible praise. None except the *Observer* signalled the author of the book for mention. Many indeed did not mention the book at all. But nearly all paid special tribute to Norman. And all next week the daily papers followed up the chant of enthusiasm : *The Times*, the *Telegraph*, the *Morning Post*, the *Daily Mail; News Chronicle; Herald; Sketch; Mirror*, the great and lesser provincials and then the highbrow and middle and lowbrow weeklies. And Alistaire Cooke, then doing the films for the B.B.C., paid it another tribute over the air, and he mentioned my name as well as Norman's, but we happened to miss the broadcast.

I was stunned. I just could not believe that the dialogue, so much of which I had written—but written without any feeling or inspiration—that the scenes I had seen shot or rehearsed in the studio, and seen in the form of " rushes " on that dreadful occasion with Norman, that the salvage sequence, the idiotic shot of Geraldine and Joan Maude in the westerly gale, could have been welded together into a coherent film that could take all these hard-boiled critics in and excite them to such adulation. Was it bally-hoo ? Had it all been put over by that very clever publicity man ? Had Corfield with his millionaire directors behind him given all the critics champagne before they saw the film ? Would the public be taken in the same way ? Of course there were the genuine out-of-door shots, the landing passage, the storm scenes, especially if those I had suggested to Norman had come out well. One or two of the critics mentioned the salvage business too, but it was clear that this was not the main thing that had impressed them. But then all these critics were land-lubbers. None of them would have noted that the wind in the Geraldine and Joan shot was west, that when Lawson and Marriott were baiting lines they were doing it the wrong way round. What would Whitby think of *Turn of the Tide*? What would Henry Lunn think of it?

A few days later the manager of The Empire Cinema, Whitby, rang me up and told me in a most respectful voice that he had succeeded in booking *Turn of the Tide* for an immediate showing. He had done this because he had been inundated by requests from his patrons, although it had meant him cancelling a famous American film. He had booked it for a week and he would regard it as an honour if I and my wife would attend the first performance for which he had already reserved me tickets. He had by the way sent tickets to all my fishermen friends who had been engaged on the film and they insisted on sitting in the ninepennys as usual. I'd know of course of the marvellous reception the film had received from the national press. It looked like being a record smasher, and he would like to take the opportunity for giving me his personal congratulations and thanks. It was going to be a good advertisement for Whitby if nothing else.

I am sure that no dramatist going to the first night of his first play could have done so with such mixed emotions as I did to the first Whitby presentation of *Turn of the Tide*. If the film was as good as the critics made out, then there'd be small satisfaction to me in it so far as my pride was concerned, for at least three-quarters of it had been made without my co-operation, and at least a quarter of it in direct opposition to how I thought it should have been made. But then if it was a success, it would mean that a considerable sum of money would come to us out of my 5 per cent royalty on nett receipts, and in addition to that it should have a good publicity on my published and future books. There was that other aspect that troubled me greatly. It had gone down with the critics. It might go down with the general public. But what about the fishermen? Would they think I had guyed them? What should I feel like if I

made a packet of money out of the film and it meant the end of my
friendship with Henry and Marney and John Lunn ? They'd seen
some of the action we had taken at Bramblewick. But they hadn't
seen the love scenes between McGinnis and Geraldine, and I'd only
seen a few of these myself and God knew what Norman had done
with some of the scenes I'd written with John Monk under the
general advice of the experts to pep the business up. I still didn't
know how the film ended.

The first house was at half-past six. We couldn't afford a taxi
but there was a bus leaving our road-end just before six which would
land us at Whitby with a few minutes to spare. Dain felt excited
and gay but I didn't. I got more and more nervy as the bus drew
nearer Whitby and started wishing I'd deferred it for a night or
two and heard first what the local reaction was. I felt indeed as
though I had an appointment with our dentist. The Empire stands
with an open square in front of it near to the Upper Harbour. The
town railway station lies opposite, and so does the bus stop. But
our road did not run through the town and it was not until the bus
entered the square that we came in sight of the Empire and saw
the biggest queue of men, women and children that I had ever seen
in Whitby. It reached from the doors of the Empire down the
harbour quay and completely out of sight. I had never been well
known at Whitby except among the fishermen. I thought when
we got out of the bus we'd be able to step across the few yards of
road that separated us from the cinema without any one taking
notice of us. But I was wrong. Some wretched boy in the queue
shouted :

" Eh—there he is. That's t'chap from Bay that wrote *Three
Fevers* ! " and a sort of wave of interest seemed to stir the whole
queue and every one seemed to be pointing at us and talking about
us. The cinema manager himself, in tails and white tie, was in the
vestibule just receiving a party of Whitby's elite from a Rolls-Royce
(not the fishermen's ex-taxi), but he moved to meet us. Thinking
of the hundreds of times we'd gone into that cinema without him
taking the slightest notice of us I thought that this was really funny,
and what was equally funny was the way the elite stared at us as
we hurried in out of sight of the crowd. All the upstairs seats were
reserved, and almost all were already full. Ours were the best, in

the middle of the front circle and of course the most conspicuous
to reach. I was glad that the Lunns had decided to take their
customary downstairs seats : gladder still when just after we had
heard shouts from outside of " House full—no standing room," the
lights were dimmed and we got the News Reel. I don't think I
saw anything in that reel. It ended and then on the screen came the
Censors' Certificate, with the name *Turn of the Tide* written on it,
passed for Universal Exhibition. There was music, music I didn't
know but noble and quite exciting, and then came the title of the
film super-imposed on a view of Whitby's twin piers and light-
houses taken from the pier extension, and showing big seas smashing
against their walls, and there came from the audience such a burst of
applause, and screams of delighted children, that my heart almost
stopped beating. Then came the title of the film again, the name
of the book and my own name. There followed the list of characters and actors. A credit to Norman Walker. Then, with the
music rising to crescendo, there was another flash of Whitby piers
with the superimposed title of

SIX MILES FROM THE PORT OF BURNHARBOUR LIES

THE LITTLE VILLAGE OF—

Which slowly mixed into an incredibly lovely long shot of
Bramblewick and Low Batts taken from the south cliff, with the
tide up and the seas crashing over the old coastguard station, and
imposed on this the title,

—BRAMBLEWICK

There was more applause and screams from the children at
recognising still another place they knew, but it died down as the
picture faded into an introductory title giving a short description
of the village and the two families of fishermen. From the dark
title background there then emerged a breaking wave rushing up
what I knew were the stones of Bramblewick Slipway and by trick
photography you saw carved on the stones in very old letters the
name *Isaac Fosdyck* 1703 which dissolved into *Jacob Fosdyck* 1752
and then into a long shot of Bramblewick Old Church graveyard

centering on a tombstone with the name *Luke Fosdyck, Drowned at Sea* 1801.

The music stopped and there came a medley of children's voices and there was a Bramblewick street with a crowd of boys slugging Derek Blomfield in the part of Steve Fosdyck and shouting,

"Go on, hit him, hit him. He's a Lunn. He's a foreigner. Black his eyes for him. Bust his nose!"

And their shouts were drowned by the screams of the real children down below. . . .

The film was on. And from that moment I surrendered my possessive literary pride in the authorship of *Three Fevers*. I forgot my feud with British National Films, my quarrels with Norman Walker, my disillusionment, my fears of what Henry Lunn and the other fishermen were feeling and what afterwards they were going to say to me. I had the immeasurable thrill of feeling that all round us and below us in the "shillings" and "ninepennies" and "fourpennies" the folk, the grown-ups and youths and children of my own town and village had, to quote the *Graphic* review, their eyes riveted to the screen, that the film had *got* them from the first title!

I gripped Dain's hand, for we had written that book together and shared in all the joys and discouragements and excitements of its creation and publication. The book and the characters in it had been very much the foundation of our comradeship. And here was reward, a more exciting reward than any money or spoken or written praise the book had brought us. The tense silences, the laughter (even at John Lunn's "I'm cutting rhubarb for your grandad's dinner"), the deafening applause when the Lunns coble got safely into the Landing through the mountainous seas, the cheers when a lobster pot was hauled into the coble with two live lobsters in it, the shrieks when Marney and Steve in their Sunday clothes fell into the beck when trying to poach a salmon, the genuine sighs from the grown-ups and the sarcastic shouts from some of the children downstairs when John gave Ruth her first kiss (this to the sound of sweet music)—all this just numbed my critical faculties. I did not consciously notice the dead smooth sea when the girls stood on the cliff edge in the westerly gale. I did not notice what someone pointed out to me later, that the lobsters that were taken out of the lobster pot had their claws tied, proof that they had been put in for the shot. But it would have made no difference if I had done, for the cheers had come from an audience that was spellbound with enjoyment.

Did it matter that Geraldine spoke " Yorkshire " with an Irish brogue ? She was lovely to look at and a perfect actress. Did it matter that Fisher-White occasionally slipped into " Devonshire," and Sam Livesey and Joan Maud into Gracie Feilds's " Lancs.", that Garrick spoke good " Yorkshire " but was B.B.C. " English " when he sang ? All of them, but especially Sam, Fisher-White and Geraldine and McGinnis had sunk into their parts, even if those parts were parts in the film and not in the book or reality. The photography was magnificent throughout. The scenery if anything was grander than the real thing, the storm effects superb. Norman's direction, especially where he had the three Lunns on the stage together, was quite inspired. In the book I had the Lunns singing in their warehouse while they feverishly fashioned new lobster pots to replace those lost in the storm. Norman had gone one better than this and given John an accordion and made him play a lilting tune which the school children of Whitby were whistling for weeks after.

I had a feeling that the salvage scene was rather slow and that Norman would have done much better if he had accepted my advice and made it a race between lifeboat and tug, but the photography in the mist was very effective, and there were some more exciting shots of the coast taken when the mist lifted, and anyway the audience loved it. But that was near the end and a sudden misgiving seized me as I saw how the end was shaping. Old Isaac had been discovered as the man who let the tug company know there was a steamer aground. In spite of him a big sum of salvage had been paid to the lifeboat crew, and Luke as coxswain had to share it out. This wasn't *Three Fevers*. Less and less was it becoming real life. Henry Lunn suggested to Luke that the two families should make up their quarrel, pool their salvage money and that they should all join in together in a keeler and (by inference) move to Burnharbour. Shades of the Fosdycks ! Luke's humble response was that even with the salvage money they wouldn't have enough brass. But he has an idea. He goes round to old Isaac's cottage, crashing in on a scene where Isaac is ordering Ruth from his home for ever and John is by her side offering to take her as his wife.

Luke charges his uncle with his treachery about the tug. Accuses him of trying to keep up the quarrel with the Lunns. Suggests that the only way for him to atone is to let Ruth marry John and give the couple their blessing, and instead of hoarding up his brass put it into the keeler Lunns and Fosdycks want to buy. And the film ended with a keeler steaming out of Whitby harbour, Luke Fosdyck at the wheel, old Isaac on the pier end with Ruth, Ruth waving her hand to John, fading out with music.

The lights went up. The applause was terrific and continued as we moved up the gangway to the exit. Many people I knew and several I didn't know shouted congratulations, and all round us we heard people saying how they had enjoyed themselves. But there were no fishermen in the circle, and when we got to the stairs I hoped that in the crowd passing out and the even bigger crowd waiting for the second house we should be able to pass unnoticed to our bus. I felt dreadful. I could think of nothing but the last few scenes, especially the last of all showing Luke Fosdyck in command of the keeler, boss of the Lunns, and of course of Henry Lunn. I thought that Henry would never forgive me for that insult.

But we had scarcely left the cinema entrance than I saw Marney Lunn pushing through the crowd towards us. Before I had time to say anything he seized my hand, and cried excitedly :

" What did you think of it, eh ? What did you think of it ? Best film that's ever been shown in Whitby ! Beats anything ! Champion. Aren't you pleased ? Come on, there's father and John waiting clear of the crowd. God—I've never enjoyed myself so much in my life."

We followed Marney through the crowd and there were Henry and John, like Marney in their best shore togs, and looking very pleased with themselves.

" Eh ! " John greeted me. " You folks ought to be on the stage bowing to the audience, and they ought to be handing flowers and chocolates to your missis. What did you make of it ? God, didn't our coble come out well, coming through the Landing. Do you think you could get us an ordinary photo of that to have framed an hung up ? I thought the steamer bit was a bit slow, but that was a fine bit of Matt Leadley's keeler steaming out of Whitby at the end. Did you know we're getting one like that, only she's another two foot longer ? "

" God ! " I muttered in astonishment. " Did you notice who was at the wheel of that keeler ? "

John laughed and I noticed Henry grin when John answered : " Aye, of course. Wilfred Lawson. He looked a bit daft, didn't he ? I didn't see them take that bit but I heard Matt Leadley himself was crouching under him doing the real steering as Lawson couldn't do it himself."

I dared to turn to Henry.

" What did you think of it ? " I said.

He answered very slowly, grinning all the time.

" It was all right. Champion. And every one else seemed to like it too. Our coble came out fine and no mistake. I shouldn't mind seeing it all over again to tell the truth, and there's never been a film I could say that about. There was a lot of daftness in it of course. Did you notice how Lawson and Marriott was baiting their lines ? They'd have never got 'em done in a month of Sundays at that rate, and pity help him who had 'em to shoot."

" But what about the last bit ? I didn't write that bit, you know. Putting Luke Fosdyck as skipper."

Henry continued to grin.

" Nay, of course not. It was daft. But it was only make-believe when all's said and done," and then he added with just a touch of the old asperity : " Luke would be about as useful at the wheel of a keeler as Lawson himself. Although he was a good fisherman, you know. It was just that he couldn't stand owt new or owt strange. Aye, it's a very good film. And I hope it will be a great success and make you a lot of brass. We made a bit out of it one way or another. Did you hear what John said about us going in for a keeler ? "

I shook Henry's hand. I felt I'd never liked him so much. I was thrilled to hear about his keeler. It seemed that at last everything had come out right for every one. But the bus was going. We shouted good-bye, but as we rushed towards the bus I sighted the Rolls-Royce taxi just outside the station, the very one the fishermen had used, and as it seemed we were going to be rich soon I hailed it to take us home.

Turn of the Tide was not a financial success of course. No one ever told us exactly why, but it had something to do with the barons who controlled the distributing and renting side of the British and international cinema industry. It had a short run at the Capitol Cinema, Haymarket, London, but only as a second " feature." It was shown throughout the British Isles, but rarely at the leading cinemas of the biggest towns, and it had further revivals at London's highbrow Studio One, at the Marble Arch, and the Polytechnic. I had a pathetic letter from a Whitby sailor who hadn': been home for three years and chanced to walk into a cinema in Melbourne where it was being shown. He said it had brought tears to his eyes. We also had a letter from a local lady who had married an Indian civil servant and had been living in Calcutta for several years. She had seen it when the evening temperature in Calcutta was over the hundred mark and she asked us to imagine what she felt like watching our north-easterly gale and snow-squalls. I believe it was shown in other British Colonies and Dominions, but not at all in the United States. Once a month for nearly two years I received a statement which had on top of it the actual cost of the production, £31,928 2s. 7d. (which I supposed included my £300), then under this were the receipts for the past month and then the total receipts to date. The first and the last figures made a subtraction sum the answer to which was given in red ink and was labelled TO BE RE-COUPED. When I got my last statement I think the total receipts were about £9000, which left £22,928 2s. 7d. to be " recouped " before I started drawing my five per cent. What happened after this I never found out, but it had many revivals, and I heard that the two " damns " that had been allowed to get on the sound track had been cut out, and that it had been used as a religious film and actually shown in churches and chapels.

What did it matter ? The film had shown to a very large number of people living in towns and inland places what the north-east coast of England and the North Sea looked like in the weather's many moods, and how fishermen lived, and what beauty as well as hardships there was in their lives. I don't suppose its backers missed their £31,928 2s. 7d. very much. Spread out the money was a benefit to a great number of deserving people. The artistes and technicians were well paid. It brought good business to the local shops, and garage proprietors and char-a-banc owners. The land-lord of one of the local pubs was able to retire on what he earned in that " off " season. Whitby got a valuable free advertisement as a holiday resort. Norman got his director's fee and laurels that he well deserved (although I still think he was wrong about the salvage sequence). Geraldine was launched as a star and in the course of her ascendancy found I believe a rich and handsome husband. McGinnis did well. The Lunns got their keeler. And we got the land for our home and our first night in the Whitby Empire to think about for ever.

THE END

Pen Pom Pren,
    Drefach, *April* 14*th*, 1944.